...The Dream

# RVing Alaska!

## (AND CANADA)

**Sharlene "Charlie" Minshall**

Gypsy Press

*...The Dream Continues*

# RVing Alaska!

(AND CANADA)

## Sharlene "Charlie" Minshall

Edited by
Janet L. Wadlington

Copyright (C) 1997 by Gypsy Press
101 Rainbow Drive, Suite 5024
Livingston, Texas 77351

All rights reserved. No portion of this book may be reproduced, stored in a retrieval system, or transmitted by photographic, electronic, or mechanical process without prior written permission of Gypsy Press.

First edition 1997

Printed in the United States of America

Library of Congress Catalog Card Number: 97-93847

ISBN 0-9643970-1-3

# NON-FICTION TITLES

by

## Sharlene "Charlie" Minshall

## *RVing Alaska!(and Canada)*
(1997)

## *Full-Time RVing*
### *How to Make it Happen*
(1997)

## *RVing North America*
### *Silver, Single, and Solo*

## *In Pursuit of a Dream*

## *Freedom Unlimited:*
### *The Fun and Facts of Fulltime RVing*
Co-author, Bill Farlow
Published by Woodall's

Order Form and More Information
(Back of book)

# About the Author

Sharlene "Charlie" Minshall began writing monthly columns, and free-lance articles, about her RV lifestyle in 1986. They range from the "how-to" to the "why-not." Sometimes, she delves into the nitty-gritty humor of real RV problems, like using the telephone, the intricacies of life with a computer, and loss of memory. She touches on the serious, the silly, and the sad side of life. A reader from Florida says her columns are more like "essays."

At present, she is publishing regular columns in Camp-Orama (SE), RV Traveler (Midwest), Texas RV (TX), RV Life (Northwest), Two-Lane Roads, plus Wagon Train Travelers Magazine in Canada, and contributes other freelance writing.

"Charlie" is the author of:

*RVing Alaska! (and Canada),*
*Full-Time RVing, How to Make it Happen,*
*RVing North America, Silver, Single, and Solo,*
*In Pursuit of a Dream,*
*and*
*Freedom Unlimited,*
*The Fun and Facts of Fulltime RVing* (co-authored)

The author gives seminars on the RV lifestyle. She tells positive, humorous, and very personal tales, of the joys and woes of life on the road as a silver, single, solo gypsy, or as she would put it...

To clarify, I do not stand before you as an expert on anything. You ask then, "Why am I here?" It is more because I am not an expert, but I did it anyway. I'd like to share my eleven years of full-time RVing experiences, and the lessons I've learned along the way (or not).

In that time, I have traveled 180,000 miles by RV, and countless miles by car, four-wheel machines, airplanes, helicopters, paraglider, ultra-light, trains, buses, dunebuggy, motorcycle, bicycle, raft, canoe, kayak, mule, horse, cross-country skis, and water skis. Let's see, what have I forgotten...oh...

*These boots were made for walkin'*
*And walkin' they have done,*
*And I may not have expertise,*
*But boy, have I had fun!*

# GLOSSARY

| | |
|---|---|
| Alaska State Park Annual Pass | $100 -- Alaska State Parks and (Most) State Recreation Sites. Available at Tok, AK Public Lands Info Center |
| Annual boat launch pass | $50 available at Tok, AK, Public Lands Info Center |
| Annual daily parking pass | $25 Available at Tok, AK, Public Lands info Center |
| Arctic Circle | Line of latitude approximately 66 degrees 33 feet north of the equator, circumscribing northern frigid zone. |
| Aurora Borealis or "Dawn of the North" | The aurora is essentially a solar-powered light show that results from interactions between the solar wind and our magnetic planet. |
| Bear Bells | Small bells that attach to your clothing or backpack to warn bears you are coming |
| Black water | Sewage from toilet |
| BLM | Bureau of Land Management |
| Blue Canoes | Alaska State Ferries |
| Boondock | Parking without amenities other than in a campground |
| Bore Tide | Steep-fronted tide crests caused by tides flowing into constricted inlets at speeds up to 12 MPH |
| "Burger Burps" | Glaciers calve and the little ice burgers burp, like popping champagne. |
| Calving | Tidewater glacier shedding icebergs off its face into the sea. |
| Cariboo, Caribou | Route 97 follows the old"Cariboo" trail to the old Cariboo gold fields (Cariboo not caribou) |
| Cats | Caterpillar -- tractor made for use on rough ground |
| Cheechako | (Greenhorn) New to come |
| Chip-seal | Oil and rock put on the surface of asphalt road to "seal" against wear and weather, usually redone every couple of years |
| Crevasses | Cracks made when nunataks disrupt the glacier's flow |
| CRS | Can't Remember Sugar |
| Denali National Park Annual Pass | $15 Covers entry into park for all immediate family traveling with permit holder |
| Doghouse | Cover over the engine inside motorhome |
| Dry camp | Without amenities |
| Dual Wheels | Back wheels on RV running side-by-side on axle |
| EMT | Emergency Medical Technician |
| Fjord | As tidewater glaciers retreat, the steep-sided valleys carved by the glacial action fill in with sea water, creating a fjord |
| FMCA | Family Motor Coach Association |
| Fresh water | Hopefully, your drinking water |
| Glacier | When more snow falls in the winter than melts in the summer, a glacier begins. Over tens of thousands of years, this snow builds up and recrystallizes into a solid mass of ice. Technically, glacier ice is so compressed that it is classified as a metamorphic rock. When the accumulation of ice becomes so great that the force of gravity causes it to move, a glacier is born. |
| Glacier blue ice | Highly compressed ice crystals. Dense crystals absorb all colors of the light spectrum except blue. What you see is reflected blue light. |
| Golden Access Pass http://www.nps.gov/pub_aff/fee.html | This is a free lifetime entrance pass for persons who are blind or permanently disabled. It is available to citizens or permanent residents of the United States, regardless of age. |
| Golden Age Pass http://www.nps.gov/pub_aff/fee.html | This is a lifetime entrance pass for those 62 years or older. The Golden Age Passport has a one time processing charge of $10. You must purchase a Golden Age Passport in person. |
| Golden Eagle Pass http://www.nps.gov/pub_aff/fee.html | An entrance pass to national parks, monuments, historic sites, recreation areas, and national wildlife refuges that charge an entrance fee. It costs $50 and is valid for one year . National Park Service, 1100 Ohio Drive, SW, Room 138Washington, DC 20242, Attention: Golden Eagle Passport |

| | |
|---|---|
| GPS | Global Positioning System |
| Gray water | Used dish/bath/cleaning water |
| GVWR | Gross Vehicle Weight Rating: (Maximum loaded weight of single vehicle specified by the manufacturer -- (Found on the Certificate of Origin and data plate.) |
| Hanging Glacier | (or valley glacier). Glaciers that flow down out of mountain valleys whose terminus is above sea level. |
| Ice fields | Large interconnecting glaciers separated by mountain peaks and ridges, called nunataks, projecting through the ice. |
| Iceworms | Thread sized Iceworms live between ice crystals near the surface of some glaciers. |
| Kittiwakes | Member of the gull family |
| Lining | Pulling the canoe along the shore by rope |
| Marge | Margin |
| Muskeg | sphagnum moss |
| Mustache | Skirt along bottom back of RV used like mudflaps |
| N.W.T. | Northwest Territories (Canada) |
| NPS | National Park Service |
| Nunatak | A hill or mountain completely surrounded by glacial ice |
| "The outside" | This is how northern Canadians and Alaskans refer to the "Lower 48." |
| Permafrost | Ground remaining frozen for two or more years. |
| Pingo | An ice-covered hill that can only grow and persist in a permafrost environment |
| Placer gold flour | Finer than dust |
| Puce | A dark red |
| Qiviut (Key-vee-ute) | Soft underwool of the musk ox |
| RCMP | Royal Canadian Mountain Police |
| Rime | "An accumulation of granular ice tufts on the windward sides of exposed objects that is formed from supercooled fog or cloud and built out directly against the wind." (Webster's) |
| RNWMP | Royal North West Mounted Police |
| RV, rig | Recreational Vehicle |
| Season | Mid-June through August |
| Seracs | Frozen spires of ice |
| SKPs | Escapees, Inc. (National RVing Group) |
| Slough | An inlet on a river |
| Sourdough | Seasoned survivor, Old timer |
| Subsistence | Rights to minimum food and shelter necessary to support life |
| Super Pass | $135 Boat launch, camping, parking: Alaska residents only |
| Taiga | "Land of little sticks," a Russian interpretation |
| Tag or Tow | Vehicle being towed behind RV |
| Tidewater glacier | (or Fjord glacier) This is a valley glacier that occupies a fjord. The terminus lies below sea level and generally has an almost vertical face that sheds huge chunks of glacial ice. |
| TLC | Tender Loving Care |
| Tsunamis | A great sea wave produced by submarine earth movement or volcanic eruption, tidal wave |
| Tundra | Dwarfed shrubs and miniaturized wildflowers adapted to a short growing season. |
| USFS | United States Forest Service |
| Utilidors | Hold water and sewer pipes |

## DEDICATION

I dedicate this book
To
The Lord,
who keeps me on, out, and in,
On the road, out of trouble, and in touch with good people
To
My brothers and sisters
Ted and Mary Stilwell
Dick and Vivian Stilwell
Leo and Pat Stilwell
Dean and Dorothy Stilwell
To
Rebecca
MBG (My Beautiful Granddaughter) and camping buddy
To
Baby Norvelle
MHG (My Handsome Grandson) who will find his way to Grandma's arms in August
To
My supportive and special sons-in-law
Bill Wadlington and Tom Norvelle
To
My treasured daughters
Janet Louise and Tracey Anne
To
Old "Gold" Friends and New "Silver" Friends
who have touched my life and my heart somewhere, somehow,
and made this lifestyle an adventure to remember forever

## ACKNOWLEDGMENTS

Special thanks
to
Camilla Bowman,
Tracey Norvelle,
Jane Parker,
and
Duane and Marilyn VanderWater
for their "time-under-pressure" reading of *RVing Alaska!*
It was tremendously helpful to have different points of view.

    I can always count on constructive criticism and loving encouragement from daughter, Tracey. Via telephone, E-mail, and Priority Mail, from Virginia to Washington, she held my hand as I progressed through two books. Thanks, Love, you're the greatest.

    Daughter, Janet, was so much more than an editor. As a computer consultant, she often rescued my sanity after I had lost 298 pages of a 192 page book, to what I feared most, oblivion. She was the calm and the hugs in the midst of my mental storms. She was my joy and laughter when all systems were go. Thanks, Honey, I couldn't have done it without you.

    Thanks to Claudia and Robert Fay for allowing me to house-sit in their lovely chalet in Leavenworth, Washington, for the winter. It gave me the needed space to spread out, and a magnificent panoramic winter scene to inspire me, while I created *RVing Alaska!* and *Full-Time RVing, How to Make it Happen.*

# CONTENTS

| Chapter | Page |
|---|---|

Glossary..................................................................................

Introduction ........................................................................1

1    Preparation ................................................................3

2    More Preparation ....................................................17

3    Beautiful British Columbia.........................................31

4    Golden Circle Loop Trip and on to Fairbanks............44

5    The Spell of the Yukon .............................................54

6    Flying with the Eagle-ites..........................................66

7    The Mighty Yukon River ...........................................74

8    Chicken Tracks Through Homer Spit........................93

9    The Bear Facts .......................................................111

10   The Hope of My Universe .......................................131

11   The Fair and the Fireweed.......................................138

12   Doing the Dempster ................................................148

13   Headin' Home .........................................................162

14   Parting Thoughts ....................................................174

Resources..................................................................................

# INTRODUCTION

### It charms me! It excites me! It overwhelms me! I love it!

## ALASKA!

You might say I'm a fan of William H. Seward, Secretary of State to Presidents Lincoln and Johnson. He arranged for the purchase of Alaska from Russia. "Seward's Icebox," as many Americans called it in 1867, was purchased for $7,200,000. We paid a whopping two cents an acre for this amazing land of 100,000 glaciers and over forty mountain ranges.

Alaska was declared the 49th United State in 1959; and in the process, it became not only our largest, but our northernmost, westernmost, and easternmost state. Honest! The Aleutian Chain extends into the Eastern Hemisphere.

It isn't just Alaska that thrills me; it is the getting there as well. The route across Canada is equally as beautiful as Alaska. Crossing the border into Canada and knowing I'm on the way to our Great Frontier, gives me goosebumps.

It has been my privilege to visit Alaska three times, totaling nearly a year. Each trip I have returned to favorite haunts, discovered different places, met delightful people, and experienced new adventures. This last five-month trip began on April 26, 1996, and it was to be my farewell to Alaska. I was certain I would get the far North completely out of my system. Ha! The longer I stayed, the longer I wanted to stay. Given my druthers, I know I'll go back.

In the night, when my mind wanders over the places I've visited, I wonder at the audacity that allows me to feel so comfortable traveling alone. I suspect it's just plain blind faith in the good Lord, that He will look after those of us who are as dumb as rocks about mechanics.

I've learned enough over eleven years of full-time RVing, to know a macerator from a Michelin, but not much more. I rather envy my four brothers who grew up taking things apart (probably without permission), and putting them back together again. In the process, they learned how things worked, or why they didn't.

Perhaps someday I'll solve the puzzle. What was I doing while they were getting down, getting greasy, and piecing engines together? All those who know me well, will vouch for the fact I can't cook. Maybe I was gardening, or uh, maybe wool-gathering. Hmmm.

Because I drive the Sprinter almost every day, I'm very aware of what it sounds like, and feels like, as it bounces down the highways and byways. When it doesn't sound "right," it is my first inkling of a problem. I fix it or have it fixed. The Sprinter has 145,000 miles on it. I am replacing it bit by bit. By the turn of the century, don't you know, I'll have a whole new motorhome!

This book began life with the Sprinter perched on a leveling rock, twenty feet from Resurrection Creek near Hope, Alaska. Its teen years evolved, while I experienced my first volunteer house-sitting, in Leavenworth, Washington. Finished, it wobbled off the computer, as I listened to swollen Peshastin Creek rush past the Sprinter, at Blu-Shastin RV Park, fifteen miles from Leavenworth.

Since I'm a full-time RVer, and my home base in Livingston, Texas, is only a mail-forwarding, license-bearing, insurance-qualifying, absentee-voting place, I'll base mileage from the Washington border. It is roughly 2,500 miles from Seattle to Anchorage, Alaska. Give or take a few miles to see everything, you could easily add 8,000--10,000 miles to your odometer. If at all possible, plan this trip for no less than three months. If you love it, you won't regret it. If you hate it (I can't imagine), you can always leave early.

My purpose in writing this book is not to pass myself off as an expert. Perhaps, even more, it is because I'm **not** an expert. I'm an every day Jill who loves Canada and Alaska, and I've told you the good, and the bad, and the straight of it. The book is meant to give you, not only an insight into RVing, but, to extend your possibilities into canoeing, flying, and playing with the grizzlies.

If you aren't contemplating a trip to Alaska, please settle back with a cool drink, and we'll go for an armchair adventure you won't forget. Actually, it might be more apropos to get a hot drink, we're leavin' for glacier country.

If you're driving an RV, the ideas, suggestions, and strong comments, are to make your RV trip smoother, and more fun. The added personal experiences, are to encourage you to visit our forty-ninth state, before it changes any more than it already has. I hope before another year goes by, you'll be

RVING

ALASKA!

(AND CANADA)

God Bless!

"Charlie"

> I drove up in the April snows,
> when the frozen lakes and streams were beginning to melt.
> Spring and summer arrived in
> a dazzling array of wild flowers.
> Autumn was yellow, orange, bright red...and glorious.
> The Sprinter pushed snow through
> the mountain pass returning from Inuvik in late September.
> I knew, then, I had come full circle...
> and I definitely, did not have the far North out of my system.

The Sprinter In Winter, Chilkat State Park, Haines, AK

# PREPARATION

## Hi!

**Special note:** If you didn't read the Glossary pages, a few pages back, you might want to do it before you start through the book. It will answer a lot of questions right off the bat.

My first trip to Alaska in 1987, was in the back of a pickup truck! Honest, it was better than it sounds. Dick and Mary Carr were checking out an itinerary for their caravan company, and took me along to do photography, and write a brochure. They stayed in the travel trailer they were pulling, and I lived under the cap of their truck. I was grateful for a taste of Alaska. In 1992 and 1996, I drove my Sprinter motorhome for two extensive trips. I haven't been cured yet.

I thought these ideas and strong suggestions would help RVers be less overwhelmed by miles and possibilities. Actually, many of these things you should do before you leave your driveway, on your way to anywhere. As you read further, you will realize I didn't necessarily follow my own advice at all times, and I did have a few problems, but that's par for this Silver Gypsy's course. Let's begin.

## How do YOU feel?

We will discuss extensively the health of the chassis and the RV, but they are both secondary concerns, to **your personal health**. There are doctors, clinics and hospitals; but, remember, the distances between places are often great. Places listed on the map, are occasionally only that, listed. In the lower 48, when a place is on the map, it might have some substance. In North country, it could be a store or gas station, or it might be closed for life, because it's historical...and you'll be hysterical.

If you have existing health problems, check with your doctor. Plan to stay in campgrounds, or towns. Take **prescriptions, insurance papers, and cards** with you (Are they good in Canada? Check with your insurance company). As with any trip that takes you many miles from home territory, give thought to insurance for emergency medical care. If you become ill, you might have to be flown to a major city (or another country), for special care.

It is scary enough to be ill, but if you are "Goin' in the brambles where the rabbits wouldn't go," it can be terrifying. There are few things I fear in solo RVing. Getting sick when I am alone, is one of them. It is frightening. It hasn't happened often and it won't stop me, but it **is** frightening.

Do you have any physical limitations? Think ahead and ask questions before going on tours. With serious considerations out of the way, let's get on to the fun.

## What should I do ahead of time?

## GET THE MILEPOST MAGAZINE!!!!!!!!!!

The most important advice I can give you, is to buy the Milepost Magazine. **Don't leave home without it.** New ones come to the book stores in April. It is a guide filled with **priceless information,** milepost by milepost, throughout Canada and Alaska. Truth is, the Milepost is all you need, but then again, this book is more fun. They can lead you, but

## I have walked the walk and driven the miles.

Even if you are using a Milepost that is a year old, it will give you most of what you need to know. Businesses open and close quickly; information can't always make the latest issue. One more thing about the Milepost, study it before you go. It can be confusing, but it will all become clear if you ruminate it, and cogitate it, and all those good things.

While I consider the Milepost to be the greatest all-time guide, not everyone advertises in it. Many more facilities and services are available, than what you will find in the Milepost pages.

When I stop for the night, I like to go through the Milepost, and get an idea what I'm going to see the next day. I check ahead for services, like gasoline (Can I dump or get water?). Will I need propane, car wash, campground, grocery store, pizza fix, or whatever?

If you will be hiking, biking, **exploring beyond the main highways**, or taking cruises to see glaciers, I also recommend buying the

## Alaska Atlas and Gazetteer,

which has topographical maps of the entire state. Even though the cruise companies include small maps, the topo maps give details of all the nooks and crannies where you are going, or where you have been.

I am not one for nitty-gritty trip planning years in advance, but a trip to Alaska requires thinking ahead. Yes, there are stores and mechanics and supplies, but still, the distances are great and the prices are high.

### Get Maps and information!

The best overall map of Canada and Alaska, is the one that comes with the Milepost magazine; however, I like individual large maps of each territory. I don't find Atlas maps as detailed as I like, although they are great for quick perusal.

Send for maps and information from each province, territory, and Alaska. You will be inundated with material. They will send good maps, and let you in on festivals, holiday celebrations, and whatever is unique in their area. Trip routing and material are usually available from your RV organizations, FMCA, Escapees, Good Sam, Coast to Coast, etc. Computer buffs can do a keyword search, and find tons of information on the internet. (See Resources)

**I use a highlighter pen to mark where I'm going, or where I've been. (Sometimes I use a different color for each direction, because most of the time, I don't know whether I'm coming or going.)**

The fun of a trip to Alaska, is the anticipation. Pour over maps, brochures, go to slide shows or lectures, watch programs on TV, read books (please), and talk to people who have been there. They can tell you whether the Moose Dropping Festival at Talkeenta, Alaska, or the International Gold Show at Dawson City, Yukon, are farces or fun. **But**, be careful, it is **their opinion**.

I can't count the number of times I would have missed something I really, really enjoyed, because someone else didn't like it. We all have different ideas of fun. Check it out yourself if you have a real interest. (Then you can tell someone else it was a farce, and ruin their day!)

If you know you are going to be somewhere specific for a few days, request material from the Chamber of Commerce of a nearby town.

Keep in mind, because of weight restrictions, everything you take into an RV, should have a dual purpose. A map is a stupendous conversation starter. Open a map on a picnic table, or carry one to the recreation hall or laundry. You will soon have numerous RVers draped over your shoulder. They'll point to where they have been, where they want to go, and give you advice about which route to take, whether or not they have ever been there. (Great Uncle Herbert was there ten years ago and the road was lousy.)

If a map doesn't clue you in to your destination, and it doesn't work initiating a conversation, use it as a fire starter.

Visit all the information booths, centers, and kiosks. The free information and maps are invaluable. (Sometimes maps are kept behind the desk, and you have to ask for them.) If not during the trip, it is nice to have this knowledge when you identify your slides, or pinpoint something in your log.

Information centers are also great places to meet other RVers, and exchange road conditions, and possibility information. **But**, don't forget, it is **their opinion**. Take it with a grain of salt. Mix it with your own knowledge and desire, then toss out what you don't want to hear, like my taking the road to McCarthy. Two out of three told me the road was nearly impassable. I chose to believe the one who said, "It isn't so bad, if you're careful." It was the worst washboard gravel road I had ever traveled, but then again, I would have missed a fantastic experience, if I hadn't followed my own desire.

Keep material organized. Keep it handy. I've never done this in my life, but it's a **great idea**.

## When should I go?

The general tourist tends to go mid-June to mid-August because the attractions are open; and generally, the weather is at its best then. I like going in April, before everyone else goes, but then I like to see the mountains in snow. It's great for slides. You will very likely drive or sit in snow for a few days, if you go early or stay late. I figured if anybody was going to keep their roads clear, those in the far North, would have the equipment for it. They live with snow. I like experiencing the seasons.

During the season you will see hundreds of RVs on the Kenai, around the loop, and on the main highways. Because I have gone up for longer periods of time, when everything gets clogged with RVs, I find a nice stream to camp beside, or do some backroad exploring. The sheer number of RVs, of course, is a good case for taking a tag with you. You can get around better and quicker, find parking, and...

## How long should I stay?

**As long as possible!** It is a long journey. Give it time. Don't try to do it in less than six weeks. Yes, it is possible; but personally, I like to see where I am traveling, talk to people, and get a feel for the communities. It's fun to take side trips or flights to places and cultures I couldn't see anywhere else. Possibilities are limited only by your imagination.

If you enjoy scenery, you will be thrilled with the whole trip. If, God forbid, you should get up there and not like it, you can always head for home earlier than you planned. You might even get hooked, like me, and go back for longer periods of time each trip. I think three months is the least amount of time anyone should take for the entire trip. If you are someone who sees Europe in a weekend, three days would work.

## Where will I stay?

The choice to drive up early and return late, means I boondock (dry camp) a lot. The Milepost will tell you where the campgrounds are, fees, and usually, when they open and close. Most of them do not open until mid-June and they close by September. However, there are many places to park. Private parks are definitely not open, until the main season. Public parks are sometimes open for parking, but have no facilities.

I choose a wide spot next to a lake or stream, if I can find one where it's feasible to park. There are many rest areas, official and unofficial. If you are stuck without a campground, and you are apprehensive about doing this, ask if you can spend the night in a business parking lot, or near an information center. Be sure you are not on private property, or obstructing anyone or anything. It all comes down to using good old common sense.

It is against my religion to make reservations, except at a really busy tourist site during high season (Denali - Anchorage - Fairbanks), then reservations are probably best. Parks fill up by late afternoon. Don't expect to always find top-notch parks. You are in North country. Both Canada and Alaska have some very nice parks, but many are forged out of the countryside; and even if they have the amenities, they are not fancy by any means. If you **must** have electric, sewer, and water, I suggest you do some good planning.

I really like camping near water, trees, and nature, in the recreation areas.

---

**My rules for boondocking outside designated camping areas are:**
**If it is posted, don't stay**
**Don't block anything**
**Don't knowingly park on private property (without permission)**
**Be unobtrusive**
    **Don't dump anything**
    **Don't leave a mess**
    **Leave it better than you found it**
**If it is a public area (Rest area -- Wal-Mart, etc.), don't stay more than one**
    **night.**
**Get there after 7 p.m.**
**Leave early**
**Keep a quiet, low profile**

Do not, I repeat, do not, go to northern Canada and Alaska, expecting major RV resort facilities like you find in Arizona, Texas, California, or Florida, although some of them are very nice. You are going to North country. Relax, enjoy what the North is all about. I go there because I love the scenery, and away from Anchorage and Fairbanks, the slower pace. That doesn't mean drive your RV on a busy main highway, going 35 miles an hour, gawking at the scenery. It means stop in the pull-outs, or stop early in the day, or stay a couple of days in one spot. Don't rush it.

Someone wrote to me recently, asking if they would have problems getting into campgrounds with a 37' rig. If your RV is ultra big, check the Milepost or campground directories, for sizes. Some campgrounds and/or gravel roads cannot accommodate, and are not advised, for large vehicles. I don't think you will have any problems, if you are on the main roads. There are size restrictions in some recreational parks.

## What should I take to wear?

The weather varies, even during July and August. Elevations and the time of day, make a lot of difference in your personal comfort. Take cool and warm clothes, and dress in layers. Take good walking (or hiking) shoes, warm socks, boots, rainwear, and a windbreaker. I wore hiking boots almost the entire time. They looked horrendous by about the third month, but that was when they were just getting comfortable.

## Break your shoes in before you need them!

I broke in my leather hiking boots by putting them on, lacing them up, and getting them soaked. I wore them until they were completely dry, and had conformed to my foot. I got rid of them when they fell apart.

It wouldn't hurt to have some dress-up or semi dress-up clothes, depending on your choice of activities. Casual dress goes **almost** anywhere. I did take off my hiking boots to go to church, but I wouldn't have been the only one with hiking boots on, if I had chosen to wear them.

## What other "Stuff" should I take?

You know what you and your spouse (or your family) have on hand to keep plugging along (or perhaps unplugging). These are only suggestions of what you might take. Your list will depend on your individual needs, and the type of activities you will be involved in.

**Ace bandages**
**Antacids**
**Anti-diarrhea medicine**
**Antibiotics**
**Antihistamines**
**Aspirin**, or whatever you use for a painkiller. Certainly, if you have a favorite brand, take it with you. *Vanquish* is the only thing that will stop a headache for me, and I can't get it everywhere.

Band-Aids
Dressings
Extra pair of glasses (and a copy of your prescription), (Repair kit)
Eye drops
If you are allergic to anything, take the remedy and prescription with you.
Insect repellent
Laxatives
Liquid antiseptic
Mosquito netting (if you are really bugged by bugs)
Sleeping remedies (A mask to keep out all that daylight wouldn't hurt!)
Something for motion sickness?
Sunscreen
Tick repellent

If you are already an RVer, you probably have everything you'll need in your medicine chest already. I carry only a few basics; Pepto Bismol, Vanquish, Bag Balm, Hydrogen Peroxide, and Alka Seltzer for the sewer tank (Yes, it works to put a couple of packets into the sewer tanks to clean the corrosion off the indicator light, even if the tech writers say it won't work!).

### Repellent

Take plenty of mosquito repellent. No one believes me when I say I used repellent only two or three times last summer. Bugs are worse in some areas than others. One of the places they were the worst in 1992, was in Fairbanks, at the Chena River Recreation Area. They were so thick, their landings and take-offs kept me awake every night.

Mosquitoes and I don't generally get along, and I didn't look forward to bugs of any kind, but I spent plenty of time outside, and wasn't bothered that much. Take the repellent. Everybody is different, and you'll probably need it. Some of the hints from the National Park Service are:

Don't wear perfume or other scented products.
Wear light colors or pastels. Bright, patterned, or dark clothing, attracts insects.
In grassy, brushy, or wooded areas, wear tightly woven fabric.
Tuck your pant legs in your socks, and your long-sleeved shirt into your pants.
Wear a hat.
Check yourself after every outing, for ticks.
Only female mosquitoes draw blood. If you see one wearing a skirt, smack her before she gets ya.

Alaska has black flies and "no-see-ums," as well as mosquitoes. You no see um the no-see-ums, but if you suddenly start dancing "The

Chicken" when you ain't in Chicken, you'll know they are about. Wearing long sleeves and long pants, with cuffs tight to your body, helps. I was also not bugged by black flies and no-see-ums. Maybe it was a light year.

I've come to the conclusion, since I didn't have a problem with bugs, maybe I'm not sweet enough, but then, who'd believe that? It could be propaganda to keep the tourists in the lower 48. Those Alaskans are sneaky. They tell everybody Alaska has two seasons, mosquitoes and no mosquitoes.

## Logs

I keep a log for mileage, repairs, and gasoline, plus costs and receipts, and another for activities, places, weather, and thoughts. It is fun to read it after you get home. You'd be surprised how often you refer to it for clarification (or to win an argument). One thing about traveling solo, I win most of my arguments.

## Photography

If you're into photography, take lots of film. It is easy to find print film, but I have a hard time finding slide film, unless I'm in a bigger city.

---

**Take your telephoto lens. This will allow you to get good animal (or scenery) shots without getting too close**
**Frame photos with trees, branches, flowers, people**
**Flash photos do not work for distances**
**Include people or rocks or trees, for perspective**
**A tripod is nice to steady the camera, for low-light shots**
**In the foreground, capture sand, footprints, a brick wall, etc.**
**Take a couple disposable panoramic cameras**

---

## Companions

This is a good time to mention companions. Should you choose to take someone with you in your rig, or caravan with one or several rigs, remember it is a long trip. Are you super good friends, who can be honest with each other? Do you like to travel long days, or stop by 2 or 3 in the afternoon to relax, and enjoy your surroundings? Is your dawn's early light at 5 a.m. or 11 a.m.? Be sure you are compatible.

If you would enjoy their company, but you don't want to wait at every turn, consider meeting them at a pre-designated area by evening. That way you can all enjoy the trip, and keep your sanity (providing you had some before you left).

Fellow caravaners, or companions, or a commercial caravan, are the greatest, if you are the least bit apprehensive about driving anywhere on your own. (See Resources)

Now, let's get more serious here.

| **What is the condition of your RV?** |
|---|

How good, or how old, are your fire extinguishers? Notice, I said extinguisher**s**, as in plural. You should have one for your tag, as well as however many you need, for the size of your RV.

Check out your water heater, furnace, and refrigerator. How is your water pump working? How old are your house batteries? (Do they have enough water in them? (I have a tendency to forget the poor things, because they are under the bed pedestal, and hard for me to reach.)

Do you have repair material if your roof leaks?

| **Your RV and chassis should be in as good a condition as possible.** |
|---|

### Begin your journey with a vehicle that's in good condition.

Your immediate enjoyment, and fond memories, of this fabulous trip (or any other), will be enhanced a hundred-fold if you

| **BEGIN YOUR JOURNEY WITH A VEHICLE THAT IS IN GOOD CONDITION!** |
|---|

### What should I take?

Many RVers are making the trip to Alaska these days; consequently, towns have increased in size. RV repair facilities and parts stores have proliferated. Still, distances are great, and it is wise to have some items for your specific RV.

Take extra engine and transmission oil; power-steering and brake fluids; gasoline and oil filters; air cleaner; headlights; and a variety of belts (air-conditioning, alternator, fan) and hoses, (radiator, heat and A/C) with you. Whatever is on the vehicle, should be new or nearly new, before you drive a mile down the road (A good idea, no matter where you are traveling).

Even if you can't replace parts yourself, you might find someone who can, easier than you can find the needed parts.

Take two spare tires, if possible. If you are traveling April or before, or September and later, be prepared to do some driving in snow. Have all-weather or snow tires, or tires with good tread, and traction devices. Are they properly inflated? Do you have a tire pressure gauge? It will make a difference in your gas mileage.

| **Don't forget the little guy you are towing behind you.**<br>**Are you packing a few extra parts, and a GOOD tire, for him**<br>**(Not one of those *puny* things**<br>**that hides under the mat)?** |
|---|

Windshield wipers should be in excellent condition. Take extras; I

never did find replacements in Alaska. Pack extra windshield cleaner. Check fuel and water pumps. How is the exhaust system? How are your brakes? Is your cooling system OK.? How about in-house, outhouse, and hazard lights? Does your cruise control work properly? With the great distances, you'll want your cruise. Make sure your radio works. In some areas, you can tune in for road, park, or travel conditions.
How old is your engine battery? Do you have jumper cables?

Everybody wants to know the answer to the all-important question,

## "How are the roads?"

Don't let stories of the Alaska Highway scare you to death. Have you driven our Interstates down here? What do you do when you hit a stretch of bad highway?

**If you have the sense God gave you, you slow down and take it easy, until the road improves.**

That is precisely what you do, when you hit questionable highways in Canada and Alaska.

Yes, the Alaska Highway is completely paved, as are the Richardson, Tok, Parks, Glenn, Seward, etc., but all have at least occasional stages of "heavedom." Except for the road from Tok to Glennallen, which has been mostly bad any time I've driven it, the other roads have bad *sections*.

Narrower, winding gravel roads, such as the Cassiar and Top of the World, in Canada, and Taylor Highway, in Alaska, are being widened, paved, and/or chip-sealed. Curves are being straightened and shoulders added. You'd better get up there, before they ruin the whole blanketyblank place!!!

Frost heaves will be a seasonal problem, until such time as the powers that be can overrule nature.

**Rough spots in both countries, are marked with flashers, flags, or signs. Trust me; when you see a marker of any kind, there is a reason -- *pay attention*!**

Also, if you travel really **early** in the spring, road crews will not have had time to repair the roads. The roads get better as the season progresses.

Phone numbers for road and pass conditions, are listed in the Milepost; however, I found most of them had been disconnected sometime between information gathering, and the printing of the magazine. Look in the phone book or newspaper when you are in town, or ask someone. People in the North live by the weather. They know where to check conditions. Definitely do this, if you are traveling early or late in the season. Even better, get a hand-held, battery-powered, weather radio. A friend gave me one, and it has been invaluable.

As with the traditional frost heaves, you should cut your speed with bad weather conditions. Ice, snow, mud, and rain, make road surfaces potential skating rinks. Gusts, or wind devils, hitting the nice broad surface of an RV, can throw you. Northern Canada and Alaska have mostly two-lane roads; and of necessity, you should travel slower under bad weather conditions.

This means you will have unhappy campers behind you. Use pullouts to let people by. If possible, stay off the road during bad weather, or at least, during the busiest times of the day. Be even more mindful, if you are towing a tag.

Now,

## What about the rumors I hear, concerning broken axles, springs, etc.?

What about them? Certainly you can have a flat tire, or break down, under the most normal of circumstances, no matter how well prepared you were when you started, or how good a condition everything was in, when you crossed the border. **But**, if you are very aware of conditions (watching those flagged bad sections), and your speed is reasonable, you probably won't have problems.

If you are going to be in such a hurry, why go?

To me, it is not the flagged sections that are the worst. I hate the "swells." These are generally not marked, because they are not a "break" in the pavement. Watch the road ahead of you. If the white stripe at the side, takes on a "wavy" appearance, that is your first clue to slow down, and quickly. If I take these at just a trifle of an angle, I can get past them without a problem (after I've slowed down).

If you do hit one head on and at full speed, you will get a teeth-rattling jolt, as your front end connects with the returning pavement.

Somehow, somewhere, and I don't remember doing it, I must have hit the pavement and bounced. When I got back, I realized one of the steel holders that hangs down from the undercarriage, for towing, was creamed completely. I also may have hit it coming out of a steep highway entrance.

Speaking of which, watch what you are turning into (a witch or a warlock??). Driveways into businesses are sometimes extremely steep (definitely not RV friendly). Especially if you are towing, but even if you are not, either find another entrance, another business, or drive up or down at an angle, to keep from bumping or dragging.

## Please remember, speed is directly relational to anguished springs, broken axles, chipped windshields, and creative alignment.

Anyone can have problems, no matter how carefully they drive. But...the biggest gripers are blustery, hot dog RV drivers who forgot a long time ago, what "vacation" or "leisurely trip," meant. They stop late. They start early. In between, they drive like a bat out of a very hot place. They aren't getting anything out of the trip, wouldn't dream of going back, can't see what anybody sees in the place (probably because they missed the whole thing), and will be dag-nabbed sure whoever is with them, isn't going to enjoy any of it either.

I've run into people like that. Their description of the trip always made me wonder what trip to Alaska they were on. It never resembled any of my trips to Alaska, and it was the same route.

## What happens if I do break down?

### Communications

Do you have a CB? A cellular phone? Are you carrying flares or flags? How about a big sign for the window that screams for "HELP?"

For crying tears in a bucket, if you have major problems, don't let it ruin your trip. Plan in a little extra moola, or a little leeway on your credit card, or last, but not least, a rich relative you can call, in case something does go wrong.

First of all, spend **$69** and get a towing service that will pick up **anywhere** without an extra fee (covering both RV and tag), and take you to a good repair facility. If you don't carry towing insurance anywhere else, carry it when you travel Alaska and Canada (Does it cover you in Canada?). One tenth (or less) of any long-distance towing bill, will take care of the cost of a year of towing insurance.

### WORST CASE SCENARIO

You are returning from Heaven only knows where, and you break down. Unless you are traveling unusually early or late in the season, other cars or RVs will be on the road. Use the CB or cell phone, to call your RV tow service, or a repair facility in the next town. If all else fails, flag someone down, and ask them to make a call for you.

If you are truly apprehensive about going somewhere, but you want to go anyway, call a friend or relative, and tell them when you are leaving and when you will be back, or leave word with the RCMP, a ranger, or the police. Stick precisely to that schedule. If you don't call them, or return within a specified amount of time, someone will look for you.

OK, what if the repair facility or wrecker, can't possibly get to you before tomorrow (either because of distances or time)? Are you off the road? Did you set flares? Once you are off the road as far as you can get, and you've put out the flares, or you have driven to a pullout, relax, you are fortunate, you are already at home.

> All the poor earthbound souls zooming by in cars,
> can't go to the refrigerator,
> mound a bowl with non-fat frozen yogurt
> plus non-fat chocolate syrup,
> or sprinkle it with 25% less fat, dry-roasted peanuts.
> You can.
> Relax. Watch the marmots sleep or the flowers grow.
> I <u>told</u> you to take at least three months.

Don't yell at your mate. Chances are they didn't have a thing to do with the problem. Even if they did, be magnanimous, try not to notice.

After you are in town, and you find you will be there a couple of days in the repair shop, don't do something really boring, like being bored. **Look at it as an adventure**. Walk (You've heard of that mode of transportation, haven't you?) around town, visit the information center, or a museum, or have a cup of espresso in the cafe where the locals hang out. Pick up a local newspaper. Find out what's happening in that community.

Go to church. Go to a movie. Go to a garage sale or flea market. Church, garage sales, and flea markets, only happen on weekends. Not to worry. It is written on the road somewhere, in big black letters, that RVs only have major break downs on weekends. So, you see, you're all set. This scenario, of course, is another reason for pulling a tag.

Before you know it, your RV will be fixed, your bill will be paid, and you will be on your way. You might as well let it be an adventure, as a frustration. I do all this, honest. Of course, first I cry in frustration, stomp my feet in anger, pray for forgiveness, and ask for help with the problem, **then** I relax and go from there. **Life is good**.

## A piece of advice

If you have had **major** repairs, and it is at all possible, drive in the area for a couple of days, to see if everything is working as it should. More than once I have traveled 500 miles, only to find the fix wasn't for real, or it went awry. After driving that distance, I paid to have the problem fixed somewhere else, rather than return.

The same is true, if you have things done before your trip. Drive your rig a few weeks before starting the trip to Alaska. You can't always detect problems ahead of time, but this gives you a fighting chance.

I asked to have my brakes and fluid checked. After the brakes went out on Suicide Hill on the Alaska Highway, I went back to the job list, and found that the fluid was checked, but not the actual brakes. That was clearly my fault, because I didn't spot it. There is a definite advantage to, "Making a list and checking it twice" with the mechanic. Brakes are, obviously, a major concern.

Wow! My brain is on overload (It doesn't take much). Continue to the next chapter for more Alaska/Canada suggestions. In the meantime,

## Remember

1) You do not <u>have</u> to get off the main highway to see the beauty and excitement of Canada and Alaska.

2) Be aware, listen, carry the essentials with you. Make sure you, and your entire vehicle, are in good working order.

3) Use common sense when it comes to your health, RV, dealing with people, and driving the roads.

4) Instead of griping because it's more expensive, or the roads aren't perfect, or it "isn't like in the lower 48," thank God it isn't. Appreciate the scenery, the people, and the different cultures. Relax! Enjoy!

Cassiar Highway, British Columbia

# ...MORE PREPARATION

## TLC (Tender Loving Care) anyone can do a lot to ward off PROBLEMS

### "Walk-a-bout"

Watch your mileage. This is not the time to neglect getting your oil and filter changed. Check the transmission oil, the brake fluid, and the air filter. If you travel gravel roads, you may want to take the air filter out once in a while, and tunk the dust out of it.

Check your engine oil every day. Thump your tires several times a day. I have gotten into the habit of doing a **"walk-a-bout"** around the RV and tag, almost every time I stop. It stretches my legs, and tells me if everything looks OK. I have discovered more than one dead dual (tire) I didn't know about.

Travel with your lights on, it may not help you see, but you will be more easily seen.

### Bathing your baby

Even when you are traveling the main roads, you may have a few miles of dusty, dirty, road construction. If you are driving gravel roads during dry weather, expect mucho dust. If it rains, expect mucho mud. Some gravel roads may be impassable. Calcium chloride is sometimes used for dust control. Your RV will occasionally need a bath. RV washes are listed in the Milepost, or advertised on highway signs. I used a pressure wash for the first time, and it worked great. A portable unit was set up in Hyder, Alaska. For $1 a foot, they did the work, and a better job than I could do.

### How should I protect my vehicle?

I have named the elaborate rock guard on the front of my motorhome, *Overkill*. It would have been perfect twenty years ago, but no longer needed to the extent it was then. Most people limit their guards to protecting the headlights and grill. I haven't driven the haul road (Dalton Highway), but I have driven almost all the other major gravel roads. If you share them with trucks, you are more apt to get chips. I have *Overkill* and I still got a chip (in Mexico). It flew right over the rock guard. You can never be fully protected.

If you have a full-length mustache on the back of your RV or truck, or mud flaps, that will help protect your trailer or tag. Most shields I see for RVs and tags, are plastic covers, or screens made of PVC pipe and wire mesh, or hardware cloth. Just for pulling, fasten carpeting over the complete front of your tag.

You might also consider protection over the cabover window, if you are driving a truck camper, or Class C motorhome.

The Sprinter and *Overkill*

## Safety Devices

Propane sensors, smoke alarms, and flat-tire detectors, are great safety devices. Tire alarms should be on both RV and tag. They let you know when a tire has blown or gone flat. A flat dual tire, is a fire waiting to happen. I know. I check my tires often, but I have found some heavy-duty blue smoke a couple of times, because I didn't realize a dual had met its demise.

### Should I take my tow vehicle?

I didn't take the Little Lynx, my tow vehicle. Many people take tags because they set up in campgrounds, and drive the tow everywhere. I'm spoiled. Because I choose to explore washboard, bumpy roads, to out-of-the-way places, where the Sprinter has better clearance than the Little Lynx, I like driving the motorhome. If I have the Sprinter with me, I always have its convenience and safety, and I can choose to stay a day or a week. It is pretty much a matter of personal choice.

### Where can I...
### Dump sewage--Fill with water--Get propane

The Milepost magazine has this information, or check at information centers.

Think ahead about dumping and filling needs. Running out of propane is only a problem, if it is the middle of the night, forty miles beyond nowhere. It is available in most towns. Keep track of your gauges.

Some towns, such as Dawson City and Homer, have public water and dump stations. Gas stations advertise them. Some are free; others charge a fee. Gas stations usually offer the service free, if you get a fill-up of fuel.

If you are off-season, the facilities may not be available because of the weather. Give yourself leeway. The Fred Meyer store in Soldotna is kind enough to have overnight RV parking, and a free dump station and water. (Buy something if you take advantage of their amenities.)

The information centers are only open from June through August, but people are friendly (if you're friendly). All you need to do is open your mouth and ask. If the first person can't answer your question, they'll likely point you to someone who can.

If you get lost as much as I do, this is really important.

### How do I get there?

People with limited time, fly into Anchorage, rent an RV, and make "the loop," seeing the main attractions. This is OK, but you miss the beauty and excitement of Canada, and a whole lot of Alaska.

Those who do not want to drive their big rigs, or subject a new RV to trip rigors, fly in and rent, or buy a truck and camper to make the trip.

RVing by ferry is a great way to get to Alaska. If possible, drive one way, and ferry the other. Ferrying both ways leaves out some interesting country.

Should you decide to use the Alaska State Ferry system,

### MAKE YOUR RESERVATIONS MONTHS IN ADVANCE!

Marine Access Routes: SOUTHEAST Ferry System: Alaska State Ferries leave from Bellingham, Washington, **or** Prince Rupert, British Columbia. The Ferry from Bellingham **does not stop in Canada**. It goes to Skagway/Haines, Alaska. The Alaska State Ferry from Prince Rupert, BC, also goes to Skagway/Haines.

You cannot use your RV as a base, while you are on the ferry. Cabins can be rented, or reclining chairs are available in an enclosed observation deck, or semi-open solarium. Except for the short distance between Skagway and Haines, I have not used the ferry system with my RV. It was a pleasant experience when I did. The big blue canoes are very nice.

### Driving to Alaska is a long way, but don't let distances intimidate you, they are just roads!

Roads must be driven mile by mile with a smile, just like anywhere else. If you look at the map from the Washington border, through Canada, and to and through Alaska, you will see two distinct loops. One loop begins at Prince George, and follows the Alaska Highway, eventually coming back along the Cassiar to Prince George. The other major loop is from Tok, Alaska, to Fairbanks, Anchorage, and back to Tok. I've made a list of places where you might make decisions.

# POSSIBLE ROUTES AND DECISIONS

In the massive amounts of material you have gleaned thus far, you will have descriptions of roads: gravel or paved, narrow or four-lane (well, occasionally), etc.

**Decision time: Prince George, British Columbia, Canada**
North to the Alaska Highway via Dawson Creek on Highway #97 **or**
**Alternate:** Highway #29 along Peace River, Hudson's Hope, connecting with Alaska Highway north of Dawson Creek
**Alternate:** West to the Cassiar Highway (Route 37)

**Decision time: Watson Lake**
West to Whitehorse and Skagway
**Alternate:** to Dawson City via The Campbell Highway

**Decision time: Whitehorse**
Alaska Highway to Tok
**Alternate:** North to Dawson City via Klondike Loop (Hwy #2), Top of the World and Taylor Highway to Tok
**Alternate loop trip:** Klondike Highway to Skagway

**Decision time: Skagway**
Return to Alaska Hwy to Whitehorse
**Alternate:** Ferry to Haines/Haines Junction, Alaska Hwy to Tok
**Alternate:** Ferry to Haines/Haines Junction. Complete Golden Circle Loop. To Whitehorse and north To Dawson City

**Decision time: Dawson City**
Cross Yukon River to Top of the World Highway, Taylor Hwy, Tok
**Alternate:** North to Inuvik, NW Territories (Must return same way)

**Decision time: Taylor Highway**
Continue on to Chicken and Tok
**Alternate:** To Eagle, Alaska (Must return same way)

---

**Tok:** Whether you choose to leave Tok on the Alaska Hwy or Glenn Hwy, either direction will eventually take you around the Alaska loop (with alternate side trips) and return you to Tok. My personal preference is Fairbanks first.

---

**Decision time: Tok**
Alaska Hwy to Delta Junction (Official end of the Alaska Highway) and continue to **Fairbanks** via Richardson Highway
Glenn Highway (Glenn cutoff) to **Glennallen** then Anchorage or Valdez

**Decision time: Fairbanks**
Parks Hwy to Denali Nat'l Pk/ Anchorage, Kenai Peninsula
**Alternate:** Dalton Highway to Prudhoe Bay along Trans-Alaska

Pipeline (Must return same way)

**Decision time: Glennallen**
Continue Glenn Highway to Palmer/Anchorage
**Alternate:** Richardson Hwy to Valdez (Must return same way or ferry to wherever)
**Alternate** from Richardson Hwy: Edgerton Hwy to Chitina, McCarthy, Kennicott (Must return same way)

**Decision time: Palmer:**
Parks Hwy to Denali Nat'l Park and Fairbanks and back to Tok
**Alternate:** Glenn Hwy south to Anchorage and Kenai Peninsula

**Kenai Peninsula:**
Anchorage: Seward Highway to Hope/and or Seward
  Sterling Highway to Homer Spit
  Back to Anchorage
**Decision Time:** To Fairbanks/Tok
  To Glenallan/Tok

Now we've completed the "loop" one direction or the other, and we are back at Tok. If you came up the Alaska Highway, now is decision time to go to Dawson City, or continue south on the Alaska Highway until just before Watson Lake.

**Decision Time:** Junction 37 - Continue Alaska Highway south
  Alternate: Cassiar Highway south to Yellowhead Highway

**Decision Time:** Turn to Stewart/Hyder at Meziadin Jct.
  (Must return same way)

**Decision time:** Yellowhead Highway
  West to Prince Rupert
  East to Prince George and home (Depending on where that is)

**Decision time:** North of Cache Creek on Hwy #97
  Continue on #67 and cross at Sumas, WA.
  **Alternate:** #99 west to Vancouver (15% grades) and cross border at Blaine, Washington

## Pets

Are you going to take Little Lulu along? Again, I'm not saying this to scare you, but you are heading for the North, where wild animals are "king." Any animal, but especially **little** dogs and cats, are vulnerable to eagles and bears. Don't let them **roam** outside. Keep them on a leash and stay with them. Don't leave them outside on a leash by themselves. Keep an eye on your pets.

Properly tag and license your pet. This will help if it does get lost. Does your pet get motion sickness? You should stop often to stretch your own legs, and it is good for your pet, too.

If you take pets aboard the ferry system, they must stay in the RV. You are allowed feeding and exercising times with them, throughout the day.

## "Lions and Tigers and BEARS, Oh My!"
### (Well, maybe not lions and tigers)

The North country is bear country. There are three kinds, but you are most likely to see black or brown bears (hopefully, from a distance).

> **They are wild!**
> **They are dangerous!**
> **Their presence is not to be taken lightly!**
> **They do not like surprises!**

I don't say that to scare you so much as to make you cautious. Bears are majestic and exciting. They are curious and intelligent. They will **usually avoid** people. If you are hiking, make your presence known with singing, speaking loudly, or using bear bells. If possible, travel in a group. **Do not ever get between a baby and its mother.** Always look to see if there are more babies. They frequently have multiple births.

If you are in a vehicle, and you see any animal by the side of the road, take its picture from inside. Do not get out of your vehicle. Do not send your children (or spouse, <sub>unless his insurance is paid up</sub>) to stand by the bear for a picture (If you think that is obvious advice -- I have seen people make some really stupid moves to get a picture).

### Do not give them food.
### "A fed bear is a dead bear"

Do not be guilty of helping them become dependent on human food (or even food not so human, like mine).

Now, God forbid you should ever come nose-to-nose with a bear. Nose to nose **is** unlikely since black bears are five feet in length (150 - 250 pounds), and brown bears are seven to nine feet in length (400 - 600 pounds). You can imagine how tall that makes them when they are standing on their hind legs...as in **v e r y  t a l l**!

Chances are quite good you never will, but as you will see while reading this book, there is **always a possibility**. What do we teach our children about possibilities? Know what to do, **just in case.**

### DO NOT SCREAM AND RUN!
### YOU CANNOT OUTRUN A BEAR.

> **IF YOU START RUNNING, IT WILL CHASE YOU**
> **BECAUSE IT THINKS YOU ARE DINNER.**
> **DO NOT CLIMB A TREE**
> **BLACK BEARS CAN EASILY CLIMB TREES**
> **GRIZZLIES CAN SHAKE YOU OUT OF THEM**

**As in all emergencies
(and this is classified as an emergency),
remain calm.**

Let the bear know you are human by speaking in a normal voice. Wave your arms to help it identify you. If it cannot tell what you are, it may come closer, or stand on its hind legs to get a better look or smell. A standing bear is **usually** curious, not threatening. Back away slowly. If the bear follows, stop and hold your ground. (By then, I will have fainted.)

Continue waving your arms and talking. If it gets too close, raise your voice and be more aggressive (Yeah, right!). Bang pots and pans; use any type of noisemaker. Never imitate bear sounds or make a high-pitched squeal. (Scream in bass??)

Now we get down to the nitty gritty.

---
**If a BROWN bear
(grizzly -- the one with the hump behind its head),
attacks you,
fall to the ground and play dead.** (As if I'd be playing!)

---

Lie flat on your stomach, or curl up in a fetal position, with your hands behind your neck. **Usually** (that word is used a lot), a brown bear will break off its attack, once it feels you are no longer a threat. Remain motionless for as long as possible. If you move, a brown bear may return and renew its attack, and you must again play dead.

---
**If you are attacked by a BLACK bear,
fight back vigorously.**

---

Don't think I am not serious because my asides are cavalier. I can do that because I am safe behind my computer, inside my cozy home on wheels. One time, a woman became quite upset with me, because I was RVing alone through the wilderness and thus, hiking alone at times. She was quite indignant, and said, "Just what **would** you do if you were confronted with a bear?" I answered her in one extremely truthful word, "Defecate!"

My biggest fear is that with my advanced CRS, I would forget which color of bear I should fight, and for which I should curl up and pretend to be dead. I think the second would be an unpicked choice, and I wouldn't be pretending!

Living in an RV, doesn't mean you can be a careless camper. **Never leave anything outside**, anywhere (even in a campground) **that even has the smell of food on it**. They sometimes shred coolers. I have seen only a few bears, however, packing can openers, so you are relatively safe, in the confines of your tin can on wheels.

**Moose**

**Moose are also dangerous.** Moose cause more injuries in Alaska each year than bears. An Alaska moose is the world's largest member of the deer family, tipping the scales at up to one-half ton, and standing over seven feet tall at the shoulder. As with all animals, they are extremely protective of their young. **Do not get between them.**

As I said somewhere in the book, if you share the path with a moose, you are the one that needs written permission to proceed. They sometimes attack vehicles. Don't do anything to try to intimidate them.

> **As always, remember, we are the visitors.**
> **This is their land.**
> **Look, laugh, photograph, but leave alone.**

There, now that you are completely discombobulated, let's continue. Just remember that I am the world's biggest wimp, so if I can make three trips to Alaska and manage, you can, too (Of course my hair is already silver). Animal information, and how to cope with them, is available at all information places.

As a bumper sticker in Wenatchee, Washington, put it, "**One thorn of experience, is worth a whole wilderness of warning.**"

## Miscellaneous Tips

If you aren't happy with where you are parking for an activity, and you have no choice, leave a light on, play a radio talk show, leave of the drapes closed.
Always be aware of your surroundings.
Never display your money in public. You never know who is watching.
If you don't have a deadbolt lock on your RV, put one on.
Do not leave anything valuable within sight from a window.
If you sleep with the window open, wedge a bar in the track, leaving the opening small. Sleep with your head at the opposite end.
If you use an ATM machine, find one that is inside a business, or in a well-lit area. Hide Your PIN number as you enter it into the ATM. Be exceptionally aware of your surroundings.
Park with your RV door toward the business you are going into.
Lock your RV when you are filling with gasoline.
Shut off all propane before you go into a station to fill with gasoline or propane
Never open your door until you know who's there. Look through the window. If you still don't know who it is, talk through the window.
Extra rolls of paper towels are great for stuffing in places to eradicate a rattle, or protect something fragile (You wouldn't take anything too fragile, would you?)
Have your keys already in your hand, and the right key ready, as you reach your RV or tag. Lock the doors once you are inside.

## EXPENSES
My expenses: April 26 through September, 1996
Mileage from border to border: 9,612 miles

| | |
|---|---|
| Gasoline: | $2,243 |
| Major Maintenance: (tire & brake) | $1,340 |
| Regular Maintenance | $ 627 |
| Camping fees: | $ 238 |
| Annual Alaska State Park camping sticker: | $ 100 |
| Propane/sewer: | $ 215 |

Propane is high because it was cooler up there
I was there early and late
I like to be warm
Relatively little of this was sewer, a couple of dollars occasionally. I took advantage of going to gas stations that offered a dump station free with gasoline purchase.

## Choices

| | |
|---|---|
| Food/restaurants | Do you want a little bill or a big bill -- eat in or eat out? Top-o-the-Mark Vs Grizzly's Cafe |
| Entertainment | Two hour, l/2 day, all day, two day excursions; night life in Anchorage; Photo journey??? |
| Admission fees/tours | Free museum, hike, scenery, floor show, day cruise, flightseeing??? |
| Parking/Ferries | Big blue canoe ride or drive; small ferries are free (Across Yukon/Mackenzie/Peel) All-day parking, or tour and park in their lot |
| Laundry | Don't do it in Dawson or Eagle -- if possible, wait for bigger towns. |
| Film/processing | You could wait until you get back, but if you're there long, you may want to see what you have, and ID them. Do this in a bigger city. |
| Souvenirs | Will this excite you as much when you get home and start dusting it? Do you really want your granddaughter to have a fur bikini or your grandson, an Ulu knife? |
| Misc. expenses | Postage/telephone/newspapers--why? |

All your expenses except gasoline and maintenance, are subject to the choices you make.

## CROSSING BORDERS

They ask different questions each time I **cross the border**. This time, the border guard asked if I had firearms, fruit, plant materials, and what route I was taking north.

I have heard a lot of grumbling about crossing the border into Canada.

On one occasion, the guard asked me the same questions over and over. He didn't seem to believe my solo traveling or my destination point. I haven't figured out yet, why he thought that I was so suspicious. He had someone come to check the inside of the Sprinter, but she only gave it a cursory glance as she walked through, and asked, "What is he looking for?" I figured if they didn't know, I didn't know.

Don't get smart with them or kid around. They have a job to do, and they usually do it without smiles or a hint of personality. As innocent as we might be of breaking the rules, they often deal with the seamier side of humanity.

### Credit Cards and Cash

**Most bigger** businesses throughout Canada and Alaska, now accept major credit cards. The thing I appreciate about using credit cards, is that you receive the rate of exchange, for the day you are making the purchase. You are not subject to a business giving you only 15% or 20% of a 30+% exchange rate.

Carry Canadian cash with you. Again, **most** places accept credit cards, but some places are just plain too small. Exchange your money at a national bank when you cross the border.

Carry US cash with you, too. Some of the smaller places in Alaska don't take credit cards, and they certainly don't all have banks or ATM machines.

### Laws (1997)

**You must cross the borders when they are open, and some of them are not open twenty-four hours. Watch your timing. It is illegal to cross without going through customs.**

**Remember that purchases legally made in one country, may be illegal in the other. Check out hand-crafted items, such as ivory, seal products, feathers, whalebone, fur, etc., before buying them.**

#### GOING INTO CANADA

Passports are not required for United States Citizens to enter Canada, or return to US.
Proof of citizenship must be carried:
    Birth or baptismal certificate, with photo ID, such as driver's license.
    Proof of residence may be required.
Minors: In addition to above, must have notarized letter of consent by
    both parents or guardians.

**MEDICINE:** Properly identify any medicine containing narcotics or habit-forming drugs, and carry the prescription or doctor's statement, as proof that you are using them under a doctor's direction.

## EXEMPTIONS: Keep your sales receipts.

United States: **If you have been in Canada 48 hours or more**, you may have $400 US duty-free exemption (Every 30 days). There are limitations on alcohol and tobacco.

Canada: You are allowed necessary personal effects, duty free. You may have, duty-free, certain amounts of alcoholic beverages and tobacco (40 Imperial ounces of alcoholic beverages, 12 oz bottles of beer or ale, 200 cigarettes, 50 cigars and 2.2 pounds of manufactured tobacco). You are allowed gas to a normal tank capacity of the vehicle. (Gas is sold by the litre: 1 US gallon = 3.78 litres.)

## GIFTS:

Canada: Bona fide gifts may be imported by visitors, duty and tax-free, provided the value of each gift, does not exceed $60 (Canadian) and the gifts do not consist of tobacco products, alcoholic beverages or advertising material.

## SPORTING GOODS AND EQUIPMENT:

Canada: Visitors may take the usual personal sporting goods and equipment, i.e., boats, motors, camping equipment, cameras, TVs, etc., into Canada by declaring them on entry.
   In RVs, we have TVs, VCRs, computers, etc. It wouldn't hurt to list everything, especially large items such as boats, motors, golf equipment, etc., along with the approximate values, or have the receipts.

## PETS:

Canadians: Dogs and cats, over the age of three months, need a health certificate signed by a licensed veterinarian that clearly describes the animal, and declares the animal has been vaccinated against rabies within the past 36 months. The animal must be healthy, under control, and on a leash at the time of entry.
Americans: Rabies vaccination certificate issued within the past six months.

## SEAT BELTS:

**Required** for all passengers **in Alaska, Canadian Provinces, or Territories**. Child restraint laws vary according to age or weight. Check it out.

## TAXES:

Alaska: No statewide tax. Cities and boroughs may levy a sales tax up to 6%, plus special taxes on goods and services.

British Columbia: Provincial sales tax is 7%. Also, room & lodge taxes.

Northwest Territories: No territorial sales tax.

Yukon Territory: No territorial tax.

## FIREARMS:

Canada: **All firearms must be declared** when you enter Canada. If undeclared firearms are found, they will be seized, and possibly criminal charges filed. **This includes possible seizure of the vehicle in which they are carried.**

Visitors are prohibited from transporting handguns through customs, unless specificially authorized by the Bureau of Alcohol, Tobacco, and Firearms. Other firearms are allowed if they have legitimate sporting or recreational use. All types of firearms must be transported unloaded. They must be kept out of sight and locked up.

Firearms fall into three categories, non-restricted, restricted, and prohibited weapons. The list of rules and regulations for firearms, is as long as your long gun. I am not going to list them here. If you have weapons of any kind, or have question, send for the booklet through Revenue Canada.

In addition, **they will not allow mace, pepper spray, or stun guns**. The long list of no-nos in this category also requires that you get the booklet, if you intend to carry such things. It would take me four years to list them, and I don't even know what some of them are (nor want to!).

The Milepost has comprehensive information on border rules, and information is also available on the internet. (See Resources)

## PLANTS, FRUITS, VEGETABLES:

Some fresh fruits and vegetables commonly grown in Canada, may be taken away from you. I had to throw a lovely new bag of potatoes into Canada's trash bin. Think twice before you stock up previous to crossing the border.

**House plants** (rolling houses, too), supposedly do not need to be declared.

## VEHICLES:

Registration is a must, or a contract, if it is rented. Non-Resident Inter-Provincial Motor Vehicle Liability Insurance Card from your insurance
    company. (It is proof of financial responsibility.)
    Trip accident policy recommended

Apparently at least a few people towing tags across British Columbia have run amuck of the authorities. The following information is straight off the presses and out of a letter from Claire B. Eraut, Executive Director of Vehicle Policy and Standards Department of the Province of British Columbia as of April, 1997.

Until recently, towed motor vehicles had to be equipped with coordinated brakes and an emergency breakaway device if the weight of the towed vehicle exceeded 3,087 pounds. In the context of this Ministry's primary commitment to the safety of British Columbia roads, the Motor Vehicle Branch reviewed requirements in comparable jurisdictions across North America. It was subsequently determined that this regulation should be changed to more accurately reflect the safety requirements and travel conditions facing motorhomes that tow motor vehicles in this province.

**The British Columbia regulation change, which took effect on March 26, 1997, increases the weight threshold to 4,400 pounds for motor vehicles towed by motorhomes.**

This means that coordinated brake control and an emergency breakaway device may only be required if the laden gross weight of the towed vehicle is 4,400 pounds or greater. However, the new regulation adds a requirement that any towed motor vehicle weighting 40% or more of the motorhome's gross vehicle weight rating must be equipped with coordinated brakes and an emergency breakaway device.

In conjunction with the new 40% weight ratio, the higher weight threshold of 4,400 pounds for towed vehicles achieves an enhanced balance of safety and mobility objectives, while corresponding more closely with towed vehicle requirements in jurisdictions with similar highway travel conditions.

## **GST TAX:**

This 7% Goods and Services Tax is applied to most items and services in Canada. Non-Canadians may apply for this GST rebate on some items.

**You qualify for the 7% tax refund if**:

You are not a resident of Canada

Have your **original** receipts (Credit card slips are not acceptable)

Your total refund claim is a minimum of Canadian $14 for each tax you are claiming; for eligible goods, each individual receipt has to show a minimum of Canadian $3.50 for each tax you're claiming. You can apply for cash refund up to a maximum of $500 Canadian.

**The refund doesn't cover**:

Restaurants/meals
Tobacco products
Transportation
Alcoholic beverages
Certain services (entertainment, parking, shoe repair, etc.)
Auto repairs (but it does cover parts)
And no such luck -- it does not cover the biggies: food, camping, cruising, rentals, or fuel.

Does that thoroughly confuse you? Well, don't panic. Keep your receipts; the GST tax is listed on it. If you don't understand it, they are most gracious in helping you. You can claim your refund at any participating Canadian duty-free shop. You can also do it by mail with the appropriate application. There are many stipulations, and you need to get a brochure with all the details, so you will know what is covered and what is not. (Resources)

OK, I'm brain weary again. I'll mention other things as we get "on down the road." Hey, if you can't keep up with me, I'll meet you in a month or so for milk and home-made pie, at the Seaview Cafe in Hope, Alaska.

## Drive with your lights on at all times

**Boarding the Blue Canoe**

# BEAUTIFUL BRITISH COLUMBIA

I have crossed borders at Oroville (Osoyoos, BC), Sumas (Huntingdon, BC), and Blaine (Vancouver, BC), in Washington. It was the most quiet at Oroville but not bad at Sumas. It was a zoo at Blaine since it is near Vancouver; however, it was noon, and I usually cross as early in the morning as possible. Sometimes the chaos is part of the fun.

Many routes lead to Prince George, British Columbia. This is the jumping off place, and decision time, for anyone going to the Alaska Highway via Dawson Creek from the south. Anyone coming from the East through Edmonton, would likely go directly to Dawson Creek. Don't be confused by the two Dawsons. Dawson Creek is in British Columbia. Dawson City is in Yukon Territory, 1,195 miles farther northwest.

A number of interesting attractions are in lower BC, but I have rarely looked them up. I can see this area sometime when I am not going the long distance to Alaska. If you have plenty of time, and you want to see everything as you travel, read The Northwest Milepost or the CAA (Canadian Automobile Association) TourBook. They will give you all the information you need.

Since I had traveled on the usual roads going north and south on other trips, this time I took alternate routes wherever they presented themselves. The first one was going north from Sumas to Mission, British Columbia, and turning right on Highway #7, eventually meeting up with Trans-Canada Highway #1, near Hope.

Mission was having spring, big time. Flowers, bushes, and trees were in full bloom. Since it was April, and I was traveling north, I looked and sniffed and enjoyed, knowing I would see little of spring again until June. Highway #7 is a leisurely route following the north side of the Frazer River. Both #7 and #1 to Hope go through beautiful farming country. I had every intention of stopping in Hope on my way back, to see the wooden chainsaw sculptures the town is famous for, but I returned a different route. Ah, next time.

I was on a decided high after crossing the border. Surely the clouds were playing hopscotch in the blue skies as I drove through the Frazer River Canyon. Cement barriers kept the road out of the river, and spring landslides off the road. A fresh dusting of snow crowned the mountaintops. The afternoon warmth added more snow melt to falls already gushing down every gully, gap and crevice.

At Old Alexandra Bridge, I hiked over the Frazer River near Hell's Gate, the narrowest part of the canyon. This beautiful old rainbow bridge is only for walking across, since the new bridge was built in 1962. Giant logs and debris swirled in runoff turbulence, a little unnerving with giant cracks at one end of the bridge. It looked like it was separating from the riverbank.

Hiking unknown territory is a little like driving down a new road. A short hike becomes "over the hill and around the bend" to see where the path leads. This led to a gigantic landslide and washout. On the way back, I found a Jeep parked with its lights on. It had locked doors. I hoped someone wasn't hiking long enough to return to a dead battery.

Canada's provincial parks are great. I sometimes pull into campgrounds to see what they offer, even if I'm not staying. I took advantage of dumping and filling with water at Skihist Provincial Park. Firewood is always provided but it is usually in large pieces. Some parks have a fee; some are free; others are on the honor system.

The warmth of mid-day drew me to an early stop at Goldpan Provincial Park on the Thompson River. After collecting tinder and kindling, I sat beside a crackling fire and enjoyed the surrounding scenery. The trains running occasionally on the other side of the river, weren't obnoxious, just interesting, perhaps because I was in a state of euphoria.

It was really cold in the night. Flannel sheets kept me cozy and nobody, except God, knew I was sleeping past 6 a.m. I prayed for everybody in the world, so I could stay in my comfortable warm bed a little longer, without feeling guilty. Guilt does strange things.

I wear three sets of clothing in a day's time. I dress for the day, change into ratty clothes for dirty chores, and wear still others for around smoky fires. Three pairs of shoes also got a workout. I was breaking in hiking boots, that I wound up wearing almost the entire trip. A pair of scroungy tennis shoes lounged by the door for around the campfire. Black boots were at the ready so I could look like something other than a bag lady, if I wanted to dress up. Dress up, meaning a pair of clean jeans and a reasonably unratty sweatshirt, or a long skirt and top for church. They aren't too formal in the North country (neither are most full-time RVers).

A train came along, as I stepped out the door for a walk. The engineer opened his window to wave at me. It was a nice communication for 7 a.m. in a strange place. Bouquets of growing daisies made me aware of spring wonders. Snow plows coming south just made me wonder.

It was a magnificent first full day in Canada. Orchards hovered on the edge of the canyon, along the Thompson River Valley's curvy scenic route. Smoke shivered and curled from cabin chimneys into the cold morning air. Cowpaths wandered through the meadows looking for cows. A tiny church awaited Sunday. The wind tilted at windmills. One white-paddled windmill, more patriotic than the rest, proudly sported a red Canadian maple leaf in its center.

A hitchhiker gave me a beautiful smile. I waved. No way, Jose. On the other hand, if he had been a little more appealing -- say with gray hair and blue eyes. A caution sign warned of mountain sheep on the highway. Immediately beyond the curve, two sheep munched by the roadside. Obviously, they read signs in Canada, eh? I knew I was deep in Canada. I stopped at the Goldpanner Restaurant for breakfast, and the owner's sentences all ended with "eh?" I love it!

I turned north on Highway 97 at Cache Creek, and saw black plastic mesh tarps covering crops of North American Ginseng. I hadn't seen ginseng growing since a trip to Korea. A sign, "Cariboo Community Project," preceded miles of people clearing roadside debris.

Many towns along here were stagecoach stops. Their names reflect the distances along the Cariboo Wagon Road to the goldfields from Lillooet, i.e., 70 Mile House, 100 Mile House.

At Williams Lake, I paid $107 Canadian for gas at 57.9 per litre.

**Fuel stops (and rest areas, if the weather is bad) are a good time to clean your windshield and fill the windshield washer reservoir. While you're at it, wipe off your headlights, tail-lights, and reflectors.**

The sign over a deeply wrinkled, flashy red Mustang, said, "120 -- 0 in 3.1 seconds. Speed is killing us."

The animals are another reason to travel in early spring. A tiny colt tried out his newfound legs. Deer and moose-warning signs cropped up at about the same time. A horse ran down a hill with a long stick in his mouth, playing, like a dog.

Quesnel is a bustling community in historical Cariboo gold territory. The museum at the information center has the history and artifacts. I once met Santa Claus there! The town celebrates Billy Barker Days in

July every year, commemorating this Cornish miner's finding of the first gold in the rush of 1862.

This is a decision stop for an interesting side trip to Barkerville Provincial Historic Park, on Highway 26. Tours are available during the season, but it is a beautiful 102 mile round trip through Devil's Canyon and along the shores of Jack-of-Clubs Lake. It also passes Cottonwood House Provincial Park that includes a restored 1864 log roadhouse.

Barkerville is a restored Cariboo gold rush town. When I was there in 1992, CBS was shooting the TV special, Jack London's "Call of the Wild" with Ricky Schroeder. The park is open all year. The buildings and history are interesting, and the bakery has fresh goodies and coffee (even more interesting). During the season, costumed interpreters and street performers, add to the daily drama. It is worth a side trip.

The road to Barkerville also leads to Bowron Lakes Provincial Park, one place I'd like to kayak (when I find a partner...or a guide). It is a series of connecting lakes, creating a 72-mile, canoe-kayak loop trail.

Back on Highway 97, Cinema Second Hand advertised a free RV overnight. It is a general store with souvenirs, groceries, videos, new and used furniture. You name it; they've got it. Vic and Theresa Olson, the owners, provide overnight parking with picnic tables and firepits. Vic said he had provided free campsites for years and planned to upgrade them. I browsed several floors of nooks and crannies; but being a full-timer, I rented a video rather than buying something I had to store.

All I had were US funds, but he paid me the exchange rate. Most businesses take a percentage if you don't have their currency. Vic said he didn't think it was right when his fellow Canadians didn't give the rate of exchange. God bless him.

They are open every day from 9 to 9. He enjoys people and thinks it is fun offering something free. Of course, it is impossible for RVers to bypass browsing any more than I did.

Prince George is a city of 75,000, and the last really big one until you reach Fairbanks (85,000), or Anchorage (260,000). At this point, continue on Highway #97 to Dawson Creek, the beginning of the Alaska Highway, or turn west on Yellowhead Highway #16 and go north on the Cassiar (Highway #37). The Cassiar is a shorter route (123 miles), but it works well to go up one direction and return the other. For first-timers, I recommend Dawson Creek first (By then you'll have driven some of the rougher roads, and you'll think it is a breeze).

In 1992, I drove west to Prince Rupert, B.C. This city of 18,000 is a main port for the Alaska Marine Highway, along the Inside Passage. It is an alternate route with connections, rates, and descriptions, well documented in the Milepost. Some folks drive one direction, then return by ferry.

> The Alaska Marine Highway ferries are available between
> Prince Rupert, British Columbia, Canada
> and Skagway, Alaska
> or
> Between Bellingham, Washington, and Skagway, Alaska
> Alaska State Ferries leaving Bellingham, do not stop in Canada

**British Columbia Ferries provide service throughout the coast of British Columbia.**

I returned east to the Cassiar Highway, along the beautiful Skeena River and headed north. It was too early in the season. Almost everything was closed. At that time of year, the road wasn't in very good condition. Besides, I drove most of it in a blizzard and...I'll tell you about it when I bring you back down the Cassiar in the fall.

In 1996, leaving Prince George, I continued on Highway 97 (Also called John Hart Highway), toward Dawson Creek and the Alaska Highway. All the highways you'll be on are named after someone; but, they also have number names. It can be confusing.

This is a good time to tell you that I avoid cities like the plague, unless there is something within its limits that particularly calls to me. I prefer small towns, villages, and the country; therefore, my stories tend to cover those areas.

Gasoline was running consistently 57.9 or 58.9 per litre. I was seeing the first frozen lakes and ice-clogged streams. The rock and roll had begun. The bad spots were flagged. I knew from that point on, I would have to watch the road ahead of me.

Have you ever noticed how we North Americans always have the tallest, lowest, highest, sweetest, biggest, or mightiest? Mackenzie's population of 6,000 is no different; they think big. They have two claims to fame: North America's largest man-made reservoir at the south end of Lake Williston, and another, that I wanted to take with me.

The Latourneau Tree Crusher is the World's largest tree crusher. It is a big yellow hummer that weighs 1,175 tons (about the same as the Sprinter, loaded), and powered by two Cummins V12 Diesel engines. It was built especially for crushing trees and undergrowth beneath its massive rollers, to clear the flood plain, under what is now Lake Williston.   I envied its 1,880 gallon fuel capacity, but I suppose signing a VISA slip for filling it would bring on instant cardiac arrest. I envisioned my Latourneau Diesel Sprinter scaring little old ladies who pull in front of me going three miles an hour. On the other hand, now that I am one, I might have to revise that thinking.

Turning north again on Highway 97, I followed two small moving vans and a car who were traveling together, s l o w l y. I didn't really mind, since giant Cats lurked on every curve across Pine Pass and snail's pace driving was necessary. They were pushing aside mud and snow and building a new road.

> Another reminder, don't Tailgate! It is irritating to have someone chewing on your bumper, not to mention dangerous. If possible, pull over and let a tail-gator pass. Go and do likewise, if you have even a small train of vehicles behind you.

The neat thing about RVing is that after a spell of white-knuckle driving, you can stop in one of many pull-offs. My notes on April 30:

*Time for a coffee break. Took garbage out, and boy, is it cold out there. Sunshiny day, hot cup of coffee, bumpy roads, fantastic scenery, what more could I ask for, except maybe a moose, but please, God, not right in the center of the road, unless I see him first.*

It was thirty kilometers into Chetwynd when I saw the herd of buffalo. I had two thoughts, buffaloburgers, because I was hungry; and if I ran out of gasoline, I could become Buffalo Gal and ride one into town.

Let's see, if I guessed right, I had roughly seven gallons of gasoline times six miles per gallon. All right. I would have about a twenty-two mile leeway.

The gas pump wasn't working right. I kept the young lady company for the forty-five minutes it took her to pump gas into the Sprinter. She was from Russia. I noticed she didn't mind the bitter cold. She said that Pine Pass was a super highway that day, compared to what it was throughout the winter. Good grief.

When I commented that I hadn't seen many animals, she asked if I was a hunter. I said no. She pointed to the mountain above us and said they usually see lots of bear and moose up there. She said, "I won't tell that to a hunter, because one guide alone took sixty bear last year, and we have five guides in the area." It won't take long for them to disappear at that rate.

Since it would take me into new territory and cut off about thirty miles, my route this trip would turn onto Highway 29 at Chetwynd and follow the Peace River. I would later connect with the Alaska Highway north of Dawson Creek.

> **I forgot to tell you to take stock in Kodak or Fuji, as one of your preps for this trip.**

A major Kodak Moment is having your picture snapped in front of Milepost "0" at Tenth Street and Alaska Avenue in Dawson Creek. The Tourist Information Bureau, a restored railway station, and the Dawson Creek Station Museum, are in NAR Park near the traffic circle. Nearby is a favorite haunt, a restored wooden grain elevator turned into the Dawson Creek Art Gallery. It was rescued from demolition for one dollar and revamped to the tune of $250,000.

Often people spend a few days making sure everything on their RV is copacetic with a long trip ahead. This is also where the caravans usually gather their RV trip people.

Returning to my turn at Chetwynd onto the Hudson's Hope Loop route, many turnouts beckoned, but I stopped for lunch and a VCR movie on the shoreline of frozen Moberly Lake. Some confused Canada geese with ruffled feathers, wandered about looking for open water. I overheard one of them, "I told you so, Myrtle. We're too early. We could be..."

Many large deer herds roamed throughout the Peace River Valley. Individual deer grazed peacefully with horses or cows. This would not be a road to travel at night.

A side road led to the Peace Canyon Dam. At Hudson's Hope, it was a fifteen-mile drive off the loop, to the 600-foot high W. A. C. Bennett Dam, that holds up the eastern arm of Williston Lake. It is one of the largest earth-filled dam structures in the world, and Lake Williston is BC's largest body of fresh water. The "biggest and the largest" but alas, I can never see it all.

The Hudson Bay Company opened its first trading post at Hudson's Hope in 1805. That was well after the mammoths called it home. The museum, with the artifacts, fossils and the 11,600 year old mammoth tusk, was closed. Instead, I took pictures of the little log St. Peter's Anglican United Church next door. An automotive shop had a sign, "Grizzly Repairs." I'd like to see them repair a grizzly...or could it have referred to the results? Hmmm.

I thought I had found the perfect place to spend the night on a cliff above the river, well away from the road. There were trees and a place for a fire, but then I discovered a smelly deer carcass thrown over the edge. It was a little too fragrant for my taste.

A 10% grade took the Sprinter past some major washouts, to a nearly 3,000' elevation, with a magnificent view of the Peace River Valley and the snow-covered mountains.

Ah, we meet up again at the junction of Highway 29 and the Alaska Highway. Did you stop to see the (didn't I tell you about this tendency to hyperbolize?) World's Largest Glass Beehive in Fort St. John, north of Dawson Creek?

I stayed in a rest area for the night and woke up to several inches of snow. I stayed put until about ten o'clock. A snow plow came in and when he left, I followed. How much safer could I be? He turned around about three miles up the road! I ran in and out of heavy snow, according to the elevation I was driving. It was May 1, and shades of the Cassiar Highway and the blizzard I drove through on May Day in 1992. The weather wasn't my worst problem; the brakes were failing.

At Pink Mountain, the mechanic said the Sprinter might need brake fluid. He said the place to check it was up under the side of the motorhome, and he couldn't do it in that weather. I couldn't blame him for that, but I was just as sure the brake fluid reservoir was inside under the doghouse.

Alas, I wasn't going to argue with him, and it was against the law to put a gun to his head. He said he didn't know of a place I could get help before Fort Nelson. That was 143 miles away. I asked him if there were any really steep hills in between (since I didn't remember). He said the only bad one was about twelve miles ahead. He didn't tell me it was Suicide Hill. With hot coffee in hand, and a prayer on my lips, I took off.

The snowflakes were getting bigger. One great flake covered the entire windshield, not to mention the medium-sized flake behind the steering wheel. A truck flew by me, throwing rocks and just missing an oncoming car right off my bumper. Where is the World's Largest Tree Crusher when you need it?

Signs warned of dangerous curves, avalanches, and breaks in the pavement (as in, the pavement disappeared entirely). The wet gravel was slippery. A heavy snow sheet slowly slid off the roof, loading my windshield wipers to the point they were doing little work. Other than the slippery mud, curvy roads, steep hills, the blizzard, and my brakes going out, the Sprinter and I were cool. We maneuvered down Suicide Hill. I just hoped it wasn't a harbinger of things to come.

Obviously, I survived Suicide Hill, but by the time I saw the Buckinghorse River Lodge, I figured it was time for some C & C (company and coffee). Right here is a good time to share one of life's lessons.

> **If you find lemons in one place, drive down the road thirty miles and you just might find a lemon drop.**

Over a delicious cup of hot coffee, served by Dave. I shared the whimsical view of my day, thus far. He worried about my trying to make it all the way to Fort Nelson. "Why don't you let me look?" he said. As I thought, the reservoir was under the doghouse, in a very awkward spot that I couldn't have reached if my life depended on it (and it did!).

He used his own equipment and brake fluid. It was only a little low. As we walked by the hood, he asked if I had checked the engine oil. I guess he figured if the brake fluid was low, I hadn't checked anything else either. I can *reach* that.

He refused to allow me to pay for his time or the brake fluid. In the course of further conversation, he discovered I was a writer and wanted to see my three books. I bought coffee and postcards, and he bought a book (I tried to give it to him, but he refused). We both paid in Canadian, but somehow I think I got the best of that deal. I meet the nicest people. By the way, they also offer free camping for the night at Buckinghorse River Lodge. I looked at it as I pulled out. The sites were filled with deep snow.

Unfortunately, the brake light came back on. Fluid wasn't the problem. I continued to Fort Nelson.

At Trutch Mountain, the powers that be have eliminated the route to the top. At 4,134', it was the second highest summit on the Alaska Highway. As so much of the original road has been straightened, leveled, rerouted, or improved, so this mountain was bypassed. With the Sprinter in his brake-weary condition, I should have been grateful.

It's unreasonable, I know, but I feel that every curve that is straightened and every hill that is cut down, somehow takes away from the adventure of traveling it. Case in point, 132 curves were eliminated in one area between here and Fort Nelson. Certainly no one could drive it with an RV, if it hadn't been improved immensely since 1942, but hey, don't get carried away.

It was 4:30 by the time I drove into Fort Nelson, too late to get anyone to fix the brakes, even if they were so inclined. Now I'll share an RVing lesson with you.

> **Whenever I am in strange territory and I need repairs, I stop at a parts store, usually NAPA, for their recommendation of someone local.**

This has never failed me. They gave me two names. I hit the jackpot with Harry's Auto Repair, Ltd.

I figured the brakes would get fixed about three weeks from the following Tuesday. Smack me for being so negative. Harry Clark scheduled me in for 8 a.m. The shock must have been evident on my face. He said he keeps one bay open for people passing through. He gave me permission to park next to the shop for the night.

I cooked dinner and watched TV. The weather outside was frightful but the RV was cozy and delightful, at least until 2:30 a.m., when two youngsters banged on my door. Another lesson:

> **Don't ever open your door to anybody unless you know who it is.**

I opened the window a crack. They asked for a tomato. Several other kids were lurking in the shadows. I told them I had eaten my last tomato, they all should go home, and I slammed the window shut. When I didn't act frightened or rise to their bait, apparently it discouraged them. They left. Another lesson:

> **Park so you can move forward, in case you need to make a fast getaway.**

Harry and crew began work at 8 a.m. I stayed in my office and worked. The day warmed considerably. Except for buying a few needed items, I stayed in the Sprinter.

Every once in a while, one of the guys would knock on the door and show me what needed replacing, or tell me what they were doing. By 4:00, they had replaced one drum completely; replaced pads, rear shoes, and seals; cleaned my windshield and wiper blades (he said I didn't need new ones), and declared me roadworthy once more. Also a spring had lost its clamp, and he showed me where the spring had rubbed against the tire.

They fixed that, too.

Since I knew I would be leaving the territory that afternoon, I requested a test drive, with Harry as my passenger. Wow! I had brakes. I didn't realize how bad they had gotten. When I pulled up to let him out, he said, "You know how to handle this thing pretty well, don't you?" I considered that a high compliment.

The bill, $936.95, translated to $693.02 US. On my return to the Canadian border the end of September, I received the entire GST tax back.

In my defense, several months before I left for Alaska, on my list to be checked, were the brakes and the brake fluid. It was my fault for not asking, but only the brake *fluid* was checked, not the brakes. Lesson:

> **Start making a list and checking it twice...**
> **once when you take your RV in to be fixed,**
> **and once when you get it back.**

It will make a difference in whether your trip is naughty or nice.

An interesting side trip might have been visiting the chopsticks manufacturing company, just outside of Fort Nelson. They produce six million pairs of chopsticks a day. What an unusual place to find chopsticks manufactured. You need an appointment for a tour and since I didn't have one, I was out of luck.

The next hundred miles didn't disappoint me. The rugged, jagged peaks of the Rocky Mountains were smothered in snow. Streams breaking loose from their icy shackles, were making their way through deep mounds of snow and ice in the valleys.

Drunken sailor-type animal tracks wandered across an ice-covered lake. Caution signs warned of caribou, but the tracks were empty. They don't read as well as deer.

I drove in and out of paved highway and gravel road. Did I mention steep and winding, my favorite kind? The Sprinter groaned a couple of times in the soft dirt. The Cats were busy again, reworking the road and rescuing it from the ravages of winter.

Summit Lodge advertised grizzlyburgers. My stomach growled, and I looked forward to a treat. The lodge, the highest point on the Alaska Highway at 4,250 feet, was closed tighter than a drum. The provincial campgrounds were sleeping in deep snow.

It was extremely cold hiking near the stream at 113 Creek Provincial Campground (more of a rest stop next to the highway), where I parked for the night. I thought I was going to have it to myself, but before I went to sleep, a motorhome and a truck camper pulled in.

I love getting up in the early morning. Actually, that isn't true. I like *being* up in the early morning. The physical act of *getting* out of a warm, cozy nest, is questionable. In this case, I had help. It came about 3 a.m. in the form of another adventurer off to see the world. This traveler was tiny compared to humans, and carried his own warmth on his back. He wasn't an animal activist; his coat was genuine mouse fur.

Although I'm usually a friendly sort, I draw the line at visitors in the middle of the night. Having had major experiences of this type previously, the wee scrambling sounds in my rolling mansion brought a whimper to my lips and a groan, "Oh, no, not again." I prayed that I was wrong, that I had an overactive imagination instead.

Finally, I got out of bed, turned on the light, and there he was, in the middle of the motorhome. We stared at each other. He moved toward me. Now, I am this fearless, brave, I-am-woman type traveler, right? Wrong! When he headed toward me, I screamed and climbed up on my bed. There was no way I was going to take a chance he would run across my bare feet. When he disappeared, I put on my hiking boots, and went out in the frigid cold to fetch the mousetraps from the hold.

He avoided my traps, and continued to make so much noise, I wondered if he was accompanied by a herd of elephants, but then I concluded it was more than one mouse in my house. I filled a wastebasket half way with water and pasted some cheese on one side, posted a "Ye Olde Swimming Hole" sign, and hoped the whole gang would go for a swim. Fat chance. By 4:45 it was getting light. Since I couldn't sleep, I took off.

Despite everything, it was a gorgeous morning. The sun painted the mountain peaks with pink frosting. The sheep, caribou and moose were hiding, probably because of the deep snow. I followed the Toad River until it turned. I traveled on alone, until I reached Muncho Lake. It was no surprise that it was frozen.

This has to be one of the most beautiful areas I have ever seen, in any season. The elevation here is almost 2,700' with the mountains above it ascending to 7,000'. The road barely has room between the lake and the cliffs. When the lake is clear of ice, it is an incredible turquoise color. Given the terrain, it isn't surprising that it is avalanche country. I parked to use a litter barrel, and a minor landslide scattered rocks across the road. I got out of there.

I hadn't caught a mouse yet, but as I rearranged the trap under the bed pedestal, my flashlight beam caught him staring at me. He was blatant and I told him so. Just because I jumped the night before, was no sign I was going to continue being a wimp.

Major beauty doesn't stop at Muncho Lake. It continues. That morning, six or seven caribou ran across the road. I preferred them to a belligerent mouse.

With no traffic to annoy, I stopped in the middle of the Liard River Bridge. Ice chunks floated between thick ice banks, extending several feet into the river. The owner of the Liard River Lodge, said the ice had broken up with great rumbling and drama the night before.

Over coffee, she told me they were trying to sell the lodge. I fell in love with the lodge and the Liard River, and couldn't understand their giving it up; but then, I hadn't dealt with tourists for eight years. I relayed my Mickey Mouse tale to her, hoping to find peanut butter in the small store, but their inventory was depleted. She gave me two peanut butter packets, usually given out with breakfast toast.

I returned to the motorhome. A mouse was in the trap. Ha! He was a big hummer, almost the size of that World's Largest Tree Crusher. In case he wasn't the only one, I smeared peanut butter on top of the cheese for good measure, and in sadistic delight. They can't resist peanut butter.

One place you must never pass by is Liard Hot Springs Provincial Park. Usually, moose are everywhere, last time even *in* my campsite. I must have parked on a moose trail, because he was there the next morning, too. It is at least a quarter-mile walk along a wide boardwalk to the first pool. Moose frequently feed in the wetlands nearby, but nary a moose showed his hide this time.

The hotsprings are heavenly. Alpha pool is the first one, more like a widened stream. Beta pool, a quarter-mile farther through the woods, is larger and deeper, with a view of the mountains. Another boardwalk leads to the hanging gardens. Spring plants were tiny, and nothing was blooming yet. A little snow here and there, had survived the warmth.

Both pools have change houses and decks. Long wooden benches in the pools are great for stretching out on. Oooh baby, wooonnnderful. The third time I went in, sleet and snow melted into the hot pool around me. Cool. Very.

The campground has excellent dry camp sites. It is open all year. The $15.50 per night is fair, considering the hot springs, the fun, and informative interpretive programs during season. The campground fills early in the day. It is wise to plan ahead for this stop. Bear warning signs were tacked everywhere. It is safer to *always* be on the lookout for animals. This is wild country.

Less than fifty miles up the road, I parked in an undeveloped campground on a bend in the Liard River. I sat on rock formations that looked like God upended them on a restless day. Last trip I was invited to share an evening campfire with two couples. They had seen a bear run through my site while I was sitting on the rocks, as I was doing now.

I have had two letters from the couple from North Carolina. When they first wrote, they said, "You probably won't remember us, but..." I could even pinpoint the date. They were in my notes, another good reason for keeping a log.

Mice tales were on the loose again, but I slept like limp spaghetti, a combination of no sleep and hot pools. By morning, mouse #2 bit the dust.

---

**When the traps snap, it usually awakens me.
I throw the culprit out the door, wash my hands,
go back to bed, and reclaim the trap in the morning.**

At a high point above the Liard River, I took my coffee outside to admire the view, and talked with a burly, full-bearded fellow from Hay River, in the Northwest Territories. I had wanted to drive there this trip, but decided against the turn near Fort Nelson because of the Mackenzie River. He confirmed the ice bridges were closed.

He suggested I come in early fall. I asked him what people do during the two-month interim between ice bridge and ferry. He said distances were so great, that people fly in and out most of the year. I forgot that the airplane is a major means of transportation in the North country.

Fritz came from Germany, had traveled the world, and raised nine kids alone, giving them all college educations. As we surveyed the magnificent scenery in front of us, he said, "I don't understand people looking at something like this, and not believing in God." Amen.

While we talked, his friend, who had been down to the river, returned with two five-pound pieces of jade and other unusual, colorful rocks. He had scales in the back of the truck. If he did that at every stop, they were going back with a lot of weight.

Mile after mile of blackened trees were evidence of a 1982 fire that destroyed more than 400,000 acres. Often signs tell the fire stories. It is interesting to know when fires occur, when the land is replanted, and how long it takes for the forest to grow back.

> **Although history reveals that fire is nature's way of cleaning house, don't be guilty of starting one through your carelessness in campgrounds or along the road, please.**

From spring through fall, the fireweed flowers are in some stage of beauty. They are the first to show promise after fires burn and blacken the countryside.

Watson Lake was flying both the American and Canadian flags on every pole. Neat.

### Decision time

**Skagway, Whitehorse, Tok, and Fairbanks, continuing on the Alaska Highway**

**or**

**North to Dawson City and Top of the World Highway to Chicken and Tok, via the Campbell Highway**

**We're going to do both**. Someday we'll return through Whitehorse, almost to Watson Lake, and head south on the Cassiar Highway. Right now we'll **fast forward** to about fifteen miles south of Whitehorse, and turn off the Alaska Highway for **Skagway, Alaska, and The Golden Circle Loop trip**. Isn't this electronic age marvelous!

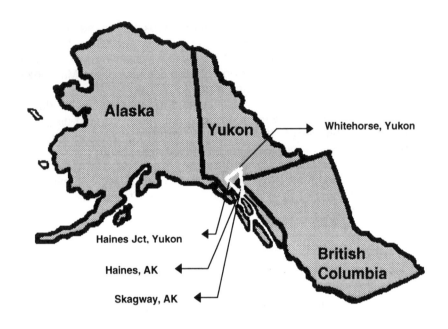

# THE GOLDEN CIRCLE LOOP
## and
# ON TO FAIRBANKS

You could turn off the Alaska Highway at Jake's Corner and take a short shortcut down to Carcross, but I haven't traveled that section yet. You can also reach Atlin from Jake's Corner.

I have traveled Klondike Highway #2 to Skagway twice, first in the green of June, and the last time in the white of early May. Road crews were knocking loose rocks off the mountainsides and "netting" the cliffs so debris wouldn't fall on tourists who would come along later in the season. Yellow Cats were clearing rockslides.

Other tracks were deep indentations in the snow on their way to places I couldn't follow, filled with animals I couldn't see beyond the ridges and rocks. A perfect stranger (He seemed perfect at the time.) I met at a pull off, offered to let me borrow his cross-country skis and return them to him in Whitehorse. I declined but appreciated the trust. This last trip I carried my own cross country skis for 10,000 miles and never used them.

Carcross is on the banks of Lake Bennett, part of the waterway the gold rushers used to eventually reach Dawson City.

In May, very little was open, and the lakes, including beautiful Emerald Lake, were still under a deep blanket of snow. The winter scenes were great for slides, but most people would prefer coming when tourist attractions are open in June.

From Yukon Territory, you drive back into British Columbia, then across the border into Alaska at the top of White Pass. The border is open twenty-four hours, during the season.

Tall poles outlined the road for the snowplows through the deep snow. From White Pass, I could see the coastal mountains still in winter sleep. I started the 11.5 mile descent into Skagway and spring.

## Skagway and Dyea

Do yourself a favor, don't shortchange Skagway. It exudes history. A good hike will take you to see most of it, but everything can be driven to as well, including the Klondike Gold Rush National Historical Park Visitor Center, a good place to start.

I parked at the Pullen Creek RV Park by the small boat harbor. It was a convenient walk uptown or to watch the cruise ships come into the Lynn Canal.

---

**Skagway (Haines) is the northernmost stop for the Alaska State Ferries (Southeast Route), following the thousand nautical miles on the Inland Passage from Bellingham, WA. You can also catch an Alaska State Ferry at Prince Rupert, B.C., to come to Skagway. Yes, this is a repeat because it was confusing for me.**

---

The former Dyea townsite is at the head of Taiya Inlet, an eighteen-mile round trip. It's a gravel road, curvy, scenic, and narrow in spots. I caught up with an organized hike. The ranger explained, "Dyea mostly washed away in the 1950s with flooding and the changing of the course of the river. An archeologist actually witnessed pine boxes washing out to sea, but was powerless to stop them. A few of the graves have been removed to Slide Cemetery."

Dyea was a trading post and Native camp, in 1897. With the Klondike Gold Rush, Dyea swelled to 8,000 and became a major port city for the arrival of stampeders. The poor harbor in Dyea, and the building of the White Pass and Yukon Route Railroad in Skagway, led to Dyea's short life. The "Slide" cemetery is the burial site for victims of the snow slide of April 3, 1898. Inexperienced gold rushers paid dearly for their eagerness to get on the gold trail, when others wisely refused.

Bits and pieces of Dyea surfaced as we poked through the woods. Everything is part of the historical site, and protected. Do not remove. The pilings of a huge warehouse are stark evidence of the prosperity of long ago. Remains of a couple of cabins and barns are all that are left.

The trailhead for the Chilkoot Trail is nearby. It was a major trading route between Indian tribes until the gold rush. It isn't long. On the Chilkoot Trail, it is only thirty-three miles to Lake Bennett, but it included "The Golden Staircase."

The Canadian government required each gold rusher to have supplies for an entire year, before entering Canada. This was carried up the Golden Stairway, steps carved out of ice and snow at a 35º angle. (This means the rushers had to step up more than a foot for every one foot forward - almost like climbing a ladder.).

Gold rushers built boats and continued by water to Dawson City. If they survived the arduous Chilkoot Trail, the winter, and the Whitehorse Rapids, they continued on to Dawson City, where they found for the most part, that the gold claims were already gone.

The Chilkoot Trail is, "The Longest Museum in the World." The ranger told us, "When the snow melts, you can see everything from the soles of old shoes to steam engines."

Skagway survived.

I was in Skagway for a week. Spring was in Skagway; but I couldn't leave well enough alone. I had to go looking for winter again.

The White Pass & Yukon Route Railroad was finished too late for the gold rushers, but it kept Skagway alive, and today, it is a great trip to make to the top of White Pass. Most of the way, we chugged along the Trail of '98. Over 3,000 pack animals died at Dead Horse Gulch trying to make it to the top. Overloaded and neglected, they died without so much as a kind bullet.

The narrow-gauge railroad goes up one of the steepest grades in North America. The track climbs 2,885' in twenty miles to White Pass Summit. I went from spring, back to snow mounds higher than the train. We waited for an avalanche clearance, went through tunnels, over bridges, and looked back from Inspiration Point toward the Lynn Canal, the Harding Glacier, and the Chilkat Mountain Range. Spectacular. It is a three-hour round trip and well worth the adventure. The train no longer goes into Whitehorse.

The Arctic Brotherhood Hall has 20,000 pieces of driftwood nailed to its front, and the Red Onion Saloon has "ladies of the evening" flouncing around in the windows, wearing fancy clothes. These "painted ladies" are just that, painted on the windows.

The stories are many; Mollie Walsh; Harriett Pullen; Jefferson R. "Soapy" Smith and his gang; and town hero, Frank Reid. You'll hear their names over and over. If you want to say hello, walk around the Gold Rush Cemetery.

Personally, I love walking around old cemeteries reading gravestones, visiting, and absorbing history. If you do, too, please remember to treat the grounds, graves, their inhabitants, and historic artifacts with respect.

Someday, we'll all be subject to grave walkers.

Well, I won't tell you all of Skagway's secrets. Take your time there. When you leave Skagway, you either return along the road you came in on, or take a ferry.

I took the Sprinter on the ferry to Haines, Alaska. It was a great hour-long trip down the Lynn Canal, the continent's largest and deepest fjord. Fort William H. Seward and the Chilkat Mountains, are the backdrop for the town of Haines, and what a view that is coming into the harbor.

Most of my time was spent seven miles out of town, at the Chilkat State Park on Mud Bay. Other than the hosts, Shirley and Victor Keitel of St. Louis, Missouri, I was the only one there. They kindly shared campfires and information with me. During the day, I parked down on the water across from a hanging glacier. Porpoises played in the inlet, and thousands of Arctic terns gave me background music to work by.

**Shirley and Victor Keitel, volunteer hosts**

I was in Haines only a couple of days but would like to explore it more. I really wanted to go there in October of 1996 on my way back, but my "intestinal" feelings were that snow was not far from my bumper. My reason for wanting to stay, was to see the eagles return to The Alaska Chilkat Bald Eagle Preserve, just outside of Haines. I saw a lot of eagles at the park but the preserve, in October, is far more dramatic.

Four thousand American bald eagles gather along a five-mile stretch of the Chilkat River, each fall. It is the largest gathering of eagles in the world. Warm water upwellings in the river bottom, keep stretches of the Chilkat river ice free through the winter, providing salmon carcasses when food supplies elsewhere, are exhausted.

The adult eagles have the distinct white "bald" head and tailfeathers but the immature eagle has mottled brown and white plumage. They can fly at thirty m.p.h., and dive at 100 m.p.h. At one time, I thought about getting one to keep my in-house mouse population down, but then I discovered their wing span is six to eight feet, and their average weight is thirteen pounds. So much for that thought.

**Eagles are federally protected.
Possession of any parts, including feathers, is illegal.**

During season, you can see the Chilkat Native Dancers and hear the Tlingit legends. A self-guided walking tour is available through Fort William H. Seward, a Historic Landmark. The military post, permanently established in 1904, has an interesting history.

Haines is famous as an Alaskan artist community. I watched Gresham Gregg woodcarving at the Sea Wolf Gallery. I also recommend the Sheldon Museum and Cultural Center, for the pioneer history and Tlingit Indian Culture. If you're lucky, they'll serve you "Russian Tea."

It was early May as I drove Haines Highway (Alaska Route 7). The area was bursting with snowshoe hare that year, and that brings on the lynx. A lynx bounded to the edge of the road, and put on his brakes at the same time the Sprinter did. I have never experienced anything quite so thrilling. His blue eyes met mine for an instant, then he was gone like a shot.

I took off on a side road to Mosquito Lake and found a delightful State Recreation campground, to wile away a few hours. It was too early for mosquitoes, or else they were taking pity on me.

The scenic Haines Highway goes past the Tatshenshini-Alsek Wilderness Provincial Park, and over Chilkat Pass into British Columbia, then into Yukon Territory, following a portion of Kluane National Park Reserve. Dezadeash Lake is a good place to stop, and don't fail to walk the boardwalk at the Million Dollar Falls. Both places have campgrounds.

Whether you camp or only admire the scenery, don't fail to stop at Kathleen Lake. When Perry Como sang, "The bluest blue is in Seattle," he obviously hadn't been to far North county. It is a glacier-fed lake, and an incredible turquoise blue. The setting is really exceptional.

At Haines Junction, stop at the Kluane National Park and Yukon government visitor information centre. Always take the time to drive around these small towns. You'll always see something of interest. Many of them have used leftovers from the Alaska Highway construction in unique ways. Our Lady of the Way Catholic mission is in a Quonset hut surrounded by flower gardens.

I returned to Whitehorse on the Alaska Highway, completing "The Golden Circle Route" (Whitehorse, Skagway, Haines Junction -- approximately 362 road miles).

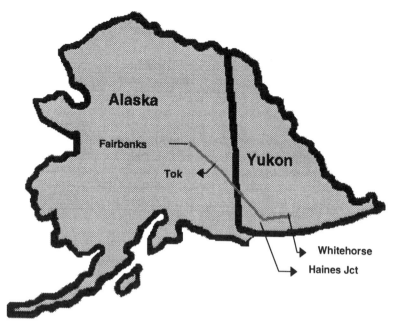

### Whitehorse

With a population of around 23,000, the capital of Yukon Territory, Whitehorse, is the biggest city until you get to Fairbanks. Whitehorse was named after the frothing, churning Yukon River rapids, that resembled charging white horses.

That rapids put an end to big dreams of getting rich for many Klondike gold rushers who chanced going through Miles Canyon, rather than portage around it. Some gave their lives to it. The rapids disappeared when the river was dammed to form Schwatka Lake. I've cruised the lake in the M. V. Schwatka. It is a pleasant, scenic, two hour trip.

If you're into hiking, trails lead along both sides of Miles Canyon with a connecting bridge.

You can find just about anything you need in Whitehorse. They have nice campgrounds, restaurants, and entertainment. The stern wheeler, SS Klondike, is permanently berthed on the banks of the Yukon River. It plied the Yukon from Whitehorse to Dawson City, from the mid 1930s until the 1950s. It is a National Historic Site, and tours are available.

I always enjoy the live shows. The Frantic Follies is a vaudeville revue with music, dancing, singing, comedy, Robert Service skits and poetry. There are other shows, as well.

The MacBride Museum has exhibits of Native culture, the RCMP, wildlife, and the Klondike Gold Rush of 1898. They also have an outdoor museum that includes Sam McGee's cabin (The Cremation of Sam McGee), stage coaches, and steam engines. All of the Yukon is celebrating the gold rush over the next few years so they will be having special exhibits.

I like the log skyscrapers downtown, and the Old Log Church Museum. The church is a Territorial Historic Site, but Episcopal services are held there on Sundays.

You won't want to miss the Yukon Transportation Museum with the amazing story of the building of the Alaska Highway, and other methods of northern transportation, including dogsleds, stagecoaches, planes, trains, and riverboats. It is impossible to miss this place. It is on the Alaska Highway, across from the Whitehorse International Airport. You can find that by the weathervane in front, a Douglas DC-3 on a stick.

The city has the feeling of excitement about it, maybe because it is growing. It seemed a great deal bigger than when I was there in 1987.

### North to Fairbanks

It is 633 miles from Whitehorse to Fairbanks. The Alaska Highway ends at Delta Junction. You continue on the Richardson Highway to Fairbanks. You'll often see signs for "old" sections of the Alaska Highway.

---

**If you haven't read the history of the Alaska Highway, take some time and do it. It is absolutely amazing that the U. S. Army Corps of Engineers built 1,523 miles of road across Canada and Alaska in just eight months.**

---

(Was that before boondoggling became popular??)

You, as an RV traveler, some 55 years later, driving 55 mph (in places!), have no idea what it was all about, unless you study the interpretive signs, or visit the museums or visitor centers along the way. I urge you to do that.

As you get closer to Haines Junction, the fantastic Kluane National Park comes into view. You can sometimes see the Mt. Kennedy and Mt. Hubbard peaks of the Icefield Ranges in the interior of the park. Spectacular mountain views, providing the weather is reasonably clear, will be with you for many miles north. Kluane National Park, a World Heritage Site, has the highest mountains in Canada, the second highest coastal mountains, and the largest non-polar icefield ranges in the world.

You'll never really lose mountain views. The views will change. Eventually, you'll see the mountains in the Wrangell-Saint Elias National Park and Preserve in the distance. This park includes nine of the sixteen highest peaks in the United States. It is our largest national park, the size of **six** Yellowstone parks. The Bagley Icefield is the largest subpolar icefield in North America. In conjunction with Kluane National Park in Canada, it is also a World Heritage Site.

Then you begin to see the Alaska Range (Mounts Hayes, Deborah, and Hess). Look at your map; magnificent mountains are in every direction. Heck with the map, throw it away, and look out your window!!

**Look in your rear view mirror once in a while. The difference in your view can be startling** (Especially if there is a semi in your sights).

Stop often. If you're like I am, you can't resist framing the spectacular mountain scenes in flowers, trees or clouds. Great photo opportunities (everywhere).

If you enjoy scenery, you could easily take a month driving from Whitehorse to Fairbanks. Mucho campgrounds are available, many are private, but also many recreation type sites park you near a stream, or lake, or in the woods (Get out that gallon of repellent!).

This trip, I didn't drive the section from Whitehorse to the Taylor Highway Junction near Tok. I continued to hear about bad sections of highway from Destruction Bay, through Beaver Creek, to the Alaska border. I know it is different each year, according to the frost heaves, but I remember driving through a very long section of construction in 1992. Even though the driving was rough through the construction, there is equipment there to pull you out, should you get stuck.

Kluane Lake is the largest lake in Yukon Territory, and you will follow its beautiful shores for many miles. I turned off at Milepost 1020 to go to Silver City. It is a little over six miles round trip on a gravel road. There isn't a lot there any more, but the fireweed and the ruins of an early trading post, made for great slides.

You'll go through Destruction Bay and Burwash Landing. The Kluane Museum of Natural History is worth a stop at Burwash Landing.

Beaver Creek is Canada's most westerly community (100 miles west of Victoria, B. C.). Twenty miles northwest of Beaver Creek, you'll hit the Alaska-Canada International border. There is a pullout where you can see the narrow swath cut across the countryside to mark the border. Bill (Yukon guide) said they clear it every ten years. You'll also be changing to Alaska time, as you cross the border. You'll now be four hours different than the east coast. This border is open twenty-four hours a day.

Outside of Tok about fifteen miles, is the junction with Taylor Highway (toward Chicken).

## Tok

You can get most necessities in Tok. It is a small community, 1,405, in the off season. Tok gets all visitors "coming and going." Tok, is a Native word meaning "Peace crossing," apropos, since you must drive through this town to reach the rest of Alaska. Tok is called, "Mainstreet Alaska."

Tok is also known as the "Dog Capital of Alaska." It is a center for dog breeding, training, and mushing. The Burnt Paw gift shop has a free Dog Team Demonstration in the evenings at 7:30.

I had breakfast at Young's Cafe, and filled up with gasoline at Young's Chevron Service. I took them up on their offer of a free sewer dump and water fill-up. They also offer free RV parking.

A number of campgrounds are in the area, Tok River State Recreation Site southeast of town, and Tok RV Village in town, among others. Tok Gateway Salmon Bake and RV Park offers a free night of dry camping with dinner. Sourdough Campground has a free nightly slide show. Check to see which one offers what floats your boat.

The Tok Mainstreet Visitors Center has wildlife displays, Alaska videos, free coffee, and a list of activities. There are telephones inside and outside. The Alaska Public Lands Information Center has a historical timeline room and displays, a wildlife museum, restrooms, pay phone, and message board.

If you intend to get an Alaska State Park Annual Pass (covers most State Recreation Sites -- $100 non-residents), get it at the Alaska Public Lands Information Center. Although I got my money back out of the pass in 1992, I didn't this last trip. Look ahead at the type of campgrounds in the area where you'll be traveling.

**Alaska Public Lands Information Centers cover National Park Service, U. S. Forest Service, Bureau of Land Management, U. S. Fish & Wildlife Service, U. S. Geological Survey, Alaska Division of Tourism, Alaska Department of Natural Resources, and Alaska Department of Fish & Game.**

They are located in **Tok, Fairbanks, and Anchorage.** It is beyond my comprehension that government agencies have come together, so you can get needed information from one place. Fantastic! If they don't have the information, they should be able to tell you where to find it.

Tok has several repair service centers, quick lube, tire centers, and places to have your front end aligned (should you have need).

South of Delta Junction there is a Bison Sanctuary. The only bison I saw were between Haines Junction and Whitehorse. Bill (Yukon Guide), as we drove from the river trip back to Eagle, told me about the roaming bison raising havoc with crops in the big Delta Agriculture Project. The Sanctuary has 90,000 acres, but so far the critters haven't read the fine print. They are still causing problems to local farmers. And who is going to argue with a 2,000 pound bison?

Stop at the Delta Junction Chamber of Commerce Visitor Center. Just as you had a picture taken at the beginning of the Alaska Highway at Dawson Creek, B. C., you'll want one taken in front of the "End of the Alaska Highway" monument.

**For $1, you can buy certificates stating you have officially driven the Alaska Highway.**

Rika's Roadhouse and Landing, is part of the Big Delta State Historical Park, and the staff wears period costumes. The Packhouse Restaurant is a good place to eat. This is the home of the Alaska Baking Company, known for their yum-yum bakery goods. Beware eating in competition with the tour bus crowd. When I was there, I could hardly find a place to sit, and it seats 150. The complex covers ten acres. It is a fun place to walk around, and the shops have unusual gifts. A campground and dump station are available.

One of the best views you will have of the Trans-Alaska Pipeline is at the Big Delta Bridge, as you and the pipeline cross the Tanana River. There is a parking area south of the bridge with interpretive signs.

Santa Claus House in North Pole, AK, is billed as "Interior Alaska's Largest Gift Shop." I've always enjoyed wandering and looking; but beware, your credit card will wiggle until it gets loose. They have Santa letters for children (or adults) for mailing at the appropriate time from the "North Pole."

This business has grown over the years and the story is interesting. They used to offer free camping. It is now a full facility Santaland RV Park and Campground, a Good Sampark. They also have dry campsites.

Later, coming from a different direction, I'll give you an idea of what you'll find in Fairbanks. For now, I'm taking you back to Watson Lake and the beginning of the Campbell Highway to Dawson City.

See you next chapter.

WATSON LAKE SIGN POST YUKON TERRITORY

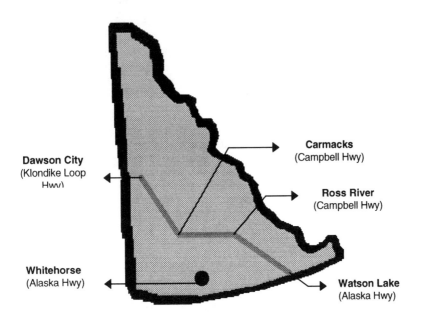

# THE SPELL OF THE YUKON

My gold panning could hardly compare to any turn-of-the-century gold rushes. I haven't gone far enough into the wilderness to experience the loneliness, the madness (well, perhaps a little of that!) or the fear. I haven't wintered in the far North or walked in a whiteout snowstorm, but the spell of the Yukon, nevertheless, holds me in its grip.

My first knowledge of Robert Service, the "Bard of the Klondike," was through a former Alaska Territorial policeman, who held me spellbound with his poetry. Now that I have traveled a portion of that wilderness, I am more enthralled than ever. The last four lines of "The Spell of the Yukon" explains very well how I feel.

> It's the great, big, broad land 'way up yonder,
> It's the forests where silence has lease;
> It's the beauty that thrills me with wonder,
> It's the stillness that fills me with peace.

I equate the word "Yukon" with adventure. My heart rate went up at least a notch, when the "Welcome to the Yukon" sign came into view near Watson Lake.

My spur-of-the-moment (the best kind) decision to take the Campbell Highway would cut off Whitehorse, and take me 373, mostly gravel miles, to connect with Klondike Loop (Hwy 2) to Dawson City. This was new territory. I was quite sure the road wouldn't be highly traveled...but then, my transmission was only a couple of months old, and I had just had an entire new brake system installed. What could go wrong? (Always a dangerous question!)

My decision point was Watson Lake, Gateway to the Yukon. Watson Lake has a population of about 2,000. During the season, the Alaska Highway Interpretive Centre, is an interesting place to visit. They have displays, photographs, and a video on the Alaska Highway construction. It was closed.

Watson Lake is the home of the famous Signpost Forest, and it is always open -- out in the open. The icy wind whipped around the poles holding roughly 30,000 signs.

If you've ever gotten lost because of the absence of a signpost, it is probably here. This amazing collection represents states, counties, towns, and most foreign countries. The tradition of leaving a geographic momento began with Carl Lindley, a WWII soldier, who worked on the Alaska Highway in 1942. Legend has it that he was so homesick, he posted a sign giving the distance from Watson Lake to his hometown in Danville, Illinois.

You wouldn't want to break tradition. Tack up an old license plate or homemade sign (not a road or street sign, please), and leave your mark.

The Signpost Forest is at the Alaska and Campbell Highway junction. It was three in the afternoon when I turned northwest. I hadn't gone a half mile, when I drove head-on into a blizzard. By the time the paved road turned into gravel, the snow stopped and blue skies prevailed. I berated myself for even *thinking* of turning back when I hit snow.

The entire route followed one river or another. All the lakes were frozen. The rivers were running through, and under, great depths of ice. It was a month and a half before I again saw completely ice-free water, especially in shady areas.

The bad road sections were flagged; but this time of year, the road was more bad than good. It was wet, slippery, and the outside edges were soft. It was narrow, often one vehicle wide, and I filled it. The road was built up several feet to avoid the water that was usually on both sides. It was abundantly clear that if I didn't want to become a houseboat (or ice house), I was going to drive in the middle, except, when I saw another vehicle.

I needn't have worried. It was slow going, but not due to heavy traffic. Over the next two and a half days, except for stops in the towns of Ross River and Faro, I saw ten cars and trucks.

The main road through Frances Lake Yukon government campground was plowed, but the sites were snow filled. At the boat launching pad, I found a level space next to shore. What a view it was of one of the Yukon's largest lakes. It wore a thick mantle of snow, as did all the surrounding mountains. I was quite certain I wouldn't be in the way of anyone launching a boat.

That night I caught mouse #3, the last one. I opened the bed pedestal and foamed it full, missing the space for the waterpump, house batteries, and inverter panel.

I foamed around the steering column. I had plugged this area during my last Alaska trip, but the carpet replacement had left holes again. If they get through there again, they'll have two feet of foam to tunnel through. I didn't have problems with mice the rest of the trip, but it took a while for my paranoia to go away. Every noise was a giant mouse looking for peanut butter.

The one foray I made into the frigid mid-day brought me another startling noise. I thought I heard a motorboat! Now, I knew that wasn't possible with ice several feet thick on the lake, then I spotted two grouse in the woods. They were the only signs of life I saw, until my first moose (this trip). I always forget how big they are. I stopped, and he lumbered across in front of me, probably disgusted with the heavy traffic.

The Sprinter and I descended into a steep ravine when I saw a black bear across from me on the next rise, probably an eighth of a mile away as the crow flies. He stopped. Even from that distance and with the naked eye, he was huge. I watched him with binoculars. Wouldn't you know it, with virtually no traffic at all, a truck load of people came through from behind him.

They were going like a bat out of a hot place, laughing like mad when they passed me, and probably thinking it was neat sport to chase that big bear into the woods. In my disappointment, I wished a pox on that load of hyenas. Another black bear and another moose eventually healed my mad fit.

Only a few of Ross River's four hundred residents were out in the cold as I went through town. I parked in the gravel lot near the Pelly River, where RVers are invited to park overnight. I bundled in layers against the Arctic air, and walked across the suspension bridge. The swollen river swirled ice chunks in its current, and pushed them on down toward the Yukon River. The bridge groaned and creaked as I made my way across to hike the mile to an abandoned Indian village on the Ross River.

It was a steep path at first, but one of those narrow ones like a cow path, that fascinates me. It wound through the trees above the river to a small cemetery where I visited for a while. I saw the village in the distance; but, I was so cold, I turned back.

The gas station wasn't open in mid-afternoon. A sign said to go next door for service. On the way, I ran into the attendant. The big news was out; a customer was at the pumps.

Faro had about four times as many people as Ross River, and was quite a bustling community. Friendly people gave directions to the driver of this usually lost "rolling igloo." They call the Discovery Store, the Case Place. They don't buy a bottle of catsup or a can of fruit in these isolated communities. Food is sold by the case.

People were walking to the movies (they did have a theatre), or other activities. I couldn't believe they were out just for exercise in that cold evening air. It might really have felt like spring to them.

On previous trips, I had seen the yellow Yukon Alaska Transport trucks, called "B-trains," originating from the Faro mine and making their way to Skagway. The Faro mine is said to be one of the largest producers of lead and zinc concentrates in the western world. They travel forty minutes apart, twenty-four hours a day, taking their loads to port. These eight-axle beasts are eighty-five feet long, and carry up to fifty-three tons of concentrate.

They advertise the efficiency, professionalism, and courteousness of their drivers. Something to remember is that each "B-train" is equipped with first aid kits, radio telephones, and "They will be more than happy to help you, should you require their assistance."

I stayed the night in a pull off, beside a half-frozen stream. If there were trucks going by in the night, I didn't hear them. I left early and connected with the Klondike Loop, north of Carmacks. I saw the Yukon River and my heart sank; the ice had already gone out. So much for that dream.

Every trip, I have stopped at the overlook above Five Finger Rapids, perhaps, because of the stories of the gold seekers who ran them, sometimes with all their worldly goods on their backs. This time, there were viewing platforms on the bluff, and down near the rapids. The mile-long path between the two beckoned to me, although I knew the 219 steps would be more difficult to negotiate coming up.

Since I had seen two black bears on the slopes above the highway a short distance back, I decided it would be prudent to be on the lookout. During this brisk, lighthearted walk, my eyes roamed back and forth across the path and into the trees, for something black and moving. My ears listened for the telltale crunch of sharp teeth on my limbs, or hopefully, a noise more distant, like the cracking of a tree limb. My nose sniffed for pungency. The experts tell me that bears do not wear enough deodorant, and tend to smell a great deal like skunk.

I wasn't wearing bear bells, and my singing would have been rather tremulous. The tape recorder became my AWS (Advance Warning System). I reversed the tape a bit, then played it really loud for a few seconds. This I did several times. Probably all present bears disliked it as well as I did, but it made me feel safer.

It was the first I had felt springtime warmth since leaving southern British Columbia. It was wonderful. Out of the corner of my eye, I glimpsed something big and dark and moving fast. My heart beat faster. I turned the recorder on loud and strong, only to realize what I had seen was across the river, a moose running. I wondered where he was going, or what startled him enough to travel that fast.

I stayed for a while on the platform next to the rapids. The miners named them Five Finger Rapids, because they looked like the fingers in a hand. I imagined how excited fellow SKPs, Scott and Karen Bonis, must have felt, canoeing through these rapids from Bennett Lake to Eagle, Alaska. I wanted to do that so bad, I could taste it.

Since I hadn't seen evidence of any animals, on my return trip I was rather blasé about making noise. When I was near the steps, I turned the recorder on one last time. Something crashed through the trees. I clutched my chest. It was a huge snowshoe hare. I had scared him almost as much as he scared me.

I had only driven 150 miles, when I turned on a narrow gravel road leading to Minto Landing Yukon government campground. It was a choose-your-own-site place. Having it all to myself, I chose a choice grassy area on the riverbank.

The lone cabin had suffered the ravages of time. It had fallen into itself, the last remnant of Minto Landing history, a halfway point for steamboats running the Yukon River, from Whitehorse to Dawson City, in the mid 1880s.

Great ice rafts nudged the heavily ice-lined riverbanks, pulling more sculptured chunks into its journey to the Bering Sea. The only sounds other than the river and the refrigerator, were the grass growing and the flowers opening.

The Sprinter and I were eleven days and 2,000 miles from Seattle, and with the warm, dry afternoon, it was an excellent time to do a more advanced "walk-a-bout."

After checking all the fluids and thumping the tires, I cleaned twenty-five pounds of mud from the generator. I sprayed WD-40 on my hold locks, and caught up on my daily log, via computer and solar energy. The Sprinter was disgustingly muddy, but I couldn't quite talk myself into a precarious thirty-foot climb down a cliff for water, and possibly flipping myself into that swirling death trap. Lovely to look at but questionable for swimming.

I took a hike upriver for a mile or so. The riverbank was grassy, and the area open enough for observing animals. The bears were out of hibernation. I felt lighthearted and free. I collected firewood on the way back.

> **Since I had already done my chores and exercised, I felt quite justified in sitting by the fire doing nothing. I kept a bucket of water, a folding shovel, and my trusty, recently-sharpened, hatchet nearby (always the Girl Scout). I poured myself a stiff drink of Nu-trisweet-sweetened, calorie-free, sparkling-flavored, Sam's Choice Free and Clear White Grape. What a life!**

I thawed chicken strips and cooked them over the fire. I rolled a potato in tin foil, but it didn't get done enough to suit me. I did what any self-respecting "camper" would do; I zapped it in the microwave. I had been so terribly good diet-wise, that I had a banana with peanut butter and fudge on it.

As the sun worked its way to the other side of the world, its low light silhouetted the wild crocuses, outlining them in silver. The sunset was a mere rosy glow by eleven o'clock. The air was frosty, and so was I. In my cozy house beside the Yukon, I was awakened only once with a loud protesting of ice on ice.

I wanted to stay a few days, but the Sprinter was in need of dumping and filling, and besides, Dawson City was calling.

Memories of previous stops gave me pleasant thoughts. I hungered for one of their delicious cinnamon buns and coffee; but alas, Moose Creek Lodge was closed. One compensation for everything being closed, was that I wasn't sharing life with bus tours, RV caravans or hungry bitey bugs.

Another plus for going early, animals were everywhere. I made my own coffee in a pullout, sharing the space with a fat ground squirrel who rose up on his hind legs occasionally, to see if the great white apparition was still there.

I almost creamed a ptarmigan. They will not get out of the way even when a ten-ton RV is bearing down on them.

I pulled off to watch a black bear. He went back and forth across the road into the woods, three times. The last time, he stopped for a couple of seconds, as though asking, "Why are you still here?"

At the junction with the Dempster Highway, I filled the Sprinter with gas to the tune of $151. It was 76 cents/liter. I took advantage of their free sewer dump and water fill-up. The fellow who pumped gas said, "The river ice is still piled up at Dawson. The Klondike River just broke up and its pushing into the Yukon, something's got to give soon." I **wasn't** too late. Yesssss! I forgot that it didn't automatically break up everywhere at once.

I arrived in Dawson City in the nick of time. The river ice had moved enough that morning to displace the tripod in the center, signaling the "official" ice breakup, with bells and whistles and celebration. People for miles around buy tickets as to the day, hour, and minute the Yukon River breakup will happen. Somebody had already won their pot of gold. The main breakup waited for me.

Dawsonites believe spring has arrived when the ice moves downstream, and they were out in number to watch it, in shorts and short sleeves. It was too cold for me. I guess when you are used to fifty below, anything above freezing is a heat wave. They sat on blankets and chairs on the earthen dike that follows the confluence of the Yukon/Klondike Rivers around Dawson City. The dike was built to prevent another major ice jam flood, like the one in 1979. The path along the top is a favorite place for walking, running, and biking.

Remember I mentioned Robert Service? Would you believe I shared the river watch with him? Wait you say, how old is this guy? He was really Tom Byrne, an actor and storyteller who relates Robert Service poetry at the Service cabin in Dawson City.

While we waited for the ice to do something spectacular, Tom regaled me with stories of local characters.

> It seems one Captain Dick, offering the best drink in Dawson City, the "*Sour Toe*," lost the major content to a bender-bent imbiber, who drank the drink and swallowed the toe. The story was a bit hard to swallow, but Tom swore the toe was real. When that toe disappeared down the hatch, Captain Dick put an ad in the paper for another. Truth being stranger than fiction, he got it!

First light follows close after last light, in the land of the midnight sun, and townspeople came early to check the river's progress. By eight a.m., the ice moved. What excitement! Many people depend on the Yukon River for their livelihood. The river breaking free, meant a great deal to them. It jammed at the bend, and water backed up alarmingly fast, but then subsided, as the chunks broke free.

The water mingled forward and backward, swirling, groaning, moaning, pulling trees grabbed from distant shorelines and river-size icebergs, into its wild journey. Desolate and dirty ice clung to the gravel bars, stranded and left to melt in the warming sun.

Locals told me it was less than a spectacular break up, but it was exciting to this Midwesterner, as is almost everything about the North.

Nearly a hundred years ago, August 17, 1896, George Carmack, Skookum Jim, and Tagish Charlie discovered gold, on what became known as Bonanza Creek. They staked the first claims and made the history that Dawson City is celebrating, the great Klondike Gold Rush of 1896-98.

As a matter of fact, once these Canadians get a party started, it's hard to stop them. They are celebrating right on through 2003 with centennials of the Palace Grand Theatre, the post office, the Carnegie Library, and numerous other anniversaries.

Over a hundred thousand dreamers set out to make their fortunes; perhaps, they were your relatives. About forty thousand survived, carrying their goods over the Chilkoot and White Pass Trails from Skagway and Dyea, Alaska, and the Whitehorse Rapids on the Yukon River to the gold fields. By the time most of them arrived, the creek beds had already been staked with claims from end to end.

Relatively few became rich with first-hand gold, like the 72 ounce gold nugget that, with today's prices, would be worth $30,000. Second-hand riches were made in services, uh, perhaps some are unmentionable here. Saloons, restaurants, and shops opened, and Dawson City transformed from a tent city, to the largest city north of San Francisco, with running water, telephones, and electricity.

Good gravy, we didn't have those amenities in the southwestern Michigan log cabin where I was born, a whole lot (a whole lot) of years later.

A good place to learn the details, are at the Dawson City Museum. The movie shows Dawson during the Klondike Gold Rush days, after it had fallen into decay, and during its slow restoration.

A few historic ruins are precariously propped with posts. Walking the boardwalks to avoid the dust and mud, you would never guess that behind business walls, lurks a computer age about to on-line its way into the twenty-first century. The 1898 population of nearly 30,000 people, has stabilized to a lively 2,019 (The population of the entire Yukon is only 31,349).

In the meantime, I met several people at the Community Gospel Church and through a writer's group at Yukon College.

Jack said his family had owned a gold mine for many years. "They exposed old sealed mine shafts, tunneled through the pay gravel. They found a post with a hat still hanging on a nail and tools leaning against the wall. In the frozen muck, were perfectly preserved cans (with readable labels) which rusted immediately when exposed to air. A man's boots were beside a woman's tiny high-button shoes. A variety of bones have appeared as well." History revealing itself.

Doreen was a retired teacher and world traveler. We became friends and went to an Up With People program together. This was a first for that kind of production in Dawson. We couldn't get much more uplifted than by this group of talented students, who were pure dynamite. These performers, ages 17 to 25, travel all over the world, singing and dancing in traditional costumes that represent twenty different nationalities. Wow!

We attended the season's opening and Silver Anniversary of Diamond Tooth Gertie's Gambling Hall. The Can-Can Dancers did somersaults, back-bends, splits, and, of course, the can-can. My back sprained just watching them. The always-buxom Diamond Tooth Gertie, belted out songs to knock your socks off, but I didn't see any diamond between her two front teeth. It cost $11.75 Canadian ($7.76 U.S.), not bad for an evening's entertainment.

The Gaslight Follies at the Palace Grand Theatre, opened as well. Tales of Arizona Charlie Meadows, who built the Grand Opera House in 1899, claim that when things got dull, he invited his wife on stage and shot glass balls from between her fingers.

Although he was a "crack" shot, one night he shot her finger off and she insisted they drop the act. Hmmm. Could it have been a finger, and not a toe, in that famous "*Sour Toe*" drink??

My emergency brake had been fixed in Washington. On leaving a gas station in Dawson, I released it. The Sprinter wouldn't move. It finally broke loose, but seized up again the next time I used it. The mechanic said the wire covering had broken off down inside, and the whole thing needed replacing. He didn't have the parts, and couldn't get them for two weeks. He suggested I be aware of where and how I parked and have it replaced somewhere more economical, as in a big city in the States (An honest man). I blocked the wheels from then on, or made sure I was on level ground.

I talked with some people visiting from Vancouver. He was very positive and loved every minute of their trip, and would have enjoyed staying longer in Dawson City. She, on the other hand, was the kind that gives tourists a bad name. Of course, I was raving about the place when she said she couldn't wait to get away. I asked how long they had been there. With a definite facial grimace, she said, "Since yesterday afternoon!"

She didn't like the dirt streets or dust, and said there was nothing to do. She said, "Dawson isn't anything like I expected. I love big cities, and I can't wait to get to Anchorage." She also griped about the nearly twenty-four hour daylight. I asked (not as sarcastically as I wanted to), "What did you expect in the Land of the Midnight Sun?"

It was totally beyond me, how she could be there less than twenty-four hours, visit none of the attractions or shows or goldfields, and judge Dawson City in that fashion. Only in my wildest thoughts could I imagine what she would think when they arrived in Chicken, Alaska, their next stop.

Please don't go from Whitehorse to Tok, via Dawson City, expecting metropolitan fare. It won't be so, and I'm grateful for it.

People in the far North country either love living there or they hate it with a passion and feel trapped. An interesting comment from a sixteen-year-old who pumped gas was, "I want to move to Ontario where I can be close to Florida." (I thought about leaving him a map.)

I drove the steep winding road up to The Dome each night, 2,000' above Dawson City, and backed into a gravel area, just below the dome. Spectacular sunsets reflected in the bend of the Yukon River at 10:30 p.m.

It was a marvelous place to hike early in the morning, with the wind threatening to unwind my muffler. The ravens flew about asking my intentions, then gathered with colleagues in the trees, discussing my answers.

Sometimes, when I walked to the top of the dome, I was in an island of fog. Other times, it was clear, and I could see deep winter snows still hugging rugged mountain ranges. Below me, great long mounds of gold mine tailings, wormed their way through the goldfield valleys.

Once, I awakened to several inches of new snow. It wasn't a hard decision to stay there for the day. I had enough propane, groceries, and water, in case the snow didn't stop. That late in the season, surely it would melt in two weeks, at the latest.

Campgrounds finally opened in Dawson, but I preferred The Dome. During the season, I'm sure they wouldn't allow anyone to park there. Only once, did I think I might have a problem.

I was reading late in the evening when a pickup truck made a bee-line to the driver's corner of the Sprinter, and slid to a stop just before it hit the bank. I stared at them for a couple of seconds, and they backed out and left. My kids would have said nobody could withstand "The Look," but what do they know.

Dawson City has a public sewer that is free to use. There is a small fee for taking on water.

> **Signs throughout the Yukon said it all,**
> ***"Bears dump in the woods...you don't have to."***

Young people (usually college students) come to Dawson from all over North America, and sometimes beyond. If you go to The Farmer's Market grocery store, Maximilian's Gold Rush Emporium, or Klondike Kate's Restaurant, and feel you are seeing familiar faces, you probably are. Most of them have two jobs. They use their talents, doubling as dancers, singers, waiters, or musicians at Diamond Tooth Gertie's or the Palace Grand Theatre.

I had quite a few groceries. I bought supplemental milk and bread. Milk was $6.14/gallon; with the exchange rate of 34 to 1, it was $4.10 U.S. Not everything was that bad, but it is more understandable when you realize shipping logistics.

A Jack London cabin was discovered in 1936 and brought in, log by log, from "the left Fork of Henderson Creek." Two cabins were built using the original logs (and a few new ones). One is at the Jack London Interpretive Centre in Dawson, and the other in Jack London Square in Oakland, California. Maybe my love of the North started way back when I read the exciting books, *Call of the Wild* and *White Fang*.

The two-room, picturesque Robert Service log cabin with a front porch, snuggles against the hillside among the willows and alders, overlooking Dawson. He wrote his first novel there, *The Trail of Ninety-Eight*, and continued writing poetry. As he created, he wrote notes on the wallpaper. He was one of the few people at the time, who could afford a telephone. According to Robert Service himself, "Everything was snug and shipshape...I would not have exchanged my cabin for the palace of a king..."

Tom Byrne mesmerized all of us with his readings of, *The Cremation of Sam McGee* and *The Shooting of Dan McGrew*. He sat on an old rocker with a huge umbrella over it. In his distinct Irish accent, he wrapped the audience in his oration. His dramatic whispers were clear as a bell. His hand movements and eye contact, kept us watching every minute. I was only vaguely aware of the small birds singing in the trees above and the ravens calling to each other a block away.

Tom owns his own cabin in Dawson. "Outsiders," as people in Alaska and Northern Canada call anyone from the "lower 48," aren't aware of the enormous permafrost problems. Tom said part of his cabin floor was rotten. He tore it out. Under that floor, he found joists of another. Before he was through, he found three floors had been built over each other as the cabin sank.

**Robert Service Cabin**
Tom Byrne, *The Shooting of Dan McGrew*

He raised it, rock by rock, with jacks until he finally hit bedrock, and the jacks started lifting, instead of sinking. After he had made some headway, three buddies offered to help. When he told them to stop jacking, one continued, and suddenly the whole thing squeejawed into itself. He said, "If the cabin hadn't been dove-tailed and pegged, it would have fallen apart." Tom started over again with jacks and a come-a-long, until eventually he had it level (by himself).

There are a number of places you can gold pan commercially, but the Klondike Visitors Association allows you to pan for gold on your own at Claim #6, above Discovery.

You can also drive yourself, via a sixty-mile loop, or a combined 102-mile loop along Bonanza Creek Road, Sulphur Creek Road, Dominion Creek Road, and Hunker Creek Road. You can visit Dredge #4, the largest wooden hulled, bucket line dredge in North America.

Worn-out rusted trucks, Cats, pipes, and pumps, compose a living history of mining claims. Tailings, with full grown trees growing in them, were evidence of the passage of time. Little cabins, houses, or mobile homes overlook mining claims. One claim had a skull and crossbones displayed at the driveway. It sounds funny, but it isn't wise to walk where you don't belong. You'll understand when I say, the gold is still being mined to the tune of nearly $40 million a year.

I did part of the route, but it was springtime, and the road was washed out. If you don't want to drive this narrow, winding gravel road yourself, commercial tours are available.

Surveying my kingdom

I visited the cemeteries on the mountain above the town, and Crocus Bluff. Càrolyn and Barb, from church, took me on a long hike on the Sancho Park Historic Trail System above Dawson. It was a great hike. Going across the old rock slide, one misstep, and I wouldn't be writing this.

You can hike to (with permission from the local Indian band office), or take a river tour to, the village of Moosehide. Where Dawson is now, the Han Indians once lived. Once upon a time, the village was below the rockslide I crossed.

Dawson is one of the few places I have visited in my travels, that is a bustling tourist town, and yet, it maintains its historical flavor. I felt I stayed long enough to feel that flavor.

Doreen invited me to dinner at her son's house one night. He was with the local RCMP. Doreen had spent a lot of time in Turkey. She asked me if I knew what happened to Mary, after Christ died and rose again. I had never thought about it before. She said, "The disciple into whose care she was handed, set her up in a house, with a beautiful view at Ephasis, in Turkey, where she later died."

The Yukon, at last, freed itself of the last dangerous floating ice chunks. The George Black, the Canadian government free ferry, and the only transportation across the Yukon River to the Top of the World Highway, slid along its wooden track, into the water. The season had begun.

I topped off the gas tank and boarded. I had mixed feelings about leaving friendly Dawson City. It was fun watching them erase winter scars and gear up for the tourists, but after two weeks in one place, my itchy wheels were singing,

## Alaska!
## Alaska!
## Alaska!

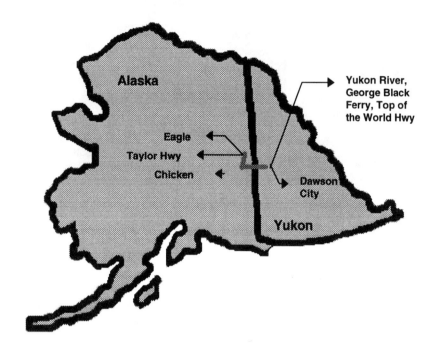

# FLYING WITH THE EAGLE-ITES

During the season, it is a good idea to get to the Dawson ferry early. It is busy, and ferrying is the only way to cross the river.

Top-of-the-World Highway has offered me fog, muddy and slippery roads, snowdrifts, and washouts, but this day it gave sunshine and flowers.

Driving on the ridge above the tree line, it feels and looks like you are, indeed, on top of the world. Although storms played in the distance, I couldn't resist stopping in an iffy pullout and hiking up to a pointy outcropping. Tiny yellow and red flowers reached toward the sun. The season is short. Even brave plants have a tough time growing.

My Julie Andrews' Syndrome took over. I felt like throwing my arms open wide and singing, "The World is alive..."

At the rest stop, and highest elevation on the Top of The World Highway, 4,515', I could see the Alaska/Canada border ahead of me. It is not open a full twenty-four hours. Be aware of your timing and time changes.

I passed a sedan, nosed halfway into a snowdrift with its windows smashed out, and flat tires. It must have spent the winter. I wondered what happened to the people who were in it. This road closes in the winter.

This is the most northerly land border port in the United States.

Population: 2. Elevation: 4,127'. The border guard came out of the Canadian Customs house, perhaps sharing his morning coffee. He was not unfriendly, but very crisp. He wanted to know what I had brought in from Canada. I told him "dust."

People, including myself, who have driven Top of the World and Taylor Highways in the past, have related all kinds of horror stories about road conditions. Top of the World, this trip, was like a super highway. It was widened, leveled, and most of it, chip-sealed.

Even Taylor Highway, except for a few miles of narrow, winding, iffy road, was in far better shape than before.

Boundary is a good place to check your fuel supply. This would be rugged country to run out of gas. A friendly fellow, Pete, worked for his uncle at Boundary Lodge. When I walked in, he said, "Welcome to the top of the world." I said, "Thank you, again."

"Ah, you are a repeat offender." He said his uncle had bought the place. They were cleaning it up and residing the old buildings. It was one of the first roadhouses in Alaska. It is now a snack type stop, but it was warm and friendly. Motorhomers were there from Germany. Throughout the summer, I ran into many visitors from other countries.

Pete had a full beard and a head of black hair that was very long in the back, with short, sort of spiky hair all around his head. He looked like he was wearing a coonskin cap. He had friendly eyes and actually was quite good-looking, considering he slightly resembled a werewolf.

After the other visitors left, we chatted. I'm always curious about what it is like to live in the far North. "I never watch TV, the view across the road is much better than TV. It changes constantly; it's never the same." He said he lived alone and liked it that way.

He wanted to know how I came to be traveling alone. I said I had been RVing solo for ten years. He said, "Sometimes, it is better to be alone. You don't have to do what everybody else wants to do." We walked on common ground.

At Jack Wade Junction, I made one of those "Decision-time stops." Should I continue to Chicken, or head north to Eagle, and into uncharted Minshall territory? Yesss! Turn north to bumpier, narrower, more-like-they-used-to-be winding roads. I wasn't kidding. It was twistier than a drunken sidewinder. Landslides were prevalent. This was springtime. Slides were expected. The road was often one lane, with a cliff to look over. Taylor Highway closes in the winter, and it hadn't been open very long.

Part of the time, the road made grand sweeping curves in treeless country, where I could see forever, or at least to Canada's Olgivie Mountains. I knew if I could see far enough beyond the mountains to the left, Fairbanks was about 200 miles directly west of Eagle on the 65th parallel. Then I dipped into valleys; "dip," meaning hairpin curves, steep winding roads, and thrills for the Sprinter and me.

At Forty Mile Bridge, with a view of the rapids, lots of trees, and nobody to break the peace, I parked for the night. The sign said "No Parking" but there were two old trucks, one with a camper on it, and an old boat. They had flat tires, and weeds a foot high, so I was sure they had been there all winter. Somehow, I didn't think anybody would mind my parking.

However, I minded it before long. A van pulled in with a couple and a dog. By that time, I had eaten a fine dinner (well, I did cook it so "fine" may be an overstatement), and was settled for the night. Their dog barked repeatedly with joy, at his newfound freedom. I climbed back in the driver's seat and drove on.

It was about 11:00 p.m. but still light. If I hadn't taken off again, I would have missed seeing the big moose ambling along ahead of me, and the little waddling porcupine. At midnight, in a rosy sunglow, and accompanied by a quarter moon, I settled into a gravel pit.

The road was narrow enough in spots, for my wide rig to need a pullout for passing, but I drove for forty-five minutes before seeing anyone. The truck driver waved. A fellow standing near a rare mailbox was startled, but waved and smiled. His tiny house was down a steep bank on the opposite side of a stream. I didn't spot his means for getting there.

Discovery Creek flowed through this narrow valley. It was nearly solid with several feet of ice. What little water I saw, was bright red. I paused to take a picture of a hiker. His red coat reflected colorfully in a mudpuddle. He wondered what I was doing, and we started talking.

Jim gave me my first Eagle welcome. A native of Wisconsin, Jim had lived in Alaska since 1969. He said he walked every morning before the dust kicked up. "I usually carry a small gun, but today I brought a bigger one. There's a moose and calf in this area. You don't know what these creatures will do when they are calving."

I talked to him again later in the day, and he invited me to come for coffee and see his cabin. Jim grinds his own beans for fresh coffee and brews homemade beer. The log cabin had beams from a miner's hundred-year-old cabin. The old logs were shaved to look new. It was a small cabin with an upstairs, totally, about the size of the Sprinter by three. He was slowly carving his existence out of the woods, finishing the cabin at his leisure.

I made my way down the long hill into Eagle. I found the post office first, then the Riverside Cafe. The cafe is in "downtown" Eagle, and has a marvelous view above a wide bend in the Yukon River and Belle Island. Marge brought me a true northwoods breakfast, big and hearty. With a touch of "outside," three weeks worth of mail, I was content.

Later, her husband, John, was doing laundry when I did mine. I asked him about the winters. "I love it," he said. "It's peaceful and quiet." I discovered that was the consensus. Eagle is at the end of the road, where they can go east, north, or west, and walk where few people have trodden, and they like it that way.

"We're quite proud of our little town."

With their only road closed October through April, he said, "The school offers various activities, and families get together more often. The library is heavily used for books and tapes."

The library is small by big-city standards. Hopefully, it will never have those standards. The barrel stove in the center, provides cozy warmth on those minus sixty, very long evenings in Eagle. What more could anyone want, than a reading room, comfortable chairs, and a book supply kept current?

To learn more about Eagle, although I didn't have a card and didn't know anybody in town, Theresa graciously allowed me to take two books written by local people, whom I later met. *Life in a Small Alaskan Bush Community*, by Reverend David Stovner, the minister at the log church, was a very personal view of local life. Elva Scott's manuscript, *Historic Eagle and Its People,* was a wealth of information.

She gave the history of the Han/Athabascan Native Americans who live three miles east of Eagle, in Eagle Village. The population has dwindled to seventeen. The road follows the Yukon River upriver, and continues ten more miles, to accommodate people building even farther away from what most people term, "civilization."

One of Eagle's most famous visitors was the Norwegian explorer, Roald Amundsen. He mushed overland from his sloop, Gjoa, icebound on the Arctic Coast, to Eagle, in December of 1905, to telegraph news of his discovery. After two months of local hospitality, he returned to his ship, and completed the first successful voyage through the Northwest Passage.

I learned a lot about Eagle as I wandered around, but a sign on the side of Elmore Enterprises, really caught my attention, "Raft through untouched Alaskan wilderness." Wow...Maybe...Do you suppose???

Bill Elmore, 46, former North Slope crane operator, jack-of-all-trades, EMT, and guide, didn't laugh when I poured out my soul's desire. "I want to canoe the Mighty Yukon River. I want to experience the wilderness. I want to see it, hear it, touch it, taste it, and smell it. I want to pit myself against nature." What I really wanted to do was erase the look on his face that said, "This woman is a nut case."

Twice, in the four years previous to this trip, I made plans to canoe the Yukon River with different male friends, who were experienced in wilderness camping and canoeing (because I wasn't). Both times, they backed out on me. I finally figured this particular dream was never going to happen. Sometimes, keeping your "Arms open to adventure" takes longer than usual. Even dreams happen in their own time.

Bill said he would "work something up." I had the choice of taking my own equipment and food, or he would provide everything. Since I had given up ever doing this trip, I was not only unprepared physically, I had little of the proper equipment needed. When I left, I was alternately elated with the *possibility* of canoeing the Yukon, and *terrified* it might actually happen.

By Saturday, I couldn't wait any longer. I went back. I was disappointed. No plans. He had been busy working on a Memorial Day speech. Later, on the canoe trip, he confessed he hadn't taken my request seriously. I guess he thought it was a passing thought, and I wouldn't be back. Ha!

Eagle has two airports, one with a grass landing field and the other with a gravel runway for the four daily flights delivering mail, groceries, equipment, or parts. It is cheaper to fly necessities in, than drive the nearly 800 mile round trip to Fairbanks.

I crossed the grassy airport, behind the "Beware of low-flying aircraft" sign, to reach the BLM campground, about a mile from town. It was free. I settled in, only to have a knock on my door at midnight. The Sprinter's lights were on. At midnight in May, I didn't realize they were on.

On my daily mile-long trek through the forest, I watched for moose and sniffed for odor of skunky bears. Visitors to the North country don't think of moose as being dangerous, like bears. I guess it is up for grabs which is the most dangerous. Bears tear you apart and eat you for breakfast, lunch, and dinner, and moose gore or kick you to death and leave you wishing you had been more polite. Some option.

| I understand that if you, and a moose, share the same path, you need specific written permission from the moose to proceed. |
| --- |

Carrying guns, is as much a way of life in Eagle, as planes, snow machines, sled dogs, and four-wheelers, but I didn't have one. My only weapons were strong lungs, and a tire-pounder. If nothing else, I could wedge it between the bear's teeth, while he ripped my arms and legs off, or maybe, break off the tip of a moose antler.

In my wanderings around town, I ran into one of Bill's four sons who said his dad was looking for me. You don't have to look too hard to find anybody in Eagle. The whole town knew he was looking for me. He had the figures. He would provide all equipment, food, and guide service for $180/day for a two-week trip from Eagle to the Dalton Highway. He asked me to think about it and let him know.

Financially, at that moment, it was probably the last thing I should have done, but since I wanted the memory more than the money, I said, "Yes," immediately.

## WOW! WE'RE GOING!

A few tourists arrive by tour bus or the Yukon Queen Riverboat, from Dawson City. Usually, they come by one means, and return by the other. They have little time to see what Eagle is all about. The more adventurous, drive in by car or RV, and stay a few days. John had said, "If you sat at the Jack Wade Junction and watched a hundred cars go by, you would see two turn up here."

The Eagle Trading Company has necessities, plus propane, a motel, and RV hookups, overlooking the river. The Village Store carries groceries and hardware. Gift shops feature creative stationary, basketry, leatherwork, beading, weaving, and quilting. The 160 residents are craftspeople, trappers, carpenters, pilots, miners, teachers, service people, and retirees.

The Sundog Gift Shop offered chocolate frozen yogurt, but I had to wait a few days. The seasonal shops were awakening after a long winter's nap, and the frozen yogurt wasn't frozen yet.

You'll find porcupine quill and moose poop jewelry at the American Summit Gift Shop. In talking with Jean, she said, "'Outside' people don't understand our need for the old-fashioned sponge bath. When you transport and carry your water from a shared well, you don't take numerous showers." She was just as unaware of boondocking in an RV, and taking a "bath in a tea-cup" to stretch the water supply.

The most important thing in Eagle is the public well. It was hand dug in 1902, and now used by 75% of its citizens. Since few have their own water, there are also more outhouses than in a "lower 48" village.

Eagle is unique. Jackie said they had to dig twenty feet, through frozen muck, to hit gravel for a septic system, and previously her garden consisted of planting it in old dirt-filled tires. The muskeg and trees were removed and the soil worked into a rich peat garden. The two months of daylight make up for the short growing season.

Gasoline was $1.83 a gallon. Washing clothes cost $4, $6, or $8, depending on the machine size. A quarter bought three minutes drying time. After $2, I finished drying in the Sprinter. It was the most expensive Laundromat I found. Even in the towns that had no roads leading to them, a load of laundry could be washed *and dried* for $3.75. Only the river trip drove me to do more laundry in Eagle.

On Sunday, I sat in the padless pews of the log non-denominational church, built by Presbyterians at the turn of the century. The original log city hall, behind the church, is still used. The school has twenty students, with a few other youngsters taking correspondence courses. Gold was discovered at American Creek, Fortymile and Seventymile Rivers. Other than privately worked claims, the only functioning gold mine now, is nine miles south of Eagle.

I started my historical tour, going through the Wickersham Courthouse. Judge James Wickersham established the first Federal court in Alaska's interior, in Eagle, in 1900. The Third Judicial District covered 300,000 square miles. Eagle was conceived in 1897, and by 1901, became the first incorporated city in the Interior.

Phyllis Hyde followed her heart to the Yukon, after reading *Coming Into the Country*. As a volunteer, she guided me through the Historical Society's walking tour. Eagle-ites say they may have more square feet of museum displays than anywhere else in Alaska. I'll vouch for it.

She took me into Fort Egbert's six preserved buildings out of an original thirty-seven military buildings. Fort Egbert was built in 1899, to maintain law and order and complete the Washington-Alaska Military Cable and Telegraph System (WAMCATS). By 1903, Billy Mitchell, known later as "The Father of the U. S. Air Force," built the final section, linking Fort Egbert to Fort Liscum, at Valdez, and Fort St. Michael on the Bering Sea. The fort closed its doors in 1911, leaving all equipment intact.

The fire station housed antiques, and the fifty-eight-stall mule barn displayed big items, like dogsleds and mining equipment. We stopped in the Customs House Museum by the river, and found the unusual, (usually what you expect in a museum), dog booties, a cabbage stomper, and an in-house, one-hole, corner-room toilet.

Phyllis pointed out the tiny cabin of Anne Purdy, a young Missouri girl, who came to teach school. She told her story in the book, "*Tisha,*" by Robert Specht. I had read that, and later read, *Coming into the Country*, and recognized the region and a few people.

Phyllis, who referred to Indiana as "out East," had settled into the harsh life of Eagle. Snowmobiling is not only a recreation in Eagle, but a necessity to get around. A few still use dogsleds, but they are mainly for recreation now. Phyllis told stories about breaking through "second" ice with her snowmobile. This is water that has frozen over, on top of the original ice.

Both Jim and Phyllis came to share evening campfires with me, giving me a chance to get acquainted, and learn their views of life in Eagle. Phyllis and I had lunch together at the cafe a couple of times, and I have heard from her since.

Jim invited me to the seasonal grand opening of a tavern his friends owned, halfway back to the junction. Taverns aren't exactly my thing since I don't drink; but in the North, they are also gathering places for a bit of social life. Jim asked if I knew what the bell above my head was for. I shook my head, thinking it was a decoration. He told me to ring it. I did, and all the locals laughed. It meant you were buying drinks for everyone. They didn't make me honor it, since I was a greenie.

A bus load of tourists stopped, and Jim and the others gave them a bit of local color. For a while I felt almost like one of the locals.

On Memorial Day, I went to the cemetery with the high white picket fence, in time to hear the bugler play *America* and *God Bless America*. Bill (the guide) told a story about another bugler, who lived at the fort in Eagle, in the early 1900s.

> "He came to visit in 1969 and told about playing his bugle when it was 79° below zero. He claimed,
> 'It echoed off Eagle Bluff and straight to God.'"

Bill said, "We should ask ourselves what we can do to help keep our freedom intact, to preserve what these people died for." He became quite emotional when he spoke of his father, who had been in three wars. You knew it all meant a lot to him; it wasn't just words. The bugler closed the ceremony, playing *Taps* over new graves and local heros, of a hundred years ago.

Afterward, Bill came to talk about the river itinerary. We covered a lot of territory in that short hour. Enough, that we felt we could survive two weeks together in the wilderness. I warned him again that I had done a lot of camping and canoeing, but nothing of this magnitude. He didn't flinch. He was a brave man.

I spent the week doing laundry, packing one tall but skinny duffel bag, writing columns ahead, and making phone calls to my daughters and brothers. They were excited for me, especially Janet, my oldest. If she could have managed it, she would have been right there in the middle of the canoe.

> On my last evening, I had a panoramic view while eating my veggieburger at the Riverside Cafe. Fresh snow covered a distant mountain. Storm clouds made quilted patterns of sunshine and darkness in the foreground. Ice chunks still clung to the shoreline of the Yukon River. The spell of the North was upon me, big time; and I knew the next day, I was starting the adventure of a lifetime.

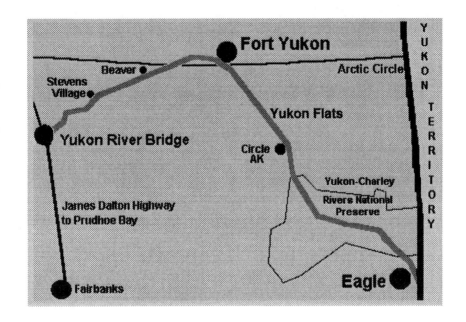

# THE MIGHTY YUKON RIVER

From my roots in Michigan soil
I sought a wilderness dream
To canoe the Mighty Yukon
And pan in a rock-laden stream

I yearned to be in the bosom of the
Birds and the bugs and the beasts
To experience the wonders of nature
In endless and infinite feasts

Beyond the Arctic Circle I canoed
I found gold in the rock-laden stream
I'll always be grateful for memories
Of living my wilderness dream

Several sources gave the length of the Yukon River, anywhere from 1,979 to 2,300 miles long. They were in agreement that it was Alaska's longest river, and North America's fifth largest river. The river has been called the "Mason-Dixon line," splitting Alaska into two very distinct halves, arctic and subarctic, with the Brooks Mountain Range to the north, and the Alaska Mountain Range to the south.

From Eagle to the Dalton Highway, the Yukon is a Class I (no rapids) area. I knew hypothermia would likely claim our lives if storms or whirlpools, or any wrong moves, dumped us in the middle of the often mile-wide, frigid (35º - 38º F) river. I knew grizzlies were a danger, bugs would be annoying, and if either of us became incapacitated in any way, we were isolated. I didn't realize how much trouble I was in, until Bill announced, "We'll have to average forty miles a day." Without batting an eye (because my body paralyzed with the thought), I still managed a resounding "Yessss!" May 31 was the big day.

I had given a great deal of thought over the last four years, to what the experience would be like. I studied topo maps (which didn't mean a heck of a lot to me), read canoeing books, books on the Yukon River, and the Indian villages along the way. I had devoured books about anyone who actually canoed the Yukon.

With all the studying, and all the canoeing and kayaking I had done over the years, nothing prepared me for how small the little red canoe looked, compared to the fast-moving Yukon River. It passes Eagle at 1.4 million gallons per second, with an average current of five to eight miles per hour.

> Only my faith in God, Bill's expertise as a guide, and my sense of the ultimate adventure, forced me into that canoe. I had goosebumps the size of cannonballs.

I don't know if Bill was aware of how inadequate I felt at that moment, but then again, I knew, absolutely, that I could do it. I had lived other dreams, and I would live this one too.

He gave me a running commentary as we passed the Riverside Cafe, the Custom House Museum, Mission Creek, and Eagle Bluff. The town is named after the bald eagles that nest on the greenstone bluff that rises 1,000 feet above the town. It dates back 600 million years. It took a while before my eyes zeroed in on the stark white head of the bald eagle in a treetop nest.

> Eagle, Alaska, was soon behind us, and we wouldn't return, until we had canoed across the
> Arctic Circle.

Our "bare bones" equipment included: two big boxes and two small coolers of food, one waterproof bag each for personal gear, a four-man tent, poles, sleeping bags, pads, tarp, maps, and freshwater jugs, packed between two lawn chairs, in the middle of the canoe.

The chairs were a stroke of genius on Bill's part. They served as sides to hold the equipment. We each had daypacks with binoculars, cameras, film, writing materials, and other *necessities* at our feet, plus lifejackets, and water sippers, to stay hydrated in the wind and sun.

Ice chunks on the riverbanks, had gathered enough dirt in their long journey from numerous tributaries, to become black. The ice snagged, and piled up on sand and gravel bars. When it broke apart, it made a clunking noise, and resembled shards of glass that were pristine sparkly. It made a tinkling sound when the river ran through the hollowed pieces.

Our first stop was to talk with a fellow who was living off the land in a log cabin tucked in the trees. He had a large dog who adopted me, but she was so friendly, she nearly knocked me off my pins. We looked out on Calico Bluff, a major landmark on the river. The black and white limestone twists every which way but loose, and lives up to its name.

Before we had gone far, a storm appeared frighteningly fast. We double-timed to shore, and Bill had a tarp shelter across a log quicker than you could say supercalafragalisticexpialidocious, all to no avail. The storm passed as quickly as it came. It was the first of many times I heard Bill mumble into his growing beard, "She wants to pit herself against nature."

We stopped at McMullen's cabin, at the edge of a slough, for lunch. It was built on stilts. During spring breakup, the river rises and backs up. We went inside. Bill reached around and closed the door after me, cautioning me to always make sure the door was shut. "Bears may come in right behind you." We were both wet from the rainstorm. He started a fire. We dried ourselves, while a dinner of Ramen noodles mixed with fresh-canned salmon, cooked. With hot tea, it was a feast fit for royalty.

Bill explained that outlying cabins are usually left unlocked. "If anyone gets caught in the wilderness and needs food or shelter, they are welcome to use them." This hospitality saves lives. They had the fanciest outhouse I had ever seen.

My excitement was beyond description...for the first thirty miles. We pulled into an open sunny area and stretched out on the ground. It was one of many breaks we would initiate over the next two weeks. I often curled up right on the bank and went to sleep, something I would never do back in my native Michigan. There were few bugs, and Alaska doesn't have snakes.

At thirty-five miles, my eyes glazed over. At 8:30 p.m. and forty miles, we pulled in for the night. Since I had agreed, with unbounded enthusiasm, that we would share the work, Bill wound me up, and I automatically carried gear and supplies to the sandbar. I didn't feel tired; I couldn't feel. My arms had dropped off at thirty-eight miles.

We had Mama moose tracks with Baby moose tracks alongside; bear tracks followed them. Bill said it was a small bear, "But sometimes they are more curious, and therefore, more dangerous."

Bill put the tent on dry sand and in the bushes, to keep out of the wind. He fastened a small attachment on the tent opening to keep wind and rain at bay, but we soon discovered that was a nuisance and didn't use it again.

A hot meal, hand-dipped into my mouth by a sympathetic and much younger guide, renewed my strength. If I had any doubts about his wilderness camping ability, they disappeared when he balanced a time-honored, and fire-blackened, kettle on the burning logs to heat water.

It didn't get dark, only darker. By the time dinner and chores were done, it was already quite late. A sleeping bag never felt so good. My arms experienced Excedrin Headache #435. I took three Vanquish. After about four hours, the aches disappeared, and I fell asleep.

During the night, we both heard wolves howling. There is nothing quite like wolves howling, to make you realize you are in the wilderness. While I have no desire to challenge one face-to-face, I thrilled at hearing them.

Morning brought a glorious paddling day on a smooth-as-glass river. By afternoon, it was quite warm.

We hadn't much more than commented on our disappointment in the lack of animals, when I saw a grizzly, padding along the river's edge, grubbing for food. We watched him as long as we could backpaddle. He sniffed the air a couple of times but didn't run away.

Less than a mile farther, Mama Moose lent us a distant view of her wobbly new twins. Later, a mother, and her yearling, ran along the river's edge, their hooves clicking against the gravel.

We stopped at several National Park Service cabins. They were similar and usually sunken into the permafrost, except for the cabin restored to its original condition to the tune of $73,000 (pricey!).

Doors were heavy and bear-proof (if anything is bear-proof). The interiors were dark, rustic with bunk beds, barrel stove, a few utensils, and table and chairs. Windows nailed shut, with the business end of the nails protruding, discouraged bears. A book logged visitor's comments on river conditions, animal sightings, and where they were from.

It was a sixty-mile haul to Slaven's Roadhouse, our second day on the river, and our only night under a roof. Slaven's is a restored roadhouse from the days when paddlewheelers plied the Yukon, and a roadhouse existed every twenty miles.

The roadhouse is on the National Register of Historic Places, named after Frank Slaven, who discovered gold on Coal Creek. Two anterooms led into one big room downstairs. Two large rooms were upstairs with kitchen facilities. The two-holed bathroom facilities were thirty running steps from the back door.

Dinner brought a spurt of energy for getting water from Coal Creek to boil, and let cool, before we poured it into plastic containers. The parasite, Giardia, is a threat, no matter where you are.

Bill slept in a bunk bed, and I had the second room, with a mattress in the middle of the floor. It was the most uncomfortable night I spent the entire trip. It was light enough all night that I could read.

We are both early risers, so we were often up and out by 6 a.m. Our one foray inland took us two miles along a curlicue path, worn into the permafrost and muskeg along Coal Creek, to see the gold dredge. The

Coal Creek Gold Dredge

NPS is preserving the dredge. It was shipped in from California and utilized until the 1960s.

It was eerie, climbing narrow stairs to the many levels, and seeing miner's tools on benches, or leaning against the wall, as if they had walked off the job two hours before. This huge piece of equipment was so far away from anywhere. Of course, the Yukon River is still a highway through Alaska's interior.

The creek was still carving its way through several feet of ice, but we managed to pan for gold in the few open gravel areas. Bill played his harmonica, and I explored and took pictures. We left, wealthy beyond measure, not in the few gold flakes we found, but in the surrounding beauty, and a perfect crisp, spring morning.

By the time we returned to the roadhouse, the river was in great turmoil. The wind whipped the water into whitecaps, and blew sand across a downriver island. While we waited for calmer waters, Bill built a fire in the barrel stove. We read and slept all afternoon.

We didn't want to spend another night in a building. We took off about 6 p.m. We paddled close to shore, but didn't progress more than three miles. The wind nearly blew us over crossing a slough. It wasn't worth the fight. The sky looked like it was going to let go any minute.

We had little cover and no choices. I found a spot in the bushes on the side of a rise. Bill cut willow branches to make room for the tent. The bushes helped keep the wind off, but we had mighty slanty ground to sleep on.

After a mad dash to set up before the deluge fell, the wind calmed, the rain went away, and the sun came out. We had a great fire, and Bill played his harmonica. We agreed the first one to awaken would check the river. If it was smooth, we would leave, *no matter how early it was.*

I woke up at 2:30 a.m. The river was smooth as pudding. With caution the better part of valor, I tapped his sleeping bag with the 44 next to it. True to his word, we were on the river by 3 a.m. Although the sun had barely dipped to the horizon, we watched it pop back over snow-covered mountains, a magnificent day on the Yukon.

Bill Elmore, Guide, Gold Panning, Coal Creek

During a slack time, I noticed Bill scribbling furiously, rewording future contracts, "There will be no paddling before my time."

Enormous ice chunks, imbedded in the river banks during breakup, had snapped trees like matchsticks and undercut the permafrost. The booming sound of trees and banks breaking away and falling into the river, startled us many times, and changed the contour of the land. Glacial silt from spring runoff, made the river gritty. The canoe sounded like it was pushing through sandpaper.

The Yukon River can change from calm and peaceful, to windy with high waves, and become dangerous in a manner of minutes. Sometimes, we went through "riffles," where the water over the rocks was only inches deep. Two streams converging caused violent turbulence, depending on the speed and volume of the water. Choppy whirlpools were a danger, and the current itself, sometimes boiled and swirled, as it moved over an uneven bottom.

Because of our early trip, we shared the river with some debris. Full-sized trees floated by. Collections of natural rubble (strainers), often forced us away from the inside bend of the river. It was really amazing that only an infinitesimal amount of it was human litter.

Bill constantly observed the weather, and I learned to do it, too. Stormy clouds were fascinating to watch, a precursor to danger. We often experienced dramatic weather changes, but the worst of the whole trip, were the last three choppy river miles into Circle, Alaska. They were a nightmare.

Though Bill was no doubt tired, his strength, endurance, and revivability, were far greater than mine. This was our longest paddling day, at

63 miles. Exhausted, I can't remember another time on the trip, when I felt more like having, "Scotty beam me up." Given terrain that didn't lend itself to camping, we knew we had to keep going. Even with a map, Circle could have been missed. It is not on the main channel. When we could finally see the town, with the wind and waves against us, it seemed like we paddled forever before we finally hit shore.

Even at that, we were fortunate. People coming into Circle from Fort Yukon, said the waves downriver were four feet high.

Circle has about a hundred residents now but, it was the largest town on the Yukon, before the Klondike Gold Rush. Looking at it in 1996, it took a lot to imagine what it was like, when it referred to itself as, the "Paris of the North."

Early miners named Circle. They thought they were camped on the Arctic Circle. They missed it by fifty miles. Steese Highway, mostly gravel, leads to Circle from Fairbanks. It was my last chance to back out. No way, Jose!

Our first stop was in the Yukon Trading Post, a combination log saloon, store, and restaurant. Bill had carried his backpack with him, so he had a chance to clean up before eating. I was a total wreck, but nobody screamed, so I didn't think too much about it. A hamburger and French fries never tasted so good.

People were friendly, and we felt quite safe leaving our belongings in the tent. Camping is free on the riverbank.

The wind was blowing so hard, we tied the tent to the picnic table. Bill retrieved a food replacement box he had sent ahead to Circle, and used it to anchor the other side of the tent.

The Circle Washeteria had hot showers. They required quarters; but, the hot water felt so good on my weary bones, I used eight of them. It took the first quarter and a half to figure out how it worked. I didn't feel so bad when I discovered Bill had the same problem.

When I went in, the doors to the showers were open, so I didn't see the labels on the doors. I walked into the first shower stall. Later Bill came in and saw only the woman's door open. He realized I had gone into the men's shower. They were the same. We later laughed about it. I had been saying, "I am **WOMAN;** I can do anything" to talk myself into ability. Now, I told him, *he* could be "**WOMAN**" as well.

After watching the wind and weather for four hours the next morning, we stayed in Circle another night. The air was frigid. It wouldn't have been a good paddling day, even without the wind.

Bill borrowed a truck to drive forty miles to Circle Hot Springs, but then we found out the road closed at Central, because of a forest fire. We could see the smoke from it.

I sat in the warm restaurant, catching up on my log, making seminar notes, and having fresh pie and milk, at $2 a glass. The rest of the time, I read in the tent, slept, or wandered around town. Houses were log, with a few frame homes. Planes tethered in back yards, strained to go flying.

Snowmobiles slept until winter rolled around again. Gasoline was $1.73/gallon.

In the wee hours, dogs barked. Shouting drunks made dirt-scattering trips through the campground with horns blasting. Mysterious bells clanged. Although we both looked at it through somewhat glazed eyes, the sunrise was spectacular. No more overnighting in villages.

Bill had never guided beyond Circle. On leaving town, we were *both* in strange territory. Since shortly after leaving Eagle, we had been paddling through the 128 mile, 2,500,000 acre Yukon-Charley Rivers National Preserve. Our next 300 miles were through the unconfined waters of the 8,630,000 acre Yukon Flats National Wildlife Refuge.

The Yukon waters became braided, and oxbows nearly touched. The river was sometimes twenty miles wide, and filled with 40,000 lakes, ponds, and islands. Despite my topo maps, we couldn't judge where we were. The maps hadn't been updated since 1955. With several feet of shoreline falling into the river daily, landmarks had to have changed a great deal in forty years.

Old fish camps and cabins were marked on the map, but what we actually saw, few and far between, were of newer vintage. Since the decline of the boomtowns during gold rush days, the river valley is less populated.

It was truly amazing that two strangers got on so well. We never argued. I considered him to have the ultimate word about all things (that in itself, amazed my children). Bill always thought about my comfort, although I occasionally questioned his advice.

> **In the land of two million migrating ducks, geese, and great supply, he said,**
> **"Use goose poop on your lips, so you aren't tempted to lick them and cause chapping."**

I wanted to hit him over the head with a paddle once or twice, but since he was behind me, he had nothing to worry about. I don't even remember what prompted those feelings, probably being tired, more than anything. I'm sure he felt the same way sometimes, but as a guide, it wouldn't have looked good to other clients.

We didn't see many flowers blooming, although Bill did find some wild roses, and we had scent of pine. We startled our share of water fowl. The geese honked; the gulls screamed; the Arctic terns squawked; and the ducks quacked up. Another strange bird softly played, *When the Saints go Marching in* and *Oh Susanna*.

We spelled each other for taking pictures, writing, or when Bill checked the maps. I had no problem holding the canoe on course in calm water, but I couldn't control it from the front, in choppy water.

In quieter times, when the water was calm, the sun was warm, and billowy white clouds floated through azure skies, we laid back and let the current turn the canoe in lazy circles. It was unbelievably peaceful. I wanted to bottle a bit of that peace to give to so many who would never know its joy.

**It was like living a prayer. I know that God is everywhere but I feel His presence more in solitude. I often talk about "Moments in time." This is what they are all about.**

One of the things I most appreciated about Bill was that he was also quiet during those times. Friends questioned my wanting to make the trip with only one other person. A group of people generates too much noise. I wanted to hear, and see, and taste, and smell, and feel everything around me, without interruption. I got it.

We exchanged stories from our experiences and backgrounds. Bill was as family-oriented as I am, and very proud of his four teenage sons. He spoke of his wife with great love and affection. We were quite comfortable with each other.

He mentioned several times around the campfire, that he was really enjoying the trip, and said I was good company. One night he added, "At least you *want to be here*." He explained that his most frequent raft trips, from Dawson City to Eagle, usually last five days. About two days out, one or two people will realize this primitive, camping, canoeing "stuff" isn't at all what they thought it would be. The rest of the trip, they are miserable and make sure everyone else is, too.

After water was heated for washing in the evening, we took turns, with one being in the tent to clean up, while the other did the same outdoors. Early in the trip, mosquitoes were not a problem although washing outside was a bit chilling sometimes.

Because I don't like to be cold, washing outdoors required what I call, the amazing Minshall "Remove your under layers, and wash under the outer layers" trick. It was fast, thorough, mosquito and wind free, and effective, sort of.

One evening it was my turn to be outdoors. The weather was warmer than usual. I took everything off as I washed, and stood there buck naked. Except for Bill, occupied inside the tent, there wasn't another soul for a hundred miles. I knew God and the animals wouldn't mind. I didn't walk around; I just stood there and let the air dry my skin, and hugged myself.

---

For all of you who are so brave as to backpack the world or live in the wilderness for months on end,
or do other things that I will never do,
you probably won't understand.
This was a wilderness "Moment" of sheer joy for the
Midwestern Presbyterian Widow Minshall.
I can't explain it, and I won't try.
Maybe it was the closest I will ever come to
"being one with nature."

After one rest stop, he couldn't find the maps. We pulled ashore, and he still couldn't find them. Going back meant lining the canoe upriver, and fighting our way back across a large slough, then overland to where we had stopped. It never looked like the current was strong until you tried to cross it. It would probably have taken us two hours. He completely unloaded the canoe and found them folded in a chair.

Since the maps didn't give us a clue as to our location, we surprised ourselves by arriving at Fort Yukon, the northernmost point of the Yukon River, in less than a day and a half.

> **About eight miles from town, we had paddled over the Arctic Circle with nary a bump for recognition or celebration.**

Fort Yukon, at the confluence of the Yukon and Porcupine Rivers, was the largest village we visited. It has a population of about 700, a mixture of Athabascan Natives and Caucasians. Two years after the arrival of John Bell of the Hudson Bay Company, in 1845, Fort Yukon was established, the first English-speaking community in Alaska.

We asked some kids if our gear would be safe in the canoe on the river. Clearly, they thought not. They directed us to the Sourdough Inn. The waitress agreed, if we left our gear for long, it would be forever gone. Bill eventually found a fellow who tied our canoe below his house. Nobody bothered it.

The Sourdough Inn was weathered outside, which wasn't unusual; everything looks weathered in such unforgiving country. It also looked like it would blow away in the first strong wind. I used the upstairs rest room, and peeked in the open bedroom doors. They were sparse but clean...and unbelievably squeejawed.

I ran into another Bill downstairs, a big strapping fellow with a full beard, coveralls, a nice sense-of-humor, and a glint in his eye. He said the Sourdough had been a brothel, a school, dance hall, barber and dental combination shop, and now, a hotel and restaurant. The building had been Officers' Quarters for Fort Egbert at Eagle. Five building parts were floated down the Yukon to Fort Yukon, in 1926. Three parts went on down to the Bering Sea. Two parts were caught in Ft. Yukon and put together in the current Sourdough Hotel. No wonder the building was squeejawed.

After breakfast (two eggs for $3, or a whole breakfast for $9), we walked downtown. It was never really hot on the river, but it was very hot and dusty in town. Bill looked for material to repair the canoe. It had a tiny hole in it, and he had been paddling with wet feet.

Ft. Yukon can only be reached by water or air. Three-and-four wheelers are a popular warm-weather transportation, ranked right up there with snowmobiles for winter. Gasoline was $2.20/gallon.

Although everyone we met was friendly, neither of us wanted to camp in town. The bucking waves slapped against the canoe, flipping water inside. We fought the wind and waves until we crossed the Porcupine River outlet, then pulled in. We were within sight of the village. The choice of campsites wasn't too great, but, it was late enough in the day, we didn't want to continue fighting the elements.

With our proximity to the trees and dry tinder, the wind was too strong to have a fire. After Bill repaired the canoe, we sat where the wind kept the mosquitoes at bay, and snacked on tuna, crackers, fruit, and a sipper. Our entertainment was watching pilots risk their lives making treeline bombing runs. They dropped red fire retardant on a forest fire that started while we were in Fort Yukon (Honest, we didn't have anything to do with it).

Beyond a curve in the river the next morning, the wind blasted us again. After several tries, Bill put up the tent. We slept and read. At 3:30 p.m., the sun was shining, and the wind seemed calmer. Ha!. Around the curve, it was waiting for us. We couldn't win. We paddled four hundred miles that day, and progressed fifteen. The good news was that the patch job worked. Bill had dry feet.

Afternoons were generally warm, but the rest of the time it was varying degrees of cool to cold, and a fire felt mighty good. Firewood was plentiful. Logs and wood floated into convenient stacks on sandbars, where we sought nightly, or breaktime refuge. I maintained my One-Match Minshall Girl Scout status, and in defending man's reputation, Bill became One-Match Elmore. The ashes of our fires built on the river's edge, would wash away in the next storm. No one would know we had passed that way.

We saw only four boats on the river. The fish weren't running yet. The fish camps, near the four villages, were empty. Fish-drying racks, benches, tables, and shelters were made of available material, with the added blue tarp. Tin cans, and any other trash the villagers had accumulated, rusted on the ground, but they did have great views.

Alaska residents have subsistence hunting and fishing rights, by permit. This means they may hunt or fish for the necessities of life but cannot sell the bounty.

On one of our colder lunch breaks, we walked back into the sand dunes and willow bushes and sat in the warm sun, watching the river in the distance. It was a popular place for Mama and Baby moose with the usual bear tracks following. Baby moose is a favorite bear snack. Bill saw a wolf track.

A fox trotted along beside us as we canoed away. When we crossed a slough, a beaver sitting on an outcropping, surprised us almost as much as we surprised him. He flipped into the water posthaste and slapped his tail, as a warning to his brothers and his sisters all over that land.

Seeing so few animals disappointed us both, but Bill had sworn to protect my life for two weeks in the wilderness. He said confrontation with a bear or moose was unlikely; but to his credit, he defended me against an extraordinary amount of tracks.

Bill followed "The high water" or main stream. Only once were we forced into a slough. We didn't start across in time and couldn't get out of its current. After several curves, it became apparent we might not be lucky enough for it to have adequate water to connect to the river again. The canoe mired in mud. Bill said, "We may have to get out and push." I said, "What do we mean '*we*,' hired guide?" Fortunately, Bill had a great sense-of-humor. We muscled the canoe out and into deeper water. We found the main channel five miles downstream.

After battling again with foot-and-a-half waves, we stopped on a high gravel outcropping on the tip of an island. The chunks of ice we had been seeing, were no longer evident on this side of Fort Yukon, but there were huge boxlike depressions in the gravel, where the ice had melted.

We sat in our chairs on the hill, surveying our kingdom. Suddenly, Bill jumped out of his chair and went pell-mell down the hill. He had put his pack on top of the other gear while he hunted for something, and didn't put it down in the canoe again. A gust of wind flipped it into the water. He rescued it, but not before it ruined his binoculars.

Many food items had a really high fat content, and I wasn't used to it. Bill obviously wasn't either. Happy hours were less champagne and caviar, more Maalox and aspirin with $H_2O$ chasers. To be fair, Bill had only five days to buy food, and that required a 400-mile round-trip flight to Fairbanks. He also had to tie up loose ends of his business and think out two weeks of canoe travel with an inexperienced partner. Come to think of it; he was pretty brave.

Sometimes it was a matter of getting tired of the same thing. He discovered the large assortment of bagels had molded, before we could possibly have eaten them. Actually, I was used to eating pretty green things from my own RV refrigerator, but.... Rather than waste them, he put them to scientific use. He threw them off the hill to see which way the main current went. Hmmm. I was trusting my life to this person.

> **I very much appreciated Bill giving thanks to God, for our safety and good health, before each meal. After several days of our combined gourmet cooking, we both considered it in our best interests for him to continue.**
> **By the ninth day, I detected his prayers becoming more frequent, more fervent, and**
> **infinitely more grateful.**

Our days started early, and by 5 p.m., I really needed to get off the river. While Bill put up the tent, I built a big fire around a tree stump and baked potatoes, made barbecue to go over them, and baked apples for dessert.

The storm in the distance was suddenly *upon* us. It is amazing how quickly two people can get inside a zipped tent when a full-blown storm descends. The tent was well staked, but even with us in it, we thought it was going to blow away. The sides were blowing in against us, so the water seeped through. After the worst was over, he opened the flap and I snapped a picture of a fantastic rainbow.

Home Sweet Home on the Yukon

Beaver was the smallest community we visited, with about seventy Eskimo and Indian residents. It had log cabins, a few businesses, lots of snowmobiles, four-wheelers, and boats. Every village had a decided hum. Enormous diesel generators provide electricity twenty-four hours a day. Fuel comes in by barge once a year.

Since the passage of the Alaska Native Claims Settlement Act, all Native villages are privately owned. Although I did take pictures, I always asked permission before taking pictures of people. I kept a low profile, insofar as a complete stranger keeps a low profile in a village that can only be reached by river or sky.

When our canoe pulled in, it was instant news. A guide led us to the showers. You might expect facilities in an isolated bush community to be primitive, at best. Not true. Each village had a combination laundromat, bathroom and shower building, operated by the local Tribal Council, and were new, well maintained and heated.

Looking in a mirror was no picnic. My face was bright red from windburn and sunburn and swollen. I had owl eyes from wearing dark glasses, and my hair resembled a fugitive from a wind tunnel. My skin had more a leathery look than its usual magnificent look of fine porcelain (?). I doubled up on lotion and Vaseline.

I think my brain was sun-fried too. I had forgotten both towel and washcloth and had to use the inside of my dirty sweatshirt to dry off.

People in the villages would always tell us that the next village was, "Really bad; you can't leave anything in your canoe." Each village had its own personality, and Bill made friends immediately. He always made connections between someone in the village, and someone who lived in Eagle, a cousin, a friend, or another relative. When it became apparent he was not an "outsider," we were accepted.

In a roadless community, where everyone depends on everyone else for survival, it is probably the only place in the U. S. A. that would open a post office on Sunday, so he could pick up a food box.

I talked with a family whose summer home was Beaver. They had come to fish. Their winter home was Barrow, three hundred miles farther north! I had been to Barrow. The wind chill factor on June 30th was thirty below zero. Beaver was definitely warmer.

Since I was part of a Nalukataq (whale-kill celebration) in Barrow, and ate muktuk, I asked them about it. The fellow fairly drooled. He loved muktuk. She said they eat it with meat but he likes it by itself. I have to be honest, I prefer pizza to fermented whale blubber. That's what is so fascinating about life in the far North; it is so different.

They told me that lots of people had died in the river, due to dumb mistakes. She also mentioned a bad spot upriver, but we never saw it.

Old Bill, who had unlocked the shower building, and showed me how everything worked, came down to say good-bye, as we shoved off. He had retired from the railroad in Fairbanks, and now, "just helps people whenever I can." Others were helping, too; eight people from Beaver were out fire fighting.

Before leaving Beaver, they warned us not to leave our gear unguarded at the next village.

The evening after Beaver was the only time I felt down, on the whole trip. I took a long walk in the sunshine, curled up on a warm sand dune, and I cried myself to sleep. I realized this fabulous adventure was nearly over, and I wasn't ready for it to end.

Everything I read while preparing for the Yukon River trip, warned of mosquitoes, black flies, ticks, and no-see-ums. Except for the times when the tent was in the trees, mosquitoes were not a problem, until our campsite after Beaver. Even then, it was more of an onslaught when we first arrived like, **"Hey gals, we've got blood!"** The fire and smoke discouraged them. I fell asleep to the buzz of mosquitoes, but they were outside. Bill accepted them in his usual laid-back demeanor. He only used his 44 a couple of times.

On that pre-trip afternoon, when we discussed the nitty-gritty details, he said he would need help with chores, since it was just the two of us. I fully agreed; in fact, I insisted I be part of the experience, not just watch it, but he had the brunt of it. He often said I was pulling my weight but then he was also very kind, so I can only hope it was so.

We started on a smooth-as-glass river at 6:30 a.m. with beautiful weather. We were beginning to see snow-capped mountains in the distance again. For several days, the highest elevation was a fifty-foot river bank. Swirling storm clouds brought whitewater and sand-filled mini-tornadoes to the islands.

We scrambled to set up the tent far enough off the river for tree protection. It thundered and rained, off and on the rest of the afternoon. In between rains, I walked the beach, following moose tracks.

We had to keep going at a good pace because Bill's son was going to meet us at the Dalton Highway. We were maintaining a day ahead of schedule, but it was always a possibility the wind would cause each paddle stroke to be a struggle, and we would need that extra day.

He said he regretted that he didn't get a hand-held instrument called a GPS, Global Positioning System, which sends a signal to a satellite. The return signal pinpoints where you are, using map coordinates. It would have been fun to see exactly where we were, but then again, it was kind of exciting not knowing. In my RVing world, I often don't know where I am.

We hadn't passed the Dalton Highway because we'd have noticed the bridge (since it is the only one crossing the Yukon River). (Unless of course, we had passed under it, thinking it was a low cloud, and we were now well on our way to the Bering Sea. Hmmm)

Bill was up at 4:30 a.m. The weather was still pretty bad. The river was smooth, but the clouds were dark and ominous. Bill wanted to stay but I wanted to go, while the river was smooth and energy was high. I was tired of laying around. I felt we could deal with the rain, if we didn't have the wind. He was restless, too. He built a long-poled teepee on the beach with scavenged wood.

We finally took off in a slight rain, then the wind hit again. As we had so many times, we paddled within ten feet of shore and kept going.

Paddling next to shore, often let us see what we would have missed otherwise. We paddled right next to two sandhill cranes. I thought at first they were herons. I had never seen them before. Where the river undercut the banks, grass and weeds caught in the roots and lay over the edge, like a great curled carpet. Underneath, was the dark frozen permafrost.

We never saw a peregrine falcon, noted in the Yukon-Charley Rivers Preserve, but we did see many bald eagles along the way. I saw two gulls harassing an eagle. They would not give up, and managed to chase him away by constantly diving at him.

The following morning, the air was still, and the river was smooth, but I didn't want to get up. I didn't want to get off the river early. I was comfortable and liked listening to nature sounds, and Bill rattling around with the fire. The perfect guide had coffee ready and breakfast made. We enjoyed a calm morning.

The days began with excitement and bravado. I shouted into the sky, "Good Morning, God, Hello World" and the first chorus of "Oh What a Beautiful Morning." A quiet voice in the back recesses of the canoe said, "*Now you know why we aren't seeing many animals.*"

Stevens Village, our last one, numbered around a hundred residents. As did the other villages, this one had a couple of churches, a grocery and supply store, a post office, and school.

While I stayed with the canoe, Bill wandered. Two men came along and told me the blue-tarped place we had seen upriver about sixteen miles, was where they were logging poles for a large community building. For food and gasoline, anyone could go work.

When Bill came back, he had Oliver Ben with him, a sweet old gent, who opened the showers for us. Bill had talked with several villagers and made connections with their kith and kin. Satisfied nobody would bother our gear, we combined our few dirty clothes in the laundromat and took showers.

Originally, I envisioned taking enough clothes for the entire trip, and washing only a few light things when necessary. I never dreamed we would have Laundromats and showers; however, the villages were interesting and the facilities welcome.

Our last stop was just before going into a long canyon, between the Ray and White Mountains. The steep banks wouldn't have lent themselves well to campsites. The wind wasn't too bad on the gravel bar, but that also meant we had nothing but smoke to keep the mosquitoes away. I learned something with the advent of mosquitoes. I leave you with this profound thought,

> **"If you moon a mosquito, repellent is the 'bottom' line for comfort."**

My female friends had asked, "How will you go to the bathroom?" I was concerned, because I figured we would be in tundra country with no trees. It is obvious to me that a great number of people have no interest in the answer to that question, as books about wilderness camping *never* touch the subject. May I be so indelicate as to answer this way.

*Going* is not a problem, since nature has a way of making everything come out in the end. Privacy wasn't a problem. Since we were both adults with adult functions, it was no secret we would have to "go" sometime. Bill stopped adequately often for such functions, because we needed to take "arm breaks" anyhow. He said, "Gentlemen to the left, ladies to the right," or I would simply announce, "I'm going to find a bush." Since we had six children between us, we even used the word, "potty," occasionally. Holes were dug, waste was buried, and any paper used, was burned in the fire.

Yes, with two people of the opposite sex traveling together, we were great respectors of each other's privacy in dressing, bathing, and finding suitable willow bushes. I never felt the least bit uncomfortable with Bill.

By the same token, the question from friends after the trip was, "Did you use two tents?" Bill had asked if I would mind sleeping in the same tent, or would I prefer a tent by myself. Since it would have meant extra gear, I told him, "As long as your wife doesn't mind, one tent is fine with me. I assume you will be a gentleman at all times," and having even a few short conversations with him, I knew he would be.

Besides, he had the gun.

Carpal Tunnel Syndrome surfaced with so much paddling. Sometimes I let go of the paddle, and vigorously shook the tingling out of my hands. Bill suggested if I pounded my hands with a rock, I would soon forget the Carpal Tunnel Syndrome. You can tell, his advice was priceless.

We had canoed beside ice chunks, through mountain passes lined with spruce, poplar, and birch trees, to the Taiga, "Land of little sticks," denoting the sparse tree growth above the Arctic Circle. We returned again to the wooded mountains carpeted with sphagnum moss. In the meantime, Mother Nature had painted all the sprouting rushes and willow shrubs in spring green.

Birds bathed in the big puddle next to the tent, all night. With all the daylight, they never seem to sleep. The last day dawned sunny and windless, but I hated getting up. It was also the end of a super adventure.

We didn't build a fire. We packed and loaded, while the mosquitoes ate breakfast, us. Two miles into the canyon, we ate ours in the middle of the river.

The canyon was long and straight, a change from the huge snaking loops we had canoed. We took our time and drifted quietly, alone in our own thoughts, knowing our solitude would soon be assaulted by *the world*.

I am a writer, and still I can't adequately express what that trip meant to me. It was peaceful, exciting, dramatic, inspiring. It left me even more in awe of God and the wilderness. Whenever I need peace in the midst of chaos, I close my eyes and remember floating in circles in the current (preferably when I'm not driving).

We rounded a bend, and there it was, the silver Trans-Alaska Pipeline perched along the top of the trees.

> We pulled out near the Yukon River Bridge at the Dalton Highway, 500 miles and fourteen days wiser.
> My terrific guide gave me a big hug and said, "We did it. I'm proud of you."

The Yukon River Bridge, completed in 1975, is impressive. It is 2,290' long with a 6% grade, and the only permanent crossing over the Yukon River. Dinner tours from the bridge, go upriver a short distance to a Native fish camp.

The "Haul Road," or Dalton Highway, opened to the public in 1994. According to the chef in the improved line-camp restaurant, a lot of RVs, bus tours, and private cars are making the trip. I was surprised it had become so touristy in only two years.

In comparison to the drab exterior, the inside of the restaurant was downtown stuff with cloth napkins, tablecloths, and candles. I had a sandwich heaped with ham on fresh bread. Yummy. Hey, I just got off the river. I was into practical and practical hit the spot.

From the river, it was 360 miles to the Deadhorse security gate at the Prudhoe Bay oil fields. The Dalton Highway doesn't go all the way to the Arctic Ocean. At the end of the line, are video presentations and exhibits. Tours are available to see the oil rigs and continue the three-mile trip to the ocean.

The Trans-Alaska Pipeline was begun in April of 1974, completed in June of 1977, and cost $8 billion to build. It is 48 inches in diameter, 800.3 miles long, has 11 pumping stations, and crosses three mountain ranges. It crosses 800 minor streams and rivers and 34 major ones. Ten billion barrels (42 billion gallons) of crude oil move through the pipeline at 6 mph and approximately 47,000 gallons per minute.* (Statistics from *Dalton Highway News*)

In September, I decided between driving the Dalton Highway and the Dempster. Weatherwise, I didn't have time to make both trips. People who had made both trips, said the Dempster had the prettier scenery. In 1992, I had ridden up the Dalton, not quite to Livingood, so most of the 140 miles back to Fairbanks, was new territory.

Bill's son, Mike, drove the 500 mile return trip to Eagle with one major stop, in Tok, for fantastic pizza at Fast Eddy's Restaurant. I highly recommend it.

At 1:30 a.m., we rode the crest of the world, witnessing a magnificent sunset. The skies immediately lightened in the red and purple and pink of an Alaskan dawn. After a few hours of restless sleep, we were both dragging, but excited about telling our stories to anyone who would listen.

Bill's wife, Terese, said several people had asked her how she could let her husband go off with a woman for two weeks. She said, "Complete trust." Amen. I said my good-byes.

Perhaps I have forgotten to mention there is one drawback to full-time RVing. You meet super people, but good-byes are frequent, and they hurt. It is Bill's business to raft visitors from place to place, and he probably doesn't get too close to anyone. He provided me with the means to live a fantastic adventure. Over two weeks, I felt we built up a very good rapport, and I would miss that camaraderie.

The sun was high in the sky when I left Eagle at 6 p.m. I stopped to fill a gallon jug with fresh water coming out of a mountain spring.

> **I spent the night at the Walker River BLM Campground on Taylor Hwy. The volunteer camp hosts, Val and Connie York, told me, "We don't have a single mosquito.
> They are all married with children."**
>
> **My next stop was even more fowl than that joke.**

## Charlie
## The Good Life

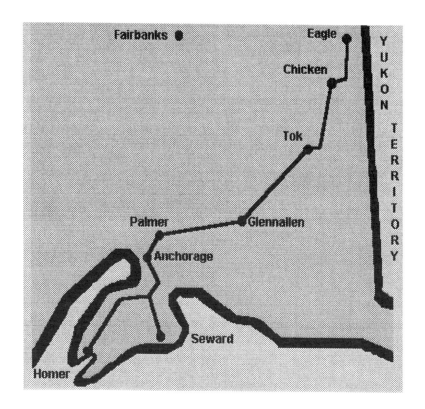

# CHICKEN TRACKS
## Through
# HOMER SPIT

    I passed the newer version of Chicken, the Goldpanner, as I drove Taylor Highway toward Tok. They offer free overnight RV parking, but I still prefer "old" Chicken up the hill. A rivalry exists between the two. They were having a gas war. I filled the Sprinter at $1.59/gallon. Maybe they are always in the middle of a gas war. The last time I was there, I filled at $1.61. The fellow who waited on me said, "You're kind of a little thing to be driving that big rig." Hmmm.

    This was my third visit to Chicken. The gift shop, saloon, and cafe are all fastened together, tiny and quaint. I am fascinated with this area and its gold rush history, or maybe it's that big "Welcome to Beautiful Downtown Chicken," printed on the end of the gas tanks, that always bids me stop.

    Chicken, population 37, is an unusual name for a town. The name was Ptarmigan originally, but the miners couldn't spell it (let alone pronounce it). They renamed it Chicken.

Susan Wiren, and her husband, own Chicken. If you don't want to get dizzy, **do not** follow her around. She is a whirling dervish of activity. I caught her long enough to tell her she was in my last book, *RVing North America, Silver, Single, & Solo*. She asked to see it, proceeded to buy several copies, and asked if I would like to sell my books out front.

I set up my book display in the good company of Anne "Tisha" Purdy's adopted daughter. It was Tisha's cabin I saw in Eagle.

It was interesting talking with RVers and bus tour people, finding out where they had been and where they were going. The Chicken Creek Cafe has good food, mostly made by Susan. I like their reindeer sausage and burgers. One tourist walked around eating homemade blueberry pie. He had a big grin on his face like he had discovered Chicken's greatest secret. Good advertising.

**Beautiful Downtown Chicken, Alaska**

The people working there were all kind and fun to be around. Jim was building Chicken's new Salmon Bake building. He had a big smile that said he loved everybody. Otis, another worker, was tall, full-bearded and really sweet. I think he lived in one of the "Chicken" houses.

At the end of the afternoon, the fellow who had pumped gas for me, asked if I wanted to see the "Real Chicken." He insisted I wear boots. I wondered why, until I realized spring melt had created a mud bog. One of the buildings was the schoolhouse where Tisha taught, and several buildings are living quarters for those working at Chicken. Guided tours are available. I am assuming that eventually everything will be restored, but little has been done to them at this point.

It was suggested I spend Saturday evening at the Chicken Creek

Saloon. Since I had a friendly escort, I decided to find out what Chicken was like after the tourists go home and the locals come out. Chicken is the only place, for miles around, for them to socialize.

My friend built a fire in the old wood stove, to ward off the evening chill. I discovered that the present Chicken buildings, including the saloon, had been there less than twenty years. The bar was tiny, crowded, and smoky. Besides the stove, it had a pool table, a couple of round tables with chairs, and the corner bar with stools. Hats and business cards were tacked to the ceiling and walls.

I met people I never would have met on my own. Chuck was tall, slender, short-bearded, blue-eyed, and had been an Ace helicopter pilot in Vietnam. He said, "Vietnam was a long time ago, and I don't dwell on it." He mines for someone else, but finds gold on his own with a metal detector. We talked about Quartzsite (AZ). He sells gold there sometimes, and I go to browse for at least a week, most winters. (A fun place to visit, if you are in the Southwest.)

Jessie was short, wiry, had very few teeth, and looked like he had lost his last dollar. Looks are deceiving. I would never have guessed he was a talented glass sculpturist. He spoke so enthusiastically about his creations, I stopped to see them at Northway Restaurant in Tok. They were tiny and exquisite. I loved the covered wagon pulled by a moose, but what would I do with delicate glass sculpture in a motorhome?

My escort and I danced, and he taught me to play pool (I actually hit the ball about three times). Mainly, we talked about what we had in common. We both had grown families, attended church (when he was home), loved to travel, and he had wanted to come to Alaska with all his heart. He was retired and worked in Chicken for the summer, doing odd jobs, loving every minute of it.

I planned to leave the next day, but my new acquaintance had the day off, and asked if I would like to go exploring and gold panning. Of course I said, "Yes."

I'll take a second here to reiterate thoughts about opening my arms to adventure. When I write about my adventures, especially from Alaska, to dear friends, Betty and George, from North Carolina, she confesses I scare her to death. For instance, when I wrote about the Yukon River trip, she said, "Sharlene, how can you go off into the wilderness for two weeks with a complete stranger?" My reply was, "He was a hired guide. It wouldn't be good for business if he molested a silver-haired grandmother."

Despite what newspapers, magazines, and TV tell you, *most* people are trustworthy. I certainly would not take off with just anybody, nor would I advise anyone else to do that. This comes under the heading of using common sense. I'm also not saying I couldn't make a fatal judgment one day, but I refuse to let the darker side of humanity imprison me behind a wall of fear. I tell my children, if somebody ever "does me wrong," I will have lived the life that God gave me, **with a passion**.

When I meet strangers, I listen. How do they speak of their children, their past, their friends, their late or ex-spouse, their God? Do they blame everyone else for their troubles? Do they pet the dog or kick it? Personally, I don't care if their relatives came over on the Mayflower. My background is all Heinz, 57 varieties. I spend time with people because they talk about interesting experiences, places they've visited, and they embrace adventure as I do. Now that you've had your morning sermon, I'll continue.

Our gold panning came to naught. We decided to drive to Eagle for lunch. People in this country think nothing of driving ninety-five miles to the nearest place for lunch. I had just been over the road to Eagle twice in the last 48 hours, but you already know it was my kind of twisty, windy road, and this time I didn't have to drive.

I was introduced to yet another interesting person. As it turned out, I had passed this person's abode at least three times in the past month, and always wondered who lived there.

Mark looked pretty grungy. When he was invited to go to lunch with us, he insisted on cleaning up. Mark lives in a brown bus, surrounded by the necessities of northern life, barrels of gasoline and equipment. It takes a second glance to realize his home and hearth is not a junk heap. He, obviously, can't store all that stuff inside so it has its place outside, and it is close by for effective use.

Talk about a metamorphose. With a bath and clean clothes, this was one handsome dude! Now, here is where I had some fun writing to Betty. I was not only going to lunch with *two* tall, dark handsome strangers, but one had a 357 strapped to his hip and the other, a 44. I wasn't sure whether we were looking for bear, or whether they thought *I* was that dangerous!

Mark has made gold mining his life. He has eight gold claims, in four different places, with teepees set up for a place to live when he isn't in his brown bus.

To my friend's urging, Mark said he once was making his way up the mountain to the road, from his canoe, when a grizzly confronted him. The bear rushed Mark, and then stopped when Mark didn't run away. The bear rushed him again, and Mark still didn't run. He had a gun, but knew it would be ineffective against the grizzly. It would only make him mad, if it wounded him. Mark stood his ground. "Either the bear would eat me or go away." The bear started eating berries, so Mark did too. Eventually the bear wandered away (Some potential dinners just aren't any fun).

He ran into another grizzly on his continuation up the mountain. The bear ran when Mark became aggressive. It seems to me it not only gets pretty dangerous out in that wild country, but it would take you forever to make it where you were going. Especially since he also said it took him six hours to canoe downstream to his claim, and twelve to come back upstream. Having seen the stream he was talking about, I couldn't believe anybody ever canoed *against* that current!

By then, we were back in Eagle having lunch. Once again, I was in the Riverside Cafe. As we ate, which probably wasn't the best time, Mark explained his dishwashing methods. He *doesn't!* Mark says the trick is to, "Let the liquid dry right away, then it doesn't create bacteria. If you let it layer without drying, then you get bacteria."

If something does start growing, he throws it away. I asked, "If I came for dinner, would I have to eat on a dish that you used for six months?" He replied, "I have plastic for visitors," and he admitted to using disposable cardboard part of the time.

After he referred to himself as the "Brown Bus Weirdo," I asked if he thought of himself as a hermit. He was taken aback, "No, I feel a hermit is anti-social, and I'm not. I like being around people sometimes."

He was enjoying lunch. He certainly was charming, and fascinated me totally. He had beautiful brown eyes, an infectious grin, and he didn't seem to mind my 1,001 questions. He was married once upon a time. Over and over again, I hear about wives who have returned to the lower 48 for a more gentle life. Living in Alaska is a hard life for women.

Then we got down to basics. He goes into town (Eagle) about four times a year, and into Fairbanks about once a year *for a year's supply* of food. I know they used to do that a hundred years ago. After talking with more miners during the summer, I realize it isn't all that unusual, in places only reached by canoe or by foot.

He mentioned buying a thirty-six-pound bucket of peanut butter and a sixty-pound container of honey. He says he gets the basics that he can fix quickly, because he doesn't like to cook. He said, "I don't get much fresh stuff, unless it's berries or something that grows near me." With that method of dishwashing (or non-method), he should have plenty of green stuff on hand.

Mark is self-taught, especially in geology, or "anything that will help me find the gold." He talked about making a laboratory to test the stuff. He certainly sounded like he knew what he was talking about.

He writes songs, and designed a recording studio into his dream cabin that he described down to the last two-by-four. It seemed rather an unlikely place to find where he intended to build it, but the dream was real, and at 41, he has a chance of making it come true.

By the time we dropped Mark off at his brown bus, I felt a real loss when I hugged him good-bye. I feel a certain affinity with anyone who is living his dream. I'll never know if he makes all of them come true because it is unlikely I'll ever see him again. The memory of our conversation about his unusual lifestyle, has brought a smile to my thoughts many times since.

By the time we returned to Chicken and said our quick good-byes, it was already evening. Another new friend, another good-bye. Given the time of year in Alaska, it was still daylight, so I fired up the Sprinter and took off.

I hadn't gone far when a fifth wheel came toward me on the narrow dirt road. About then, I hit soft dirt and thought I was going over. The

Sprinter tilted and ran along the ditch at a miserable angle, hitting brush and dragging dirt. I knew if I didn't keep moving, I would be there permanently. About thirty yards later, I was able to angle it back up over the shoulder onto the road.

When I reached a pullout, I accessed the damage. The generator exhaust pipe needed straightening, and the step was forever creamed. I pulled weeds and dirt out of a few places, but nothing appeared permanently damaged. Even the surface marks rubbed out. I was quite happy this happened where land lived and not near a thousand-foot drop.

The inside was a lot like it would be, if a mad bear got loose within the Sprinter's confines. The silverware drawer had upchucked. Everything on the counter had made a spectacular dive for the floor. Fortunately, all the computer and printer equipment, were on the side that only pushed it further toward the wall.

> This story is also to emphasize the need for safe driving practices. I consider myself a good driver, but the unexpected happened.

I have never had a problem driving that road before. It was a fluke and it turned out well. Actually, it could happen just about anywhere on a gravel road. Perhaps, by the time you drive this route, the Taylor Highway construction will be completed.

I love early mornings views, especially on a ridge. It was 4:30 a.m. I purposely moved early to avoid the construction workers. The road was a mess the last forty miles to the Alaska Highway.

A month had passed since I left Dawson City. I could hardly believe the adventures I had experienced in four weeks.

At Tok, I took advantage of the telephone (there isn't one until you get to Eagle or Dawson City) to make business and personal calls and do laundry.

It would normally be a decision time between driving the loop toward Fairbanks or toward Anchorage. I didn't have a choice. It was June 18 and I was flying out of Anchorage on the 20th.

After discovering the Tok Post Office had returned my mail, without keeping it the usual two weeks, I filled with gas, emptied the sewers, filled the water tank, and was on my way.

The Tok Cutoff is a beautiful route toward Glennallen (notice I didn't say beautiful **road**!). If it is clear, you'll see magnificent Mount Sanford, 16,237'; Mount Drum, 23,010'; and Mount Wrangell, 14,163', in the Wrangell-St. Elias National Park and Preserve. Although the area closest to the road showed signs of spring, the mountains were heavily draped in snow. Only some of it would melt before the snows returned in the fall.

Notice I said "clear." Some days you will see nothing. I'm not sure whether it's called a Kodak Moment or a Fuji Drama, but if they all come out to play, it is a breathtaking panoramic sight, stretching all the way to

Glennallen.

A side road off Glenn Highway (Tok Cutoff), Nabesna Road, will take you forty-five miles into the National Park. I haven't driven it (yet!) but it sounds like a road I'd like to take. Most of it is gravel and with no formal campgrounds but lots of places to dry camp. Information on road conditions is available at the visitor center in Glenallen.

State Recreation and private campgrounds are frequent, all the way to wherever, the Kenai Peninsula, the loop to Fairbanks, and back to Tok.

At the junction of Glenn and Richardson Highways, the people at the Copper River Valley Visitor Center were friendly and helpful.

> **Always stop at visitor centers. They are a wealth of information about accommodations, tours, and locally, "What's happenin', Baby!"**

We'll hit Valdez and McCarthy later in the trip. Now, we'll continue toward Anchorage. Look in your rear view mirror for more spectacular views of the Wrangell Mountains.

Have I said "spectacular" too many times already? Too bad. I have seen it green and I've seen it white. From Glennallen to Palmer is spectacular. You'll be driving between the Talkeetna and Chugach Mountains with many places to pull off. Please stop. Absorb the beauty; don't just fly by it.

> **If you can't get your spouse to stop, promise sex, the view will be worth it.**

After all those nearly animal-less miles canoeing the wilderness, I saw two moose munching along the green strip between the highway and the trees.

Don't fail to stop at the overlooks to the Matanuska Glacier that flows out of the Chugach Mountains. This is one of the glaciers you can get to, but entrance is through a private campground, and there is a fee. It might be worth it, because they have a trail leading right up to the glacier.

I have stayed in the Matanuska Glacier State Recreation Site and hiked their ridge trail. Great views of the glacier, and I also saw a mother moose with twins. One of them lost his footing and rolled down the steep mountain, got up, and scrambled after his mother.

You'll find plenty of activities in and around Palmer. One of my favorite stops is the Musk Ox Farm. I've always said moose are so ugly, they're cute. By the same token, musk ox also have faces only their mothers could love.

If you want a pet but can't take it with you, these shaggy beasts are available for adoption. A couple of noted surrogate fathers are Alex Trebek and Garth Brooks. The Musk Ox Farm is a domestication project started in 1954. The musk ox is considered a "Unique prehistoric remnant of the last great Ice Age." It was spring, and the babies had just arrived from Musk Ox Heaven.

Shaggy Shadows on the Musk Ox Farm, Palmer, AK

If you want to own something that is "softer than smoke," buy an item made from "qiviut." As a protection from the frigid weather, musk ox grow massive layers of soft underwool called "qiviut." They shed this in warm weather, but it is also combed out with a regular pick comb and spun into yarn. An ounce of qiviut is eight times warmer than an equal amount of sheep wool. It is knitted into clothing by The Native Alaskan Knitters Cooperative. I have never held anything so soft in my life.

It is a working farm run with the help of many volunteers (want to join?) and tours are available.

The Palmer Visitor Center has a showcase garden to walk through. It is only a few blocks from the Visitor Center to the United Protestant Church, "Church of a Thousand Logs."

The Mat-Su Valley has an interesting agricultural history. In 1935, the Matanuska Valley Project brought more than 200 families from the Midwest Dust Bowl, to the rich valley land at Palmer, to build a farming colony supported by the federal government. While the project wasn't totally successful, the Mat-Su Valley is now a thriving agricultural region.

Palmer is a decision point, but since you wouldn't want to miss the Kenai Peninsula, let's head down toward Anchorage. We'll go to Fairbanks later in the summer.

If you have an interest in Native culture, stop at the Eklutna Historical Park. More than eighty "spirit houses" are in a sacred burial ground of Dena'ina Athabascans. We listened to a talk about 350 years of culture and traditions, by a knowledgeable host. We then toured the spirit houses, the prayer chapel, and the hundred-year-old hand-hewn log St. Nicholas Russian Orthodox Church, on our own.

Originally, Native people were cremated, and the spirit houses were built as a home for the ashes, along with personal effects. Natives began burying their dead during the last half of the 19th Century, but spirit houses are still built on top of the burial site. The spirit house also shelters the departing spirit of the deceased and provides a cherished place where the Great Spirit can visit.

When an Indian is buried, the family places a new blanket over the grave, instead of flowers, as is our tradition. A cross is immediately placed at the foot of the grave, signifying the deceased was Orthodox Christian. On the fortieth day, the family erects a spirit house atop the grave, painting it in traditional colors, unique to each family. The shape and design are at the discretion of family members.

Close by is Thunderbird Falls. It is an easy two-mile round-trip hike back to the 200 foot falls. The path follows Eklutna Canyon through a birch forest to a boardwalk and viewing platform. In the same area, drive out to the Eagle River Visitor Center in the Chugach State Park.

Anchorage has a lot to offer. I was caught up in Alaska's aviation history at the Alaska Aviation Heritage Museum, at the Anchorage International Airport. They have details of the crash at Barrow of Wiley Post and Will Rogers. Other legends of Alaska history were Carl Ben Eielson, who flew Alaska's first airmail run in 1924. Many of the bush planes rescued from ravines, mine tailings, and other obscure places, are being restored. They have over thirty vintage aircraft and exhibits.

The nearby Lake Hood Seaplane Base, is the busiest, and largest, floatplane base in the world. I love to watch them take off and land. Alaska is noted for its plane population. Alaska has nearly six times the pilots, and sixteen times the aircraft, per capita, as the "lower 48." You'll probably see more planes tied down in back yards than RVs! It is not all that unusual to see signs on Alaskan roads warning of their use as emergency landing strips.

A lesser-known, but extremely busy airport to the south of Anchorage International, is run by a Michigander. It is restricted to tourist season and accommodates only 747 flights. Their business is transporting blood. Stop in and tell him Charlie sent you. His name is Moss Quido.

While I was in downtown Anchorage picking up mail at the post office, I wandered over to the log cabin Visitor Center. They were having free summer concerts. Bandstand Park has shade trees and benches to sit on and listen, eat lunch, or buy souvenirs (or food) at the nearby stands.

RV parking is $5 for all day, down on Third Avenue, across from the post office. The best information on current activities, nightlife, museums, and tours is at the Visitor Center on Fourth Avenue. The Anchorage City Trolley Tour is only $10.

If you want to see all of Alaska in less than an hour, see "Alaska the

Greatland" on the Omnivision screen at the Alaska Experience Center. I really enjoyed that. In the same building, is the Alaska Earthquake Exhibit. That was interesting to me, after visiting so many of the places affected. While you watch the story of the quake unfold in the theatre, you actually feel the rumbling and shaking of a simulated earthquake.

I stayed at Centennial Park just outside of Anchorage. Some pleasant big campgrounds, with all the amenities plus, exist within the city limits, but their prices are not as pleasant as Centennial Park. It is a dry camp park for $13/night. They have showers, dump station, and telephone. I like it because it is in a wooded area, and convenient.

Leaving my precious tin tent in the airport parking lot, I flew from Anchorage to Wenatchee, Washington. I picked up my car in Leavenworth, and drove to the University of Idaho at Moscow for the Life on Wheels Conference. In writing my plans to a good friend, I realized how often we skim, rather than read, letters. Her reply was thus, "I had no idea the Russians were so interested in RVing."

It was my privilege to be an instructor for the Life on Wheels Conference for a week. Four hundred thirty RVers or "Wannabees," came to listen to forty-one enthusiastic instructors from varied backgrounds and expertise.

> **I had two basic messages.**
> **One, life is short; live it to the fullest.**
> **Two, if I can live this lifestyle, anyone can.**

The Life on Wheels Conference was a brainchild of Gaylord Maxwell. From 6:30 a.m. "doughnut hours," to late afternoon "meet the author" sessions, people from all walks of life listened, learned, and asked questions. They were an enthusiastic group of people, and it was a fantastic experience.

When I returned to Alaska, I kept a low profile and stayed in the airport parking lot. I had paid for two weeks of long-term parking, so I took advantage of it. Without interruptions, other than constant airplanes, it was time to pay the piper. I caught up on columns, wrote about the conference, answered mail, and mailed books.

My Fourth of July was uneventful until evening, when the lady whom I call my "surrogate mother," arrived from Florida for a two-week visit. I lived with Jane and Orville Parker during the time I studied to become a Medical Secretary, more years ago than I care to mention. We remained friends through the years. She is now a widow of six years and occasionally visits me in my travels.

This was Jane's first trip to Alaska, and I wanted to show her the highlights during our limited time together. Our first direction took us to the Kenai Peninsula.

The Seward Highway is a designated National Forest Scenic Byway and rightly so. It has to be one of the prettiest routes you will be on. It has everything. Seward Highway follows the shoreline of Turnagain Arm. If the fog takes a hike, you can see down, and across the Arm, to glaciated snow-covered mountains.

Stop at one of the many turnouts and look above you to more mountains. I can *almost guarantee,* you'll see Dall sheep posing on the cliffs, and whale are often in the Arm. Your clues, unless you happen to be the first person that day, are visitors in pullouts, craning their necks looking through binoculars, or scanning the water.

When I say the sheep look like they are posing, they really do. It is great fun to watch these unbelievably agile creatures.

Of great curiosity to me, are the mud flats. When the tide is out (tide table books are available), all the water in Turnagain Arm has turned out toward Cook Inlet and, ultimately, to the sea. It looks like a great, irregular bowl, filled with lumpy, dark, chocolate pudding.

> **Do not walk anywhere on the mud flats. Some of it is quick sand and extremely dangerous.**

Several places along there are worth a stop. Potter Marsh has a long, wide boardwalk for viewing wildlife. It is a refuge and nesting area. The Chugach State Park Headquarters, Potter Section House, has an enormous snowblower on a train engine. This is a definite stop for train buffs.

A favorite stop of mine, is McHugh Creek state wayside. If you have an abnormally big rig, this won't be a stop for you. I have pulled in more than once, to park beside the peaceful falls, or up another level overlooking Turnagain Arm. When Jane was with me, I stopped to finish some work, where she could see over the Arm. We were warned by the volunteer park attendant, that a bear was in the vicinity. It had destroyed the backpack of a tent camper, an hour before.

Beluga Point is a turnout for sea and land gawkers. Informational signs fill you in on what you might see.

Dead, naked trees (ghost forests) and sunken buildings, rest in the marshes along this section of the Seward Highway. It shows firsthand, the destruction of the 1964 earthquake. The Arm dropped six to twelve feet, allowing the lowlands to be inundated with saltwater, killing the trees.

Alyeska had grown drastically since I was there in 1987. The Jade shop is still there, and a bakery with great cinnamon rolls. Alyeska is a big ski area, crowded both summer and winter. I have never yet ridden the Alyeska Tramway to the 2,300' level of Mt. Alyeska. Seven Glaciers Restaurant, and the view, are open year around. If you like crowds of people, this is the place to go in season. Many exciting activities begin at Alyeska, flightseeing trips, gold panning, etc.

On the Seward highway, you'll see a ticket office for the Alaska Railroad. The Alaska Railroad was once the only way to reach Denali National Park. The Denali Highway opened in 1957, and the George Parks Highway in 1972. I talked with some homesteaders on the 1987 trip. The husband moved to Alaska to build bridges in Denali National Park in 1937. There were no roads. They brought in a trailer by train, and lived in it, until they skidded a cabin to their homestead property.

This scenic railroad travels 470 miles from Seward to Fairbanks, with a shuttle service making several trips daily to Whittier. You can make various tour arrangements using the Alaska Railroad. This was my trip in 1992.

CHARLIE'S CRUISE

A friend and I signed up for a Twenty-six Glacier Tour on the M/V Klondike high-speed catamaran. The Alaska Railroad took us from the ticket office on Seward Highway (at Portage), through two tunnels, one 13,090', and the other, 4,910'. The trip is nearly twenty-five miles round-trip and connects with the Alaska Marine Highway.

With a population of roughly 250, Whittier is a fishing community. It is a great jumping-off place for seeing Prince William Sound; and besides, it's named after one of my favorite poets, John Greenleaf Whittier. They have an RV park for self-contained RVs who come in via ferryboat or train.

Some trips are shrouded in fog; but that day, it was as clear as a bell, with unbelievable sunshine and warmth. Our smooth-sailing catamaran took us up College Fjord, where we visited Harvard and Yale Glaciers. They began at the top of the Chugach Mountains and the great Columbia Glacier.

Along the way, we passed Wellesley, Vassar, Bryn Mawr, and Smith Glaciers. We visited Harriman Fiord to see Harriman Glacier, named for Edward Henry Harriman, father of Averell. Since Columbia Glacier was named for Columbia University, the glaciers were named after women's colleges on the left, and men's colleges on the right.

Dozens of sea otters floated on their backs, with babies resting on their bellies. Their bellies are also used as tables to crack clamshells open. If we went too close, they would dive. They are able to dive to depths of 120 feet. I'm not sure what happens to Junior when they do.

We saw an American Bald Eagle's nest and several eagles, as well as a noisy kittiwake rookery.

We returned to Passage Canal where the captain said if we could see forty miles down Wells Passage, we would see, "At four minutes past midnight on Good Friday, March 24, 1989, the tanker, Exxon Valdez, slamming into Bligh Reef, spilling over 10.8 million gallons of crude oil into the Sound." We all cringed. The brochure assured us that, "These areas are now a dynamic wilderness laboratory for recording the progression of natural changes, and the re-establishment of ecological equilibrium."

Another note of interest in their handbook was that they now believe the epicenter for the 1964 Alaska Earthquake, was on the peninsula between College Fiord (where we were) and Unakwik Inlet. This looked to be about twenty miles away, as the crow flies.

You are unlikely to remember the names of twenty-six glaciers, and one glacier will look like any other by the end of the day; but it is worth the $120 ticket. It is a narrated hundred-and-ten-mile cruise with a great crew. It would be fun, even if you weren't seeing some of the world's most spectacular scenery. I highly recommend this.

When a tidewater glacier sheds icebergs off its face into the sea, it is called "calving." To actually hear the loud boom of a glacier calving is amazing. The ice crashes into the water, leaving pristine ice, so blue you won't believe your eyes. The Twenty-Six Glacier Tour was expensive but not a farce.

Back to the Seward Highway, and Jane, and continuing down Turnagain Arm.

We spent the night overlooking the river and mountains, in Ptarmigan Creek USFS campground for $9/night. I think Jane didn't realize how different it was going to be. She wanted to phone her son to tell him she had arrived safely. Remember, folks, you will not find telephones hanging on spruce trees. Plan ahead if you are going to need a phone.

The Exit Glacier Road was paved for about four miles, but the rest of the nine-mile trip, was miserable washboard. It was under construction. Maybe it's all paved by now. It is worth the trip. I have also discovered that driving faster over washboard is less miserable, than inching my way along. Perhaps I am just hitting the peaks that way!

Exit Glacier, part of Kenai Fjords National Park, is one of the few places you can drive to, and have an easy quarter-mile walk right up to a living glacier. A paved, wheelchair accessible trail, leads to a glacier view. From there, you can walk across the gravel to the glacier base.

**It is not wise to climb on the glacier.**
**There is a longer trail to an overlook.**

A good-sized stream comes from under the glacier and warning signs advise you not to stand too close to the ice. You can't see it move but it is living and moving. Ice chunks and rocks fall. I mean, how "up close and personal" do you have to be with a glacier?

Seward, our northernmost ice-free port, and part of the Alaska Marine Highway System, has RV hook-ups and dry camping, all along the harbor. We paid $8/night for dry camping. We watched the comings and goings of kayaks, ferryboats, and cruise ships on Resurrection Bay.

Sidewalk traffic brought humanity in all its varied forms and dress, ambling, in-line skating, or biking. Harbor seals swam along next to shore.

If you have reasonably good walking skills, RV camping is close enough to walk to the many galleries, shops and the bayfront activities. This is another jumping-off place for flightseeing, kayaking trips, day cruises, fishing charters, sled dog rides, and the Alaska Railroad. July 4th, which we missed by two days, is a blast.

They have a footrace up Mount Marathon. It is a 1.5 mile climb to a 3,000' elevation on a mud-slick trail. The return, is a fast slip and slide down a gravelly decline. Anyone can get in on this, "One of the oldest foot races in the U. S." by registering. Do I see a mass exodus, as all of you register? Well, it might be fun to watch anyway.

Previously, I enjoyed driving out to Lowell's Point. The hike to Caines Head State Recreation Area begins there. I'd like to do that hike, but not alone. Early in WWII, the territory of Alaska was attacked, and occupied, by Imperial Japanese ground forces. Fort McGilvray was established at Caines Head, one of the strategic spots for defending the Port of Seward. Seward was the southern terminus of the Alaska Railroad, and a critical supply line for the war effort.

The remains of the bunkers and gun emplacements, built to guard the entrance to Resurrection Bay, are still there. Three miles of the 4.5 mile trail must be hiked during low tide.

Miller's Landing at Lowell's Point, has a campground, interesting store, and charter services. Coffee is free, and five-cent fishing advice is guaranteed. It doesn't get much better than that.

Seward has a memorial to Benny Benson, a 13-year-old orphan from Seward, who designed Alaska's deep violet-blue flag with the golden stars. He explained, "The blue field is for the Alaska sky and the forget-me-not, an Alaska flower, the North Star is the future state of Alaska, the most northerly of the Union. The Big Dipper is for the Great Bear, symbolizing strength."

The waterfront in Seward is the official Milepost 0 (Hoben Park) of the Historic Iditarod Trail. The Iditarod Trail Sled Dog Race begins in Anchorage, but the trail started here in 1908 and went 1,200 miles to Nome.

The Alaska SeaLife Center, next to the University of Alaska Institute of Marine Science near the ferry dock, is scheduled to open in 1998. St. Peter's Episcopal Church has a unique mural, "The Resurrection." Resurrection Bay is used as a background and Seward residents are models. Dutch artist, Jan Van Empel, painted it in 1925.

The Visitor Center hands out a card that you don't get just anywhere. This one lists the Tsunami Safety Rules. The strongest earthquake ever recorded in North America, 9.2 on the Richter scale, shook Alaska in 1964. Seward had an estimated $22 million in damage. The waterfront fell into the water, bridges collapsed, and oil storage tanks exploded. If that wasn't enough, the tsunami came with thirty-foot sea waves, that continuously pummeled the town until the next morning. An earthquake movie is shown at the community library, and the Resurrection Bay Historical Society Museum, has a quake display.

Jane and I opted for boarding the Kenai Star for a full-day Kenai Fjords Wildlife and Glacier Cruise, for $99. Seward is the gateway to the Kenai Fjords National Park. A National Park Ranger gave a running narration of the sights.

He explained that the sea otters, called "old men of the sea," are protected by a fur coat that they constantly groom. "The only part that isn't covered by fur, is their feet. That's why you see them swimming on their backs with their feet out of the cold water." Made sense to me.

They promised we would see cormorants, kittiwakes, and puffins. We did. They didn't promise Humpback whales. Sometimes, finding whales is a fluke, but we found several in a cove. The engines shut down and we drifted in their bath water.

Dall sheep posed on the mountain. A new mother nursed her baby on a precarious cliff, to protect it from predators. We saw bald eagles, porpoises, and a raucous colony of reddish-colored Stellar's sea lions.

At Holgate Glacier, we enjoyed our delicious all-you-can-eat salmon buffet, and the narrator explained "Burger Burps." "After the glaciers calve, the little ice burgers, burp, like popping champagne." Unfortunately, since our beautiful sunny weather had turned into "swell" weather, we weren't sure all the burps were coming from the ice burgers.

By the time we started back into the continued swells, an alarming number of visitors had turned a deep shade of puce. The helpful and sympathetic attendants handed out barf bags and ginger candy.

Our cruise was to include a run through the Chiswell Islands National Wildlife Refuge. Since the bow aimed directly into the water, then directly into the sky, the captain used good sense in turning back. Nobody objected. Funny how rough seas brought a song to mind, "The Wreck of the Edmund Fitzgerald." (Gordon Lightfoot).

We returned along the Seward Highway, following a section overlooking Kenai Lake, to Tern Lake Junction, turning left on Sterling Highway toward Homer. The big pullout at Tern Lake has a boardwalk and viewing platforms with informational signs, a good place to stop.

Because of its fame as a fishing paradise, campgrounds are abundant on the Kenai Peninsula. I don't give a whit for fishing, but the scenery is worth the trip.

We met up with another arm of the Kenai Lake. The extraordinary color is from glacial melt. We stayed overnight high above the Russian River, in a USFS paved RV parking lot for $5, and had to be out by 8 a.m. The Kenai River kept us company. It is very scenic along there and heavily fished. I once saw a mother moose and her baby swimming across the river.

Soldotna has a huge Fred Meyer Store. They encourage RVers to stay overnight in designated areas of their lot, and offer a dump station and water fill. During season, it is always jammed. The store has everything. It is a good place to replenish whatever.

The Interpretive Center for the Kenai National Wildlife Refuge is near Soldotna. It covers a good bit of that side of the peninsula. It is the largest moose range in North America, and usually, I see a lot of them.

On one trip or another, I have stopped at most of the beaches along the Sterling Highway, such as Clam Gulch. It lived up to its name; lots of clamdiggers there. Scenic pullouts on the cliff, high above Cook Inlet allow overnights for zip. You will have company if you park on any of the scenic gravel pullouts overlooking Cook Inlet. The facilities are zip. The cost is zip. The scenery is zippy.

I'll mention here that the camping has changed in the last several years. Dry camping isn't encouraged anywhere, but until this last trip, many pullouts were available for free overnights. A lot of these places have disappeared into formal campgrounds. Signs denying RV overnight parking are proliferating. This may have happened for several reasons, the number one reason being,

> **It takes only a few rotten RVers in the boondock barrel to spoil privileges for all of us.**

We can't blame the State of Alaska (or anyone else) for disallowing the privilege of boondocking, if idiots dump sewers or leave trashy messes behind. I would like to think that 99.9 percent of RVers live by the Girl Scout rule (probably boys, too),

> **"Leave it better than you found it."**

While I'm on the soapbox, I was at a stoplight incline, behind an RV last summer. Liquid was pouring out of a sewer tank. It wasn't water runoff from filling too much. That happens to me, too, and always it embarrasses me, because I'm afraid people assume it is the sewer.

Without a desire to get in a fight with anybody, I tried raising the RVer by CB. It was either turned off, or he was ignoring me. I was going to ask if he was aware that his sewer was pouring all over the street. It was probably gray water.

> **A number of people feel it is OK to let gray water leak because it is only bath or dish water.**
> **Think again!**

> I don't advise it anywhere.
> People other than RVers look at it and think the worst.

In this instance, I was hoping for a cop to pull up behind him and give him a ticket. That could happen, but not in my lifetime would justice be so timely. At least most people aren't so blatant about it; they let the water drip, not gush.

Most of the time, it just takes a bit of planning ahead to find places to empty your sewers. In Canada and Alaska, sewer dumps are listed as service station perks, offered with a fill-up. The Milepost advertisements are great places to find relief from that full feeling.

One of my favorite places to stay on the Kenai Peninsula is at Starski State Recreation Area. From this high cliff I had a panoramic view of Cook Inlet, St. Augustine, Mt. Illiama, Mt. Redoubt, and Mt. Spurr. They were all out in great splendor. To add interest, I heard a wolf howling in the night.

A lot of people zoom right by Ninilchik. It's big by some village standards, about 450 people. You can't drive into the town, but there are parking areas. Abandoned boats are near the beach, and camping is down there too. I like the view from the hill above the town. The tiny historic Russian Orthodox Church sits in the wildflowers, mostly purple fireweed. The cemetery is cuddled by a white picket fence. It is an active church, and closed to casual visitors.

It's a nice drive along Anchor River Road off the Sterling Highway. It leads to several river and beach campgrounds, but I took Jane out there just to prove she had been there. A sign declares

> Anchor Point, Alaska, is
> "North America's most westerly Highway Point."

I thought I could argue that point with the roads in Nome, but then the Milepost adds the word, "Contiguous."

On a clear day, the Kachemak Bay view from Bluff Hill, just before you descend the hill into Homer, is a Kodak/Fuji Moment. Don't miss it.

Homer has a population of about 4,500 and has most anything you might need. We took advantage of Homer's sewer dump and water fill for $2, before going out on the spit.

On Homer Spit, I drove Jane around the loop to see the private campgrounds, that have all the amenities. We spent the night in a city-run campsite for $7.

Homer Spit, extending five miles into Kachemak Bay, dropped several feet during the earthquake. It was rebuilt, mostly on stilts. Shops, restaurants, charters, and campgrounds, dominate the side opposite the huge marina that floats up and down with the tide.

We had halibut, shrimp, and scallops at the Boardwalk Fish and Chips. Food is reasonable, fast, clean, and the small restaurant sits right on the water. Actually, on Homer Spit, it's almost impossible to sit anywhere else. I had my first clam chowder on the boardwalk in 1987, during a cold, miserable, foggy day. I don't know if it was the frigid weather, or the good cooking, that made me fall in love with clam chowder.

On that same trip, I had my first halibut and haven't gotten over that yet either. Fred Cushman, one of our group of five in 1987, went on a charter fishing trip and brought back a fifty-pounder. His wife, Madelaine, baked it for all of us. He figured with all his expenses, the fish cost about $3 a pound. Not bad, considering the memory he made.

Evening time is a fun time to watch fisherpeople at the fishing hole. It was extended to accommodate quite a few more people, from when I was there in earlier years. The term "Combat fishing" could describe the people standing shoulder-to-shoulder. Fish were jumping several feet in the air. At times, there were as many as a dozen in the air at once. At that point in their lives (or deaths), they aren't interested in eating. They mostly react out of instinct, when lures pass in front of them. Three seals were swimming and fishing within the hole, too.

There are numerable side trips leading to fantastic places from Homer Spit. Keep turning the pages. I'll tell you about them in the next chapter.

**View From Bluff Hill**

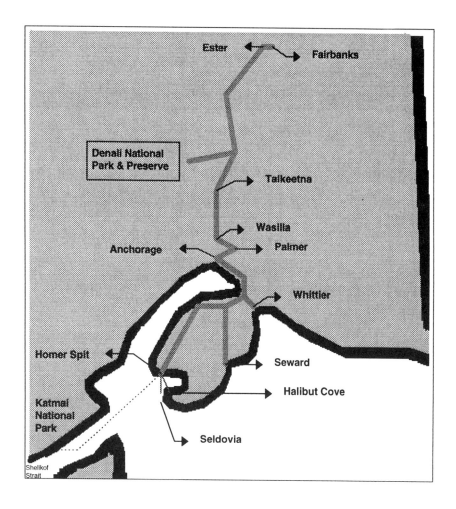

# THE BEAR FACTS

Jane had no interest in these side trips from Homer Spit, so I took them at a different time.

### Seldovia

Two times I have made the trip to Seldovia, a community reached only by air or sea. Unless you stay overnight, the tours aren't quite long enough to see everything. I like more time to inhale the fragrance of a new place. The Alaska Ferry System stops there also.

Seldovia is one of the oldest communities on Cook Inlet. St. Nicholas Russian Orthodox Church, built in 1891, dominates the scene overlooking the harbor. If you do nothing else, walk to the top of the hill. I love boardwalks, flowers, small villages, and boat harbors. Seldovia fits the bill. Sod grows its own garden on old log cabin roofs. Seldovia has art galleries, shops, and cafes, or you can sit and contemplate bright orange Arctic poppies, pushing between rocks on the harbor wall. They say Seldovia is, "Just beyond the end of the road." I like that.

Most tours include a look at Gull Island. It is extremely noisy and smelly. I saw my first puffins there. The captain told us, "They burrow into the dirt at the top of the rocks, lay one egg, and abandon the hatchling as soon as it is old enough. It is forced by starvation to come out and find its own food."

So what's new, my kids were forced by starvation to cook for themselves. (Maybe it wasn't quite that bad but don't check with them...just in case.)

He also said that since the 1964 earthquake, and the 1989 Exxon oil spill, both happened on Good Friday, "I've decided not to get out of bed on Good Friday any more."

Reflections of Halibut Cove

Russian Orthodox Church, Seldovia, AK

Portage Lake Begich-Boggs Visitors Center

### Halibut Cove

The Kachemak Bay Ferry is the Danny J, a small "classic" wooden boat, leaving from Homer Spit. We rode outside in the mist. The mountains were fogged in. We did a slow turn around Gull Island to see puffins, a few sea otters wrapped in seaweed, kittiwakes and cormorants.

The stench was bad on a cool day, and I remembered what it was like on a hot one.

Halibut Cove is on Ismailof Island. A tiny post office, with its flag flying, floated on its own dock. One of our all-woman crew, said it had many post office boxes as a requirement of the government, "The keys hang in them because nobody bought any. This aversion to buying unnecessary boxes, was known before the building was put up, but it didn't matter." She added, "No one needs them in a place where people seldom lock their homes."

After landing, we were instructed in where to find the bathrooms, the most important part of the tour. A barn-type building on the boardwalk had a rounded bottom, that made me wonder if the Ark had been greatly misplaced. The guide explained the boat was floated to its dock, and made stationary right there with the barn on it.

It was a pleasant walk to the restaurant. Starfish clung to rocks and poles under the boardwalk. Houses on stilts clung to the upper boardwalk. Curious horses lived in a pasture across from an art gallery. The gallery lady pointed out three galleries on the island. It was picturesque; the whole island was a gallery.

She, and her husband, home-schooled their children when they were small, but now they live in Anchorage during the winter, and their children to go to school in town.

It is a private island. The Danny J runs ferry service twice a day for residents, bed and breakfast guests, and the Saltry Restaurant. Private boats can come in, but their only landing places are the restaurant and the post office, unless they live on the island.

During the peak of the herring-fishery days in the early 1900s, thirty-six saltrys operated in Halibut Cove. The island also lays claim to a colorful history during prohibition, with bootleggers, stills, and revenuers.

The Saltry, the island's only restaurant, was at the end of twelve blocks of boardwalk. They bake their own bread, and I couldn't resist the nut-raisin bread with butter, a hot mug of coffee, and potato-broccoli soup. It was reasonable at $7.15, especially with the unique setting. Reservations are required.

I sat outside, overlooking the harbor. It was pleasantly cool. Raucous seagulls added their two-cents worth to the soft music and quiet conversation of my fellow travelers.

Modern houses were huge and somehow didn't fit in. The older ones were charming, with boxes overflowing with poppies, bachelor's buttons, sweet peas, pansies, and daisies.

A mother shouted to her children, who were fishing off the boardwalk, "I'll be right back." She left in a fishing boat from the dock below.

Floating stairways descended from the buildings, accommodating whatever the tide level. It was low tide at that moment, but they have the third highest tides in the world.

The sign on a picket fence surrounding a six-foot-square garden just before going through the gate to the top of the hill, said, "Please don't pick my flowers." I didn't.

The "Phenomenal Tree" trail to the natural stone arch was steep. I was accompanied by chattering red squirrels through a dense, towering Sitka spruce forest, Devil's Club plants with bright red berries, and lots of red elderberry and fern. The path ended behind a split rail fence, above the arch, on the back side of the island. A gentle breeze blew in my face. I leaned on the fence and saw Homer Spit in the distance, and a black beach below me.

I found a child's lonely grave hidden in the forest. Birds sang and bees buzzed. Water lapped at the shore below. Tall ferns rustled in a slight breeze. Perhaps it wasn't a lonely grave after all. An islander later told me the two-year-old girl had died in a fire. "All the cove felt her loss keenly. She was the only child here at the time and we lavished her with our love."

The same talkative native explained that the other grave at the top of the hill, belonged to "Ham-handed Larsen." "He was so strong, they gave him jobs that were big enough for two Swedes and one Norwegian. He was a great storyteller and a terrific dancer. He taught all the woman on the island to dance."

At Tillion's Art Gallery, they featured octopus-ink art work. One of the "washes," was of a woman walking naked along the shoreline of a lake. I wasn't the only one wanting to be "one with nature."

A number of sculptures were of island people. One was a mother nursing a baby. When the sculpture was done, the artist realized that the mother's head was falling off. It stopped toppling in time to make it look like the mother had fallen asleep nursing her baby. The sculpturist firmed it in that position. Take it from one who knows, the sculpture looked very natural.

Halibut Cove was too charming to absorb in only two-and-a-half hours. If you go, take raingear and dress in layers. Take binoculars, cameras, and wear good walking shoes or boots.

## Katmai National Park

My next adventure was with Inlet Charters, one I had wanted to do since I first read about the possibility. This trip is definitely weather oriented, both for your safety, and your pleasure. If the fog is too thick and doesn't show any signs of lifting, you wait or cancel out.

Three planeloads of cameras and film took off from Beluga Lake in Homer, with a few photographers aboard as well. The sign over the pilot's door said, "Bear Facts: Never run! Speak to the bear in a calm voice. Wave your arms slowly or clap your hands. Retreat slowly. Always give bears the right of way. Pilot Facts: Never run!! Speak to them in a calm, loud voice. Tip generously or retreat slowly and clap your hands." Hmmm.

Dale, our pilot, circled over the water whenever there was something to see below us, like the "fin whales."

Bald Mountain Air Service flew us into a bay on the Shelikof Strait at the edge of Katmai National Park, affording a view of lush green islands and great beaches. We were shuttled from the seaplanes to a base boat, where we ate whatever food we had brought. We weren't coming back for lunch and we couldn't take food with us.

THE BEAR FACTS

KATMAI NATIONAL PARK

It was difficult negotiating in and out of the skiff, wearing thigh high boots, but it soon became apparent why we needed them. Gary, our guide, instructed us to stay together at all times. "Don't let the bears get between us. They get confused. Groups intimidate bears. If we all stand up, we will look like a whole herd of bears." He also said, "These are coastal brown bears, grizzlies, just like at Denali, but they get a whole lot bigger. They eat lots of fish and berries after a hard winter."

According to the Katmai National Park Service brochure, that huge brown bear is "Earth's largest terrestrial carnivore." I wasn't sure I liked the sound of that. I found something fishy about their flesh-eating habits.

We went over the side, into the water, through the mud and seaweed. We were to kneel, bend over, or sit, at all times, so there was no chance we would intimidate the bears (who were they kidding?). The kneeling was dryer because of the long boots. Do they know how hard kneeling is?

The skiffs returned to the base boat. We were there for the duration. A good thing we didn't drink a lot, because there was no place to get rid of it, and he wouldn't allow us to go anywhere.

The bears shuffled along, peering into the water, then suddenly heaved themselves into the waves. It looked like they tried to land on the fish. They don't get their fish every time either.

Gary said the two young bears near us were probably four-or-five-years old. "They stay with the mother until she kicks them out about their third year." They looked like they were going to fight, then settled into playing, standing, biting, rolling on the ground, and chasing each other.

Obnoxious gulls flew all around the bears, picking at their fish. We asked if the bears ever ate gulls. He said they never bothered with them. I wondered if it was because it was too much fuss and feathers, or perhaps, just too many feathers?

It is illegal for guides to carry guns for protection. Gary said he had never needed one.

The bugs liked the idea of fresh blood. When Gary handed me the repellent, he said, "These are ENT bugs. They go for the eyes, nose, and throat."

Despite strict orders not to bring food, one fellow started eating a sandwich. Everybody noticed. Gary immediately told him to get rid of it. He stuffed it all into his mouth at once, and looked awful for a few minutes until he could get it down, sort of like a pelican gorging on an oversized fish.

A huge bear beyond the stream, watched us for a long time, a big furry couch potato. Gary said "The Couch" was pushing a 1000 pounds.

After a few minutes, we were surrounded by bears. The guide developed swivel-headedness. He was always very aware of what was happening. We could look in any direction and see bears. He said there were thirteen or fourteen different bears, "We get to know them by their scars, color, or actions."

The other visitors were from Switzerland, Italy, Australia, Germany, and Canada. The husband of a vivacious, sparkly Australian lady, was watching their small children, so she could come on this bear trip. Her guilt was alleviated by his planned $17,000 moose and bear hunting trip. Made sense to me.

The fog moved in slightly, and we had a steady light rain. It enhanced the scene, rather than causing a hardship or discomfort. We were asked if we wanted to leave, but nobody was interested.

---

**I hoped nothing chased me in those boots.
I couldn't have run if my life depended on it; but, of course,
I would have given it a bloody good try.**

---

We were on an elongated island, with a stream passing on either side of our small group. We sat fairly close to each other. We were each engrossed in bear activity, photographing, and conversing quietly. The closest bears were probably fifteen feet from us. The bears ignored us.

Only occasionally, would one lift his head, sniff the air and come toward us. Gary expected us to move, when he said move, then he stood up, waved his arms and yelled. The bear always ran away.

We left, following a circuitous route around the bears, that took us through swift streams, and over slippery rocks and shells that would have cut bare feet to shreds. I waited for the last skiff. I didn't want to leave. I rather envied the couple from Germany who were going to stay overnight on the ship, and go bear-watching during the evening. Someone said the privilege would cost them $1,000. Though it was worth every penny, $450 for the day, was steep enough for me.

On board the base boat, the crew served fresh deep-fried halibut. That wasn't hard to take. It was late when we shuttled back to the seaplane, and flew over the seals, puffins, lush green islands, and deep blue water, a perfect place for kayaking.

During the return trip, the clouds lifted enough to allow us views of glaciers and mountaintops, sculpted in rock and mounded with snow. We saw more whales. The three-hour, round-trip plane ride was certainly a major part of the adventure.

> It is difficult for them to have boot sizes for everyone, so if you have the opportunity, take your own thigh-high waders. Take other necessities, like cameras, film, bug repellent, raingear, lunch, and something to sit on. It is a fantastic experience.

As exciting as it was, the four-million-acre Katmai National Park, across from Kodiak Island, is much more than bear watching and scenery. It is volcanoes and history. I want to visit The Valley of Ten Thousand Smokes and -- did I say I was going back?

On our way up the peninsula, Jane saw her first moose grazing beside the road. By the time I turned around and went slowly back, we could see she had a baby with her. We didn't do anything overly exciting on the way to Anchorage, so I'll describe a couple of things from later in the season.

I drove the Skilak Loop off Sterling Highway and stayed at Upper Skilak Campground, on the lake. The sites were level and paved. The paths were gravel and paved. Picnic tables had extensions for wheelchair use. I couldn't believe so few people were using the campground.

Summit Lodge is one of my favorite stops. It is on the Seward Highway, after the turn toward Anchorage. Huge carved doors with leaded glass windows, have a bear on one and a moose on the other. I've eaten breakfast or lunch there several times with friends. Even if the food wasn't good (and it is), the view of Summit Lake surrounded by trees and mountains, would make up for it.

### Portage Glacier

At the Begich-Boggs Visitor Center at Portage Glacier in Chugach National Forest, we watched the movie, "Voices From the Ice," and walked through the simulated ice cave. If you don't believe iceworms live between ice crystals near the surface of some glaciers, a Forest Service Interpreter will take you on an "Iceworm Safari." You may never have another chance to see such wiggly wildlife, and they aren't nearly as intimidating as bears.

The glacier is receding at the rate of approximately 350 feet per year. Since I was there in 1987, it had disappeared around the bend. The narrated tour to the glacier face, aboard the MV Ptarmigan, is the only way you can see Portage Glacier. It usually costs $21 per person, but the last tour of the day was half price.

The boat stayed close enough to the front of the glacier to see the little bit that calved. It was crumbling over a huge rock formation so it was not as dramatic as calving usually is.

Williwaw USFS Campground has nice campsites. From the observation deck, you can watch salmon fight their way upstream. It is interesting, but sort of sad. The Williwaw Natural Trail hike led to beaver dams, and to the falls coming from Middle Glacier.

## Wasilla

Jane's time was passing quickly. We saw a full view of Mt. McKinley (roughly 170 miles away) as we drove through Anchorage. We made a beeline for Denali National Park on the Glenn and George Parks Highways (Alaska Hwy #3).

I am fascinated with Iditarod racing, mushing, and dogsledding. At Wasilla, it is almost fourteen miles along Knik Road to the Knik Museum. This museum has all the information on Knik, a gold rush village from 1898, and includes the Sled Dog Mushers' Hall of Fame. They have race history, musher and winner portraits, and dog-mushing equipment. It isn't open every day. Check it out before making the trip. They used to use adhesive tape or electrical tape to fasten booties on sled dogs. Now they use Velcro. Have we progressed or what?

You can also stop at the Iditarod Trail Sled Dog Race Headquarters to see dog racing memorabilia and watch a film.

Another trip off the Parks Highway will take you to Talkeetna, a small, but mighty, town. This is one of many places you can get flight-seeing tours of Mt. McKinley. There are other kinds of tours and museums, but what really interested me, was their annual Moose Dropping Festival. I had every intention of going, but Jane and I made a decision after Denali, that we would either head for Ester and Fairbanks, or go back to Talkeetna. We couldn't do both. Fairbanks and the paddlewheel trip won out. One of these days!

## Denali National Park and Preserve
### A "Subarctic Sanctuary"

In four trips into Denali National Park, I have five times driven the 14.8 miles of paved highway to Savage River. Private vehicles may not go beyond that point without a camping or special permit. My favorite time is at dawn or sunset. I've never failed to see animals.

I have taken the bus tour through Denali six times. Each trip has been memorable and different.

I've seen dozens of grizzlies, sometimes right next to the bus, and sometimes so far away, I had to use binoculars. During other trips, Dall sheep have posed on the mountain above the bus. Moose and babies are often all over the place, but nary a one stepped out for Jane to see.

On a short hike at Eielson Visitor Center, I once sat quietly on the trail, and caribou grazed close enough to touch. A dozen people watched a fluffy-tailed fox, outsmarted by an Arctic ground squirrel. I've seen eagles, wolves, marmots, and ptarmigan.

Denali Caribou

The bus makes several scheduled comfort and leg-stretching stops. The driver also stops whenever anyone sees an animal. They pull over allowing enough time for everyone to rush to the side of the bus, where "somebody sees something," to take pictures, or ooh and ah over the sights. You may not get off the bus, except during scheduled stops.

In 1987, I didn't see Mt. McKinley, even though I was within sight of it for at least five days. In 1992, I saw it from every direction. I saw it from Anchorage, Fairbanks, flying over it to Kotzebue, in the park, and when I drove over the Old Denali Highway.

In 1996, Jane and I saw it from many places, but only bits and pieces as the clouds would allow. There are never any guarantees. The 20,320' mountain, the tallest in North America, is big enough to make its own weather. If you are lucky, it will come out to play. It is a thrill you can't imagine.

Regardless of The High One's temperament, the scenery has never been a disappointment. It is so varied, with mountains, braided glacier-born rivers, and glaciers. Out of June, July, and September visits, my favorite was seeing it dressed in autumn splendor. Golden aspen trees stood against green pines with red and orange ground cover in the foreground, and a background of mountains freshened with new snow. It was almost hard on the eyes.

The roads are gravel and well maintained. When buses meet in exceptionally narrow areas, one bus stops and lets the other sidle by. The drivers are excellent and have a great sense of humor and fun.

You have to pack your own food and drink, as there is nothing available on the trip. The round-trip to Eielson is approximately eight hours (66 miles), give or take a few minutes for exceptional animal sightings. The Wonder Lake trip is eleven hours (84 miles). A shorter version goes to Polychrome/Toklat. Time goes quickly, and most people sleep all the way back.

I look at magnificent Mount McKinley (when it lets me), and I think of all the climbers on it. Controversy stirs repeatedly when climbers must be rescued at National Park Service expense. Their budget to maintain parks, is already strained beyond its limits. Climbing "The High One" is extremely popular because of the challenge. Mount McKinley has a vertical relief of 18,000 feet, greater than that of Mount Everest. According to geologists, it is still rising.

Many of these climbers are visitors from foreign countries. Unlike other countries, we, apparently, do not require special rescue insurance for them or our own climbers. Raising the park entrance fees is an option, but that answer doesn't even approach "fair," for those of us who do not choose such risks to enjoy Denali National Park.

The point has been made that not all rescues involve climbers; some are hikers. I am a hiker. If I would choose to hike on the ice, snow, and crevasses of Mount McKinley, I would be willing to pay for the privilege. OK, so I'll get off my soapbox.

---

**Take binoculars, cameras (with long lens), extra film, insect repellent, raingear, lunch, and drink. Wear layered clothing and sensible shoes,**

---

Shuttle buses cost $12 to $30, depending on your destination. This does not include the $3 entrance fee. Sign up at the Visitor Center. You can make reservations, or if you aren't too fussy when you go, you can take a chance with a walk-in reservation. I've never had a problem getting on a shuttle, even during high season, but that doesn't mean you mightn't have to wait a day or two.

Narrated bus tours are available for various prices. Multiple or season shuttle bus tickets are cheaper, if you intend to go more than once.

During Fourth of July week, we were able to get on a bus at 6 a.m. the day after we arrived. I prefer early trips, but many people like later in the day. It doesn't make a lot of difference as far as seeing animals. We took the Eielson Visitor Center trip for $20 each.

Denali has seven campgrounds, three accommodate RVs. There are no amenities, except water. Riley Creek Campground near the Visitor Center, has a dump station. The campground fee is $12 a night, with a minimum of three nights at Teklanika, twenty-nine miles into the park. At Teklanika, you are allowed to drive in and out once, and must use a ticket for the camper bus, otherwise. Towed vehicles must be left at the Riley Creek overflow parking lot.

Without reservations, Jane and I stayed in Riley Creek our second night at Denali.

If you are waiting for a campsite, or a ticket on the shuttle bus, guided hikes or hiking trails might fill your time. A free bus is provided from the Visitor Center to the dogsled demonstration.

Jennifer Reed was the ranger in charge, and did an excellent job explaining how the dogs are trained, what they eat, and answering questions. The dogs were hooked to the sled. and pulled it around the loop.. The dogs get extremely excited about running, and go lickety split. (Do not take your own animals with you.)

Denali is the only National Park that maintains a dog kennel operation with working sled dogs. This is a chance to see the kennels up close and see how the dogs live and work. Dogsleds are still used for ranger patrols to contact winter users in the backcountry, deter illegal activities by hunters and trappers, and haul maintenance and emergency supplies to remote patrol cabins.

If you still need something to do, go outside the park for river rafting, flightseeing, or horseback riding.

Several rafting companies are just outside the park. Many rafting trips are available in Alaska, but if you want an afternoon's ride with experienced professional guides, rafting the Nenana River is a good trip. Guided rafting, when they do all the paddling, is not quite as exciting as when you are helping, but not everyone needs that thrill.

I was disappointed to learn that the gravel spit in the bend of the Nenana River, about two miles toward Fairbanks, had been taken over as a private RV park. It used to fill with boondocking RVs, all waiting to get into Denali. The private park had a closed sign on it at 5 p.m. The park we paid $10 to stay in, was unlevel, crowded, and noisy. All the places where I had previously parked overnight along the river, had been signed for no RV parking.

I don't know their reasons for taking this privilege away. It surely wasn't because the campgrounds were empty, or that we didn't spend enough money in the area. I guess I'll never know.

### Ester

Jane and I continued on to Ester Gold Camp, ten miles out of Fairbanks. A lot of people flit right on by, but I love the place. Don't expect fancy. It's a miner's camp.

We paid $10 for dry camping. They had a dump station and water. Reservations for dinner, at the Bunkhouse Buffet, were $14.95 each. The menu featured good simple food like baked halibut, reindeer stew, and country fried chicken. This was my third time to overfeast. The house specialty is Alaska Dungeness Crab and costs about $4 more.

If you've never seen the Aurora Borealis, go to the Northern Lights Show at the Firehouse Theatre. It is a photosymphony, a melding of classical music and shimmering lights, on a thirty-foot screen.

According to Leroy Zimmerman, who puts the show together, "The feelings are beyond understanding when you see the Aurora Borealis. You don't know whether to cry or get down on your knees and pray." Almost to the night, two months later, I saw them. He knew of which he spoke.

Ester is the home of the "World Famous Malamute Saloon," swinging doors and all. If your table isn't full, other visitors will be seated with you. They squeeze in as many as possible, but it is a happy atmosphere. You throw your peanut shells into the sawdust on the floor. Alaskan history hangs on the wall, a hangman's noose, gold pans, washboards, picks, and axes. The bar was barged downriver from Dawson City

The performers, or "Esteroids," as they call themselves, are a bundle of energy and entertainment, and a lot of entertainment it is, for $5. Anyone would agree with their song assessment in "Dad Gum, Dad Gum, Dad Gum Govn'mint Woes," or their logic. "If you don't buy a souvenir, folks back home will wonder if you really went to Alaska."

Their scientific name for all true Alaskans is "Alaskan Basicus." "They are all crested, wear a baseball cap, and eat only stream-caught salmon, ice cream, and beer."

By the time your trip is over, you will be well acquainted with, and I hope a fan of, Robert Service. At the Malamute, they call it "Service with a Smile." You could have heard a pin drop as performers recited poetry that brought the North country to life. You could feel the cold in your very bones, and the loneliness was palpable. Oh yesss!!

Their drinks are as potent as an "Ice Worm Cocktail" or as mild as a "Prunella Pinfeather." Just don't ask the waiter if he has a "Fuzzy Navel" as I did in 1992. He said that was a dangerous question! Hmmm.

Occasionally, they throw in something serious, "Cat's been using her litter box again; winter must be coming." When we laughed, he said, "I find no humor whatsoever in the weather."

They mentioned having their special Alaskan flag, "As a reminder of the hardships we had before we became a state." As a political statement, he added under his breath, "We don't need no special reminder to remember the hardships we've had since we became a state." Hmmm.

### Fairbanks

In Fairbanks, we visited the Tanana Valley Farmer's Market. This is fun to do in almost any Alaskan community. It was small, but had great fresh fruit and yummy baked goods.

The University of Alaska Museum is a must stop. Their answer to Michigan's Babe the Blue Ox, is "Blue Babe," the World's only restored Ice Age bison mummy. (I'll get a lot of flack claiming Michigan's right to Babe the Blue Ox, but one of her footsteps did make Lake Michigan.)

An interesting display in 1996 was, "Forced to Leave," about the WWII internment of Alaskans. This is a good place to get a thorough explanation of the Aurora Borealis via video.

In the Aurora Dome, we sat for a program presented by the World

Eskimo-Indian Olympics. We saw athletes of the Northern Inua, perform traditional games, songs, and dance. It was informative and humorous. Trying their "One-foot-high-kick" would injure me for life. They jump straight up, with one foot coming off the ground, and the other kicking straight up to hit the ball. It is like doing vertical splits. The world record leap is over seven feet.

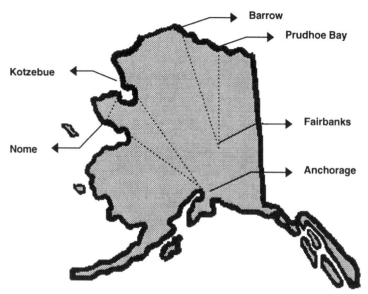

**The Outer Limits**
**Barrow, Alaska**

    This is a good place to encourage you to fly to at least one of the outlying villages. In 1987, I flew from Fairbanks to Barrow, an Inupiat Eskimo Village of around 4,000, the northernmost point of the North American Continent. It is called, Top of the World, and who would argue that, being 330 miles north of the Arctic Circle, 1,500 miles from the North Pole, and surrounded by frozen tundra. Dress warmly.

    I visited a former Girl Scout of mine, who lived up there for two years. I was able to see and do more than perhaps the average tourist, but tours cover a lot of territory.

    Lynn explained the Eskimo philosophy, "Whether it is a whale kill, paycheck, or anything else, they share what they have. They believe if they are ever in need, their friends will share with them, also." I asked Lynn how living among the Eskimos had affected her life. She said, "It helps you set priorities. You don't worry about having a Chemlawn truck in your yard. It gives you perspective in your life, after viewing someone else's culture."

    I joined Lynn's Eskimo friends at a Nalukataq, a successful whale-kill celebration. We sat in a semi-circle. Men carrying big buckets and wearing plastic gloves, placed a handful of "Muktuk" in each of our containers. The fermented whale blubber resembled bloody, uncooked liver; chewed like bubble gum; and with no disrespect to my hosts, tasted like Lynn's description, "slime."

Children were tossed high in the air from a sealskin blanket. Lynn commented, "When the adults get in on this, an ambulance is kept on hand. Adults tend to get overly enthusiastic with their tossing."

Near the airport, is a memorial to Wiley Post and Will Rogers, who died in a plane crash fifteen miles south of Barrow in 1935.

Igloo (Place To Stay), Kotzebue, AK

## Kotzebue

In 1992, I took a two-day tour from Anchorage to Kotzebue, with an overnight in Nome. Kotzebue is twenty-six miles beyond the Arctic Circle, and I thought it was the most charming of the three "far-out" villages I visited. Perhaps, some of that was due to the terrific brother-sister tour-guide combo. It is one of the oldest communities on the North American Continent and only 200 miles from Cape Dezhnev, Russia.

I learned that calling my RV a "Rolling igloo," is correct. Lahka said the word "Igloo" means, "Place to stay." A regular two-story house costs between $65,000 and $250,000.

The guides pointed with pride to the one "real" tree in town. I puzzled at all the driftwood on the beaches in that treeless tundra country, but Lahka explained, "It is transported by floods from the wooded mountains." After canoeing the Yukon, I understand.

All the distant villages have freezing and permafrost problems. Pumps within the pipes, keep water and sewage moving, so they don't freeze.

Our guides took us on a "tundra walk" and dug down into the permafrost, so we could see what it was like. They pointed out the Alaska cotton plant; blueberry, cranberry, salmonberry plants; and the plants they use for smoking food and dying colors. I'm happy to report that dandelions are alive and well in Kotzebue.

At the Inupiat Culture Camp, the Inupiat culture and lifestyle were explained. They demonstrated how to skin and tan animal hides to make mukluks and parkas. We shared Lunch and conversation with our charming guides. The reindeer stew was delicious.

The highlight of our Kotzebue visit, was the NANA (The Great Hunter) Museum of the Arctic, with animal and sealife exhibits and dioramas of the Arctic environment. After the slide show on Eskimo culture, three elders, one an eighty-eight-year-old man, played drums and sang for dancers, who told of their traditions and history. We participated in a blanket toss and danced the native dances.

Kotzebue's first mile of paved road was due in 1996. Residents were concerned about the four-wheelers and the new "strip."

## Nome, Alaska

I stayed overnight at the Nugget Inn in Nome and ate dinner at Fat Freddies, only 130 miles from Siberia. At dinner, I experienced one of those "Moments in Time" I have talked about. It is as though I am mentally backing off, and assessing what I am doing, and I can't quite believe my good fortune in being where I am. Fresh flowers were on the table but outside the window, only a few feet from me, icebergs were floating on the Bering Sea in mid-June.

The one thing I didn't realize, until during the tour the next day, was that the beachfront property is public domain, and open for anyone to pan gold. I wasted the evening wandering. Hmmm. I could have paid for the whole trip. Well, maybe not, but it would have been fun.

Lest you think that is an impossibility, the guide said, "They took $37,000 of placer flour (finer than dust) gold from the beach last year." She also added, "But we all know how miners tell tall tales." She mentioned the red garnets sprinkled on the beach. "If you find red garnets, you'll usually find gold nearby." I blew it.

If I had had extra room in my suitcase, I might have brought back a tiny, furry creature that will grow up to be a sled dog. This little guy was only a month old, and a wiggling bundle of joy. Our tour had taken us to visit Howard Farley, a musher in the first Iditarod Race. He now raises dogs and promotes what he calls, "The Last Great Race."

He gave us the history of the race, "The Iditarod Trail Sled Dog Race started in 1973. The Iditarod Trail was used previously by ancient hunters. Later, it was a supply and mail route to and from the gold-mining camps in bush Alaska. The seed for this race and its legends, was planted in 1925, when a diphtheria epidemic struck Nome. Vital serum was relayed from Nenana to this tiny Eskimo Village, by dog team. Planes in those days, were grounded in winter, due to harsh weather conditions. Twenty volunteer mushers carried the serum 674 miles in 127 1/2 hours, saving the people of Nome."

He also said, "Women winners not only dominated the scene for a while, but put the Iditarod Race on the map." The first woman to win the race was Libby Riddles in 1985. Susan Butcher became a four-time Iditarod champion in 1990, and set a new speed record for the second time.

He explained that, "The term 'Husky,' usually means any dog pulling a sled." He raises Siberian Huskies and trains them, running them in the sand when he doesn't have snow. The dogs were eager to demonstrate.

Our tour included gold panning at the Alaska Gold Company, a Historic Mine Site and still an active operation. A 108-ounce gold nugget was mined there. It is now in the Smithsonian Institution in Washington, D. C.

The population of Nome is around 4,500. They have just about every kind of store you might need. The guide said, "Nome is a pretty jazzy town, with three roads leading to small outlying communities, as far as eighty-seven miles. We have an Arts Council, a theatre group, and lots of kids. We have long winters, you know."

Tours give a good taste of the outlying communities. Overnight isn't enough time to soak in the native culture, history, or the local stories but I definitely recommend a flight to any of the bush villages.

Depending on whether you leave from Anchorage or Fairbanks, whether it is one day or overnight, etc., tours include air fares that run between roughly $350 and $500. I agree, it is a lot of money, but maybe you'll never have the opportunity again. The nice thing about flying to Kotzebue, is having a great aerial view of Mt. McKinley, depending, of course, on whether the weather is turned on or off.

### Fairbanks Continued

Fairbanks offers a lot of activities. Alaskaland is big on everybody's list. At the Alaska Salmon Bake, they have a big semicircle cooking area where you can watch them prepare salmon and halibut. The meals include salad, sourdough rolls, baked beans, and blueberry cake. I have waddled out of there four times now. Making reservations is a smart move. The RV caravans eat there.

While you're waiting, you can wander around their gold mining exhibit, and see the equipment they used during gold rush days.

The renovated twenty-nine log cabins that house the shops on the boardwalk, are authentic, donated by descendants of pioneer families. You can write postcards, eat ice cream at outdoor tables, or just soak in this historic stampede theme park. The Visitor Information Center is in the Sternwheeler Nenana, the second largest wooden vessel in existence, permanently docked only a few yards from the Chena River.

Take a whole day, or even better, two or three, to see everything at Alaskaland. Walk through the Alaska Native Village, see the workings of a mine or a fish wheel, visit the Pioneer Museum, or ride the Crooked Creek and Whiskey Island Railroad.

Stay for at least one Alaskaland evening. The Farthest North Square and Round Dance Center, offers some form of dancing each evening

**Salmon Bake, Alaskaland, Fairbanks**

**Native Fashion Show**

**Native Fish Wheel**

**Pick 'N' Poke Gift Shop, Ester, AK**

**Native Fish Camp**

during the season. You can watch or join in.

I must have been a dance hall girl in a former life. When I watch the performers at The Palace Theatre and Saloon, I am right up there doing the can-can in the Golden Heart Revue. They always have good advice for tourists, "No matter what the locals tell you, moose droppings do not taste like pine nuts."

## Alternate Activities

It used to take two or three weeks by stagecoach, to reach Chena Hot Springs from Fairbanks. Now, you can drive the seventy-five miles in a day. I rode up there with a friend in 1992, but neither of us were prepared to stay and soak. Chena Hot Springs Road is paved and follows the Chena River through, what else, The Chena River Recreation Area. There are many campgrounds along the way, and RV parking, with electrical hook-ups, are at the hot springs.

Gold miners discovered the spring in 1905, and used it to alleviate the aches and pains of rheumatism. The springs come from the center of a forty-square-mile geothermal area at 156 degrees. Fortunately, they cool it first, so your goose won't be cooked.

I mentioned Circle Hot Springs on the Yukon River trip. It is 129 miles from Fairbanks, and you could go on up to Circle as well, two adventures for the price of one.

## The Riverboat Discovery

I thought I had been on as many riverboat trips in my lifetime as I needed, but Jane and I both really enjoyed the day trip on the sternwheeler Riverboat Discovery.

The narration by Commentator, Phil Deisher, was interesting, informative, and broken up by activities on the shore. A Piper Cub took off and landed along the shore for our benefit. Phil said, "They really deliver. Recently, a pilot delivered a baby while he was flying the mother to the hospital. The bush communities live and die by the sound of the mail and medical planes flying in and out." How a pilot could deliver a baby while he is flying, remains a mystery to me. Either the mother did all the work, unaided, but encouraged, or someone else was in the plane. A taxi driver I might believe. Hmmm.

Four generations of the Binkley family have owned and operated the riverboat, for nearly a hundred years. The river history of this family dates back to prospectors, fur traders, and Native people. They all relied on the rivers as their only link to the outside world. "The old paddlewheelers used one cord of wood every hour, for 24 hours a day. Now we use diesel engines."

We left the Chena River, and went into the Tanana River, the largest glacier-fed river in the world. "The glacier rock is ground into glacier flour that causes the silt, and the gray color of the water." He said it was a completely uncontrolled river, with no navigational aids.

The river supports salmon. "The silt goes right through the gills, but because of the silt, the fish cannot see, and are easily caught." There you go, fisherpeople.

We stopped for an over-the-side visit with Susan Butcher. She talked about her dogs, and showed us the puppies she was training. She says, "It takes one and a half weeks to teach them to go, and two and a half years, to teach them to whoa."

Later on, we stopped to talk with "Dixie," a full-blooded Athabascan Indian. She demonstrated cutting up salmon, and how they dry it in the smokehouse. Salmon is stored in cache houses after it is dried. Cache houses are the tiny cabins you see at the top of four long poles. Tin cans are placed near the top of the poles, to keep animals from robbing the cache.

We watched a dog-mushing demonstration by Susan Butcher's assistant and long-distance racing team, at the Old Chena Indian Village, then we left the riverboat for a guided tour.

They showed us how the Indians might have lived, before they had contact with the outside world. They were constantly on the move, following the animal herds. Their houses were made of skin, and snow was packed around the outside for insulation. A cabin, with insulation and windows, was used after contact with the outside world.

A pregnant guide explained that diapers were made of moss or rabbit fur, "The first earth-friendly, bio-degradable, disposable diaper. After it was used, it was buried, and more moss or fur applied."

Several girls modeled clothes. "Each person had their own design, and it was always good for a husband to know his wife's design. It gets very dark here in Alaska in the winter."

All parts of hunted animals were used. Eating tools were made of bone. Moose antlers were scrapped against a tree to summon another moose. "The moose would hear it and think another moose was invading his territory." She held up a long narrow tube and said, "If you are very quiet, I'll call a moose. I have to be very careful, one might come." She held it to her lips and whispered into it, "Here, moosey, moosey."

Suddenly, as we were all getting into the hang of the ancient arts, a telephone rang in somebody's pocket. It was incongruous, there in the wilderness in an Indian village.

At the turn-around, we enjoyed complimentary coffee and donuts, and later, had canned salmon and crackers. The salmon is canned by their own company, and sold only on the riverboat. It was delicious, and deliciously expensive, but worth it.

Twelve days, 1,300 miles, and a lot of Alaska later, I said good-bye to Jane Parker at the Anchorage International Airport. By the time she flew back to Stuart, Florida, she had traveled over 12,000 miles. Jane is young at heart, one game lady, and I'm proud that she (and her four kids) lets me tell everyone she is my surrogate Mom. She is still talking about her Alaskan adventure.

As for me, I wanted to land in one place and stay there for a while. I didn't know where. As a full-time RVer, I tossed a coin and headed back down the Kenai Peninsula.

These pictures might give you a clue to where we are going next.

Summer Puddles

# HOPE, ALASKA

**Robert Salmon, Chef
Seaview Cafe
"The Chef Who Refused To Die"**

5K Run And Bazaar

# THE HOPE OF MY UNIVERSE

## Hope, Alaska

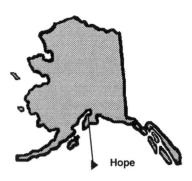

Coming from the apple-tree country of Michigan, I appreciated their claim that the first apple tree in Alaska was planted in Hope.

The road to Hope is paved, a fifty-six-mile round-trip from the Seward Highway. It passes the site of Sunrise City, a ghost town of gold rush days.

Hope is on the back side of Turnagain Arm. It is almost directly south of, and eighty-eight miles from, Anchorage. As the crow flies, the mileage is considerably less. Although I hesitate to say that anything is beyond hope, Porcupine USFS campground is. It is at the end of the Hope Highway, just beyond Hope. It is perched on the side of the mountain with great views over the Arm. It is beyond Hope's only gas station, owned by an eighty-three-year-old lady. The pump read, $1.73 a gallon.

Before Anchorage existed, and before the gold rushes happened at Dawson City or Nome, "A man named King" gave Hope the distinction of becoming Alaska's first gold rush town. He discovered gold in Resurrection Creek. It flows past Hope into Turnagain Arm. The town was named after Percy Hope, the youngest gold rusher to get off the boat.

As with all boomtowns, the gold gave out and miners pushed on to other gold rushes. It is hard to imagine Hope as a rowdy town of 3,000. It has dwindled to the 250 who live there now.

The food is good at the Discovery Cafe, a tiny one-room restaurant. If you are lucky, as I was, you can listen to Tito, the owner, telling local stories to the cheechakos. The cafe serves another purpose. Several bookshelves are filled with mysteries, love stories, stories of the North country, or whatever your interest. They are for trading and I did.

I stayed in and around Hope for the next five weeks. I camped on the Old Hope Townsite just beyond the Seaview Cafe. The best spot was at the far end of the campground. My views of the mud flats and Turnagain Arm were unobstructed.

The campground, operated by the Seaview Cafe, had electricity and a view for $12, or $7 with only the view. I went to Henry's One Stop whenever I needed a sewer dump. The fee was a reasonable $5. Henry's had a Laundromat, a small store, and a full hook-up campground in the trees. He didn't have the view I needed for inspiration.

Early in the morning, or late in the evening, I walked the path above the mud ravines that reached out toward the Arm. It paralleled the pasture where three curious horses lived. They came to greet me, until they discovered I didn't carry treats.

The mud flats and the tides fascinated me. The outgoing tide left interesting indentations and rivulets in the mud. It was usually quite windy out near the Arm. I usually wore my hair down, because I loved feeling the wind in my hair. Once again, for some reason, I felt free and uplifted and joyful.

Hope was a victim of the 1964 earthquake. Many of the historical buildings collapsed or floated away on the tide. Apple tree roots dropped into the salt water and died. During the winter months now, the water actually laps at the Seaview Cafe.

The Upper Cook Inlet has the second greatest tide range in North America (in the world, I heard) at 38.9 feet. (I had seen the highest at the Bay of Fundy in Nova Scotia.) I didn't see it, but they sometimes get "bore tides," steep, foaming walls of water up to six feet high, that go down Turnagain Arm at speeds up to ten knots.

The second highest tide of the season was expected in Hope on August 1. The water came into the campground, all over the pasture where I walked evenings, and the horses were driven back against the fence. It was up to thirty-three feet. Fishermen and campers moved to higher ground.

Linda, the postmaster, said that once a year her family puts on old clothes, and spends a day playing in the mud, choosing their tide time and place very carefully. "It ruins your clothes. You can't wear shoes because if you get stuck, you can't pull your foot out of the mud."

Playing in the mud was one thing I wanted to do before I left, but I needed to have someone pull me out, if necessary. I never found quite the right conditions.

Linda also cautioned, as everyone locally did, that the mud flats were extremely dangerous. Rising or falling water tables under their surface, can suddenly change the solid surface to quicksand. She said a newly married couple went out on the flats with a three-wheeler and got stuck. The wife got off to push. They freed the three-wheeler; but, she was so tightly stuck, the husband was unable to pull her out. A helicopter couldn't pull her out either. They were afraid they would tear her in half. Eventually the tide came in and she drowned.

In my full-time travels, I have learned, "It's a small world." Chuck Anderson was a motorhomer who parked at the Seaview Campground for many summers. On the day we met, he drove me to Henry's One Stop for milk, and then wanted to visit friends, who had been coming to Hope for thirteen summers.

He hadn't any more than introduced me, when the lady asked, "Do you know Miriam and Bob Johnson?" I went into shock. The Johnsons are friends of mine from New Carlisle, Indiana. Fran and Bodie Bodemiller had been neighbors of the Johnsons, at one time. Miriam had sent Fran my books, and told them to watch for me in Alaska. It was really amazing that we crossed paths. Alaska is a big place.

Actually, we more than crossed paths. Chuck was kind enough to take me to the Hope Christian Church each Sunday, and we always sat with Fran and Bodie. Services didn't start until 3 p.m. At first, I thought this was because the place needed to warm up in the winter; but then, I realized the minister and his wife drove from his morning service in Seward, approximately seventy-five miles away.

Through the three of them I met, and heard about very interesting people, including Billie and Ann Miller. Billie built the little church from logs he dragged down from the high country, and Ann was postmaster for many years.

Ann also volunteered at the Historical/Mining Museum, an interesting place to spend a few hours. Billie worked on an outdoor cabin exhibit. Everything he touches has to turn out "just so," probably better than the original building.

I found everything about Hope appealing. I took different routes to the post office, when I tired of staring at the computer monitor. I liked the dust smell I kicked up. Picturesque cabins hid in yards high with natural growth. Wild pink roses decorated gray, unpainted fences, and old squeejawed birdhouses perched on the posts. After a rain, everything reflected in the puddles, and the trees hung over the road and dripped. Even the mud had a fresh smell to it.

Everything was green and lush. Purple fireweed grew taller than my head and waved in the breeze. Devil's Club was thick with leaves and bright red berries. The cow parsnip that looked like an enormous Queen Anne's lace plant that we had back in the Midwest, was rampant. If you bruise a leaf, a chemical left on your skin, makes your skin supersensitive to the sun, and causes a blistered burn within a short while. Fortunately, Alaska doesn't have poison ivy or poison oak.

Hope Sunrise Library was built in 1938, and used as a one-room schoolhouse. Volunteers keep it open. It was a cozy place to go on a summer's day, and look through old clippings, newspapers, and books.

The Seaview Cafe had a warm, friendly atmosphere, and the fragrances were heavenly. The shelves held Hope memorabilia and another trading library. The walls were gray-weathered wood, and bouquets of plastic flowers lived on the few yellow oil-cloth-covered tables. Robert was a chef from Anchorage, working on his degree. His cooking did absolutely nothing for my waistline.

With camping nearly on the doorstep, it was easy to go where I could find friendly conversation, hear local stories, meet people, and eat pancakes, pies, and burgers that were out of this world. Occasionally, I restrained myself and just had coffee.

We all teased Robert. He was an accident waiting to happen, and it usually did. One day he had a black and bruised eye, walked with a strange limp, and the rest of him didn't look too good either. He and his friend, Paul, had a wreck, "We went airborne, end over end both directions, and smashed up both ends of the car. Ended up in the ditch." Chuck and I saw it later. It was completely and irrevocably totaled. I told Robert they must have something pretty special to accomplish on this earth for them to have survived that accident. He began to refer to himself as, "The chef who refused to die."

What a place to raise kids. They had the whole summer for fishing, exploring, and playing. Two little girls, about eight-years-old, walked up the street past the cafe. As they chattered, the white horse from the pasture plodded between them. He didn't even have a rope around his neck. He reached down and nuzzled one girl's hand; rewarded, he then nuzzled the other girl's hand. He was more dog than horse.

The first foray into the cafe was to have the halibut dinner ($10.95 at lunchtime). My mouth still waters. The next day, I went back for their weekend BBQ special. I had, in the meantime, become acquainted with the Williams' from Iowa. When they came in, the place was jammed. They joined me. During our conversation, I didn't notice that the husband had gone up and paid my bill, as well as theirs. When they left Hope, I was the proud owner of a big hunk of fresh filleted salmon, Howard had caught in the creek. People are kind.

Postmaster Linda, said there were nine bears poking around town when I arrived. She, and her husband, set a bear trap with moose meat. The trap was metal, strong, and supposedly, bears couldn't hurt it. That night, they watched a bear pick it up, spring it, and mangle it. He shredded a duck decoy from their pond, to the point they couldn't find it. That was one upset bear.

Another lady told me she had watched the horses chase a grizzly out of the pasture a few days before. A fisherman claimed a bear had interrupted his fishing. I asked if the bear chased him. He said, "No, I just backed away slowly." I didn't see any of the bears, but over the next few weeks, I saw a moose once in a while.

All the bear brochures warn hikers to make noise, or wear bear bells on the trails, to warn them you are in their territory. Robert's theory was that bear bells were more like "dinner bells." Having never (thank God) encountered a bear on any trails, I couldn't argue the theory.

It was always a possibility. Fran came out of their fifth wheel at Henry's campground, to go up and take a shower one morning. A bear was by the telephone booth (waiting for a call?). Apparently, neither one of them had brushed their teeth yet. They split without conversing.

The salmon were running. The place was packed with fisherpeople. I had no interest, but just in case any fishing nuts are reading this, I did hear this comment, "I get so tired catching fish; my wrists are sore."

On the third Sunday in July, Hope sponsors a 5K Run and Bazaar. It started at the Hope Social Hall, with a book sale and art exhibit. The Social Hall was built in 1902 and is still used for meetings and weddings.

The event brought runners and supporters in from quite a distance. They milled around, greeting old friends, and doing warm-ups. Others were taking pictures, eating, and enjoying the sunshine and camaraderie. After instructions via a bullhorn, and warnings that bears were in the area, they were off: old ones, young ones, hotshots, and little kids. Encouragement flowed, a pat on the backside, or shouts, "Yeah, John, way to go, good job, you're almost there." What a great summer day.

On my way through the campground one evening, I saw Gordon Bort playing a saw for a group of admirers. He made different sounds by bending the saw as he drew the bow across it. That particular saw was made especially for playing, but he said you could also build a house with it. Gordon doesn't read music. He had learned to play the saw through a correspondence course.

A buddy he had grown up with in Syracuse, New York, had come to Anchorage to surprise Gordon, and the two families were camped at Hope for their reunion. When they left, they gave me two "Conies," white hotdogs made with veal.

Next to the Seaview Cafe is the Seaview Bar. Joyce and Don own both of them, as well as the motel and gift shop. Joyce ran the saloon in the evening. It was a gathering place for leftover tourists, locals, and occasionally, nosy writers like me. Chuck helped Joyce for a couple of hours most evenings. If nobody came, they played cribbage.

One night, the Sweet Adelines, who were weekending with their leader who lived in Hope, ran a karaoke in the bar. The next day, Fran, Bodie, Chuck, and I went to the Social Hall to hear their fun program.

The railing in the front of the cafe, was a good place to enjoy the sunshine, while waiting for the phone. If you looked up on the grassy mountain meadows, you could sometimes see sheep grazing. I wanted to twitch my nose and go up there. I couldn't find anyone to hike up with me.

One afternoon, Robert sent a young lady from Anchorage, over to my RV to go hiking. Gull Rock Trailhead is at the far end of the USFS campground, and goes through a forest cathedral, across a rock slide, and down through an avalanche gully, hugging the flower-bedecked cliffs above Turnagain Arm.

Donna was 37, and in the process of getting her second Bachelor's Degree. She told me about working on a fishing boat the summer before, with three guys she didn't know. She had even more adventurous bones than I did.

She did the cooking (naturally) and helped bring in the nets. I asked how she liked the experience. She said there were only a few instances when she questioned what on earth she was doing there, but, "We saw so many animals and such incredible scenery. I realized that other people spend thousands of dollars to see what I saw."

Although I made many trips into town, most of my five weeks were parked in a USFS campground on Resurrection Creek. I hadn't shut off the engine before a fisherman gave me salmon that wouldn't fit into his freezer chest.

I parked six feet from the water. My solar purred and my computer hummed. The host couple were SKPs, and Chuck (another one) often brought other campers, or visitors, to my door to say hello. I think he was trying to marry me off.

Chuck always had interesting stories about campers. Two couples, each with babies less than three months old, were going backpacking over the mountains. He asked if they were aware of the bears. They told him about a fellow in Fairbanks, who had written a book about bears. He said that bears had never been known to attack a group of more than two people. Chuck said, "Good, you take the book and throw it at the bear, in case he hasn't read it."

The only other camper was Mike. He was from California and came to pan for gold. The campground was alongside a recreational gold panning area. He claimed he found more gold in a day there, than in all the years he had panned in California. He panned dirt by the bucketful instead of standing in the cold creek for hours at a time, and said he never failed to find something. One night, he knocked on my door to show me his treasures of the day. He had found quite a few nuggets, just smaller than peas, and wanted to share his excitement.

I tried my luck at gold panning. The water was frigid. After I couldn't feel the cold any more, I figured my feet were frozen. A champion gold panning couple from Austria, was in the park a couple of days. I watched them panning. They did it really fast. I did it their way, not knowing whether I was whishing away a wealth of gold or not.

My equipment was rudimentary, at best. I had a gold pan. Along with it, I used a steamer basket and a Tupperware dish. They helped to weed out the bigger rocks (or nuggets!). After four hours of getting my hiking boots, socks, and feet soaked in icy water, and mud up to wherever, I had about ten gold flakes to show for it. That was nothing compared to the silver flake who was doing it.

The afternoon of gold panning proved one thing beyond a reasonable doubt: I would earn more at writing than gold mining, which also meant I was destined to be poor. I found enough gold dust and flakes to see a glint in my tiny vial (if I held it in the right light and in the right position).

If you want to do serious gold panning, write, or visit, the Alaska Public Lands Information for a list of recreational panning places you can use. You mustn't pan just anywhere because you would likely cross paths with an irate miner. They get pretty touchy about anybody panning on their claims. As always, respect the rights of others. You are allowed only hand tools and light equipment for recreational panning. Check it out before you do it.

A few people came in to camp or pan for gold; but mainly, it was quite peaceful. No matter how cool it was at night, my window toward the stream was open. With the cool air coming inside and that fast-running stream outside, it was great for sleeping.

The pinks and king salmon fought their way upstream to spawn. Fishermen were elbow to elbow down on the inlet at Hope. Up there on the creek, the fish who made it through the gauntlet of inlet fishlines, fought only their battles against time.

The mountains were covered with wildflowers. As I walked around on one of my breaks from writing, I was startled to see autumn's first tinges. It was only the last day of July! That night, I saw something I had never seen in Alaska. I opened the curtains, and a full moon shown in all its glory. I had never been up there late enough to see it before.

Chuck Anderson knew I was working. He tried never to bother me, but I could count on his bringing my mail up from Hope.

Bodie, an older version of Christopher Reeve, was a retired engineer who spoke in engineereze. Most of the time I understood him. Fran and I had many good conversations. They both had a terrific sense-of-humor, and their stories of life, and characters in Hope, were priceless.

They warned me about the miner who was always looking for a new bride. He had married several times. Many years ago, he had advertised nationwide for brides for his whole mining crew, as Bodie put it, "To take care of their biological needs." Only one came. The wedding was quite elaborate with a period setting and a horse and buggy. Alas, the marriage collapsed, and he was alone once more.

One of many things I didn't find the time to do when I was in Hope, was rafting the Six-mile River. It is described as, "Tranquillity, interspersed with moments of high drama." It is a guided trip and dry suits are required, but I will do it...the next time.

I drove Chuck's car into town behind his motorhome, instead of having his kids come out for it. We had dinner at Ole's with his daughter and came right back. Everything was closed up: the cafe, the gift shop, the saloon. It was a Monday, August 19. Nobody came to visit so they closed the doors early. I was the only one parked in the campground. Chuck and I said our good-byes, and he drove back to Anchorage.

I felt pretty lonely. I left. I stopped at the post office to say good-bye to Linda, and saw Fran and Bodie at the Museum. They invited me to dinner at the Discovery Cafe. It was fun, but sad. My time in Hope had come to an end. Summer visitors were fast disappearing, and the air had a definite feel of fall.

As with all communities, Hope had people from all aspects of life. In every village where I stayed for a while, I eventually discovered the (some) town secrets. One village wasn't so different from another; only the names were changed to protect the innocent, and the not-so-innocent. Everyone has a story to tell, as with everywhere else: some were sad, some poignant, some brutal, some comical, and even a few, joyful.

I parked overlooking a lake; a scenic spot tightly held by mountains. I closed the drapes toward the highway, enjoyed my personal view from the bedroom window, and read the evening away.

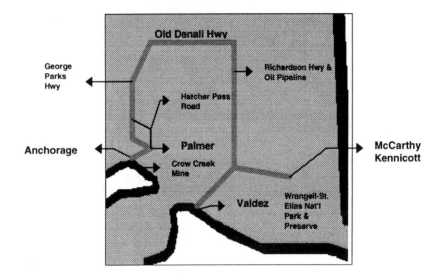

# THE FAIR AND THE FIREWEED

Ken, a good friend from California, was flying in for a sea-kayaking trip in Prince William Sound. I had only done river and lake kayaking. I was excited about trying something new, especially in Alaska. It was late late August and tourists had dwindled. After Ken's plane reservations were already set, the company canceled. When he arrived, we made other plans.

At Girdwood (south of Anchorage), Crow Creek Mine was not a disappointment. For starters, they have a campground for self-contained RVs. It is an 1898 mining camp, a National Historic Site, with eight original buildings and mine equipment. It would be easy to wander for hours looking at equipment and reading the history.

Many places offer gold-panning. They hand you a bucket of salted dirt, and you pan in a hokey sluice box. You always get something, so it's fun. Crow Creek allows you to hike back along the creek, pick your spot, and pan wherever. If you don't know how, someone will show you. We found one large flake, and some dust. It was work, but greatly rewarding.

We went through all the Crow Creek buildings after we were through panning, the Blacksmith's Shop, Mess Hall, and Barn. Barney and Cynthia Toohey, who own Crow Creek Mine, have lived there for twenty years. None of the buildings, including their personal beautiful cabin, have electricity or running water. They love it. They no longer endure Alaskan winters; however, they visit Mexico or the Caribbean.

We went on up the road to the Crow Pass Trailhead, parked and took off hiking. Crow Pass was a steep three-mile hike, following the

Historic Iditarod Trail. We left at 3:15 and didn't get to the mine and the falls, above the tree line, until six. Bright fall colors were coming on strong, but the summer flowers were hanging in there. Dark wispy clouds took turns shadowing the mountains and glaciers; but mostly, it was sunny, with fresh snow on the peaks.

The climb in the sun forced us to shed extra shirts. The views above tree level were incredible. It was hard to believe this steep trail was the original Iditarod.

We examined the mining equipment and ruins and sat for a while, surveying our momentary kingdom. With the sun going behind the mountains and a frigid breeze blowing through the pass, we didn't linger.

One activity I didn't want to miss was the Alaska State Fair at Palmer. It was celebrating its Diamond Jubilee. It was compact, with lots of activities and booths. Animals were different than at the Van Buren County Fair back in Michigan. There were llamas, alpacas, musk ox, and reindeer.

The fair is in the heart of the Matanuska Valley, famous for its oversized vegetables. Cabbages weighed in at more than eighty pounds. A Diamond Jubilee Giant Cabbage Weigh-off, offered prizes of $4,000.

Kids were getting their faces made up, hair pulled into different styles, and spray painted with sparklies. One little tyke had her face painted like a cat. She was quite patient with the whole business. When she looked into the mirror, however, the reaction was priceless. She couldn't quite believe it. She looked away and back quickly, as if the image would change. She was a wee bit awed with her image as a feline.

We ate everything that wasn't nailed down; deep-fried halibut, ice cream in home-made cones, cheesy popcorn, pizza, elephant ears, and anything else we could get. There was plenty of variety in junk food, but that's what an evening at the fair is all about.

I love being caught up in fair excitement, and it was fun having someone to share it with. The Workmen Hunk performed on guitars and fiddles. A grandmother danced to the music with a tiny tot. The name stuff on the big stage, the Soul something was just noisy and not my kind of entertainment (Am I getting old??). Listeners sprawled on a grassy embankment. Police hand-checked backpacks. Life goes on.

Their entertainment was varied: Demo Derby and stock car racing, All-Alaska Racing Pigs, Scheer's Lumberjack Show, and Bud Bog, among others. The Guess Who came (I guessed and I still didn't know who), Blessid Union of Souls (Amen!), and the Alaska Native Dancers. Alaska wasn't too far away to attract the rave of Nashville, LeAnn Rimes. Homesteader Events included wood splitting, ax-throwing, crosscut and bow sawing and other activities most of us rarely see.

It was a perfect evening at the fair and we wanted to return for the next day's activities but morning brought heavy rain with it.

**If you are ever near Palmer, Alaska the last week of August, or first week of September, spend at least one day and evening at the Alaska State Fair.**

We headed toward Hatcher Pass on Fishhook-Willow Road. The rain stopped, the clouds lifted, and the sun came out. We passed the Motherlode Lodge where I had eaten on a previous trip. I was in new territory. We continued up a pothole road at fifteen miles an hour. The Sprinter zigged and zagged, and slowly ascended through the scenery to the Independence Mine.

The Independence Mine is a State Historical Park at Hatcher Pass, elevation 3,886 feet. Gold was discovered in this area as early as 1886. It was years before independent mining claims were brought together under one company. During 1941, a peak year, 34,416 ounces of gold were mined. Today it would be worth $17,208,000.

Immediately surrounding the mine, Boomtown grew to twenty-two families. Now the mine and buildings are silent save for the conversation of visitors walking the trails, and looking into shafts, tunnels, and buildings. Interpretive signs explain the history.

The manager's family house was renovated for the Park Headquarters and Visitor Center. It was a neat building with pictures of the old days and even though it was warm outside, they had a fire going. I asked about the road over Hatcher Pass. They said it wasn't too bad. They brought out a map, and said it was another thirty miles of what we had just come through, potholes, with a couple bad hairpin curves. When they discovered I had a motorhome, they said I probably shouldn't. When they saw the size, they said, "We don't recommend it."

Despite knowing how bad the road was ahead, I hated to go back over the same territory. I decided to forge ahead. I hadn't yet seen a hairpin curve that couldn't be negotiated with backing up.

The first quarter-mile was narrow, washed out and potholed. Then it improved to potholes and boulder tops sticking out of the ground, that I had to weave around. Traveling was slow, but then again, the scenery was worth it. We looked down on lakes, waterfalls, glaciers, and streams, wending their way through the valley. Aspen groves had turned to gold. Low cranberry and blueberry plants were bright red and orange.

The hairpin curves were wide enough for a wide turn with no problem. Only a few impatient souls wanted to fly around me. I let them. We stopped several times in the valley along Willow Creek to admire beaver engineering. Active beaver houses with four, five, and six-foot dams corralled large expanses of water. Not one beaver came out to say hello. I have watched them working before, but Ken had never seen a beaver in the wild.

We found a campsite on Willow Creek, along a narrow, puddle-filled road through the bushes. It took some maneuvering to get in place. Someone had left a note on the tree, saying that anyone was welcome to the site, but the note-writer would be coming to use it on the weekend.

It was the perfect campsite with the stream rushing along just outside our windows. The next morning we reached the George Parks Highway.

At Cantwell, before turning onto the old Denali Highway toward Paxson and the Richardson Highway, I filled with gas and asked about road conditions. "Not bad," they said. I don't know why I ever ask. I know you can't take the word of a tourist who will usually say, "They're terrible;" and, the locals will always say, "Not bad."

The Denali Highway was the original road leading to Denali National Park and Preserve before the George Parks Highway was built. It has impressive views and remote places to camp but it was September, and I hadn't counted on hunting season. Trucks, four-wheelers, tents and hunting camps, were everywhere. The scenery was still impressive but the road was much worse than previously. Along with a lot of washboard, each pothole did its best to outdo the last one.

I have learned that driving faster on washboard is smoother than going too slow, but it was a challenge to fly over the washboard, and slow down quickly enough to avoid the potholes. I pulled over often to let others by, and then swallowed their dust. Gravel roads don't bother me; a certain amount of washboard and potholes don't bother me; but 114 miles of driving an average of twenty-miles-an-hour, got to me. Fortunately, the last twenty-one miles into Paxson, were paved.

I may have to revise my comment, "I've never met a road I didn't like."

For quite a distance after leaving the George Parks Highway, Mt. McKinley played in and out of the clouds. Denali Highway has everything, glaciers, archeological sites in the Tangle Lakes District, and kettle lakes left behind by blocks of glacier ice melt. Some of the road is built along "eskers," great ridges of gravel, formed by streams flowing under glaciers.

While Mt. McKinley is outstanding, the Alaska Range is no slouch. We could see Mt. Deborah (12,339'), Hess Mountain (11,940'), and Mt. Hayes (13,832'), and their accompanying glaciers, all mounded in snow, some of it fresh. On our other side were the Talkeetna Mountains. As we approached Richardson Highway, the Wrangell Mountains came into view again. Every curve brought a more beautiful sight, with the fall colors against the stark white snow.

We stopped and walked back along the one-lane multi-span Suisitna River Bridge, 1,036' long, to take pictures. Except for the Atigus Pass on the Dalton Highway, Maclaren Summit, 4,086', is the highest highway pass in Alaska.

Would I drive it a third time? Of course, but I would go during a quieter time than hunting season, and take several days to explore the side roads into the trailheads. In addition to the hunters, blueberry pickers were out in force. We saw trumpeter swans and beaver dams, but no large animals. They were hiding from all the hunters.

We camped in a pullout beside Clearwater Creek. The sun shown, but fall chill was in the air.

## Fast forward and sideways to Delta Junction

When we arrived at Paxson on the Richardson Highway, we turned right toward Glennallen, but I want to mention the Richardson from Delta Junction to Paxson. Unless you are in Alaska a long time, and deliberately seek this highway, it is probably one of the roads you'll miss. It is quite a beautiful route, a bumpy one either time I've been on it, with the usual good and bad areas.

Delta Junction, at the junction of the Alaska Highway and the Richardson Highway, is the official end of the Alaska Highway. I had driven from Delta Junction to Paxson in 1992, and experienced views of the same mountains I saw on Denali Highway; Mt. Hayes, Mt. Deborah and Hess Mountain. It is an opportunity for excellent views of the oil pipeline.

In the summer, Richardson Highway was decorated with purple fireweed and in September, it was dressed in fall colors. Along with the mountains, were Black Rapids Glacier and Gulkana Glacier; and lakes, Summit Lake, Paxson Lake, and Willow Lake. The road follows the Delta and Gulkana Rivers part of the way.

Leaving the Paxson area, west, the Chugach Mountains were in the distance, the mountains of Wrangell-St. Elias National Park and Preserve loomed to the left, Mt. Sanford, Mt. Drum, and Mt. Wrangell (again).

After passing the Tok cutoff road leading to Tok, I stopped at the junction of Glenn and Richardson Highways at Glennallen to get current information on McCarthy.

## McCarthy

We made reservations. I had driven the motorhome to McCarthy in 1992, and vowed to go back because it was such a neat trip and place. I wanted to stay at least two weeks. As good weather, and Ken's time were running out, and I wanted to stay longer if I ever drove that miserable road again, we took the $60-per-person round-trip van tour.

Leaving the Richardson Highway, I drove the paved Edgerton Highway to Liberty Falls State Recreation Site for the night. Continuing the thirty-three mile stretch into Chitina the next day, we passed Three-mile Lake, Two-mile Lake, and One-mile Lake (Does this show a lack of imagination, or am I being picky?).

The driver of the van, our tour guide, was Wen, a tall, slender fellow who, with his wife, were missionaries from Siberia, 150 mile above the Arctic Ocean. They were home for the summer and he had interesting tales to tell about their unusual life. The best part of taking the van was that I could relax and enjoy the scenery, without worrying about the Sprinter's undercarriage, or a flat tire.

Everything about the road to McCarthy fascinated me from the first time I heard about it from the volunteer hosts at Chilkat State Park, the Keitels. They had traveled it many years prior to the "improvements." The word improvement should be taken with several grains of salt; although, from the stories they told me about their first trip, improvements really have been made.

If you're driving the road, a National Park Service ranger station is in Chitina and they can tell you about current road conditions. The ranger station was closed both times I was there. I asked other people, and took the advice of the worst out of three. The Sprinter wasn't thrilled with that decision but I was.

The McCarthy Road begins just outside Chitina, at the Copper River. After approximately sixty miles of dusty, narrow, and washboard road, it ends at the Kennicott River. It follows the roadbed of the Copper River and Northwestern Railway. (The CR & NW was referred to as the "<u>C</u>an't <u>R</u>un and <u>N</u>ever <u>W</u>ill" Railroad.) This was used from 1911 to 1938 and transported 200 million dollars worth of copper ore from the Kennecott Mine to Cordova. Basically, the McCarthy road is an "improved railroad bed."

Although the rails and ties have been removed, sometimes old railroad spikes surface. For that matter, I've seen some of those "removed" ties underneath the dirt, that got scrapped to the surface. At any rate, it is a dirt road, narrow enough in spots to require waiting at iffy turnouts, for a vehicle to pass. On my two trips, I never saw a great deal of traffic on it.

The Chugach Mountains are on the right and the Wrangell Mountains on the left. The McCarthy Road is surrounded by the twelve-million-acre Wrangell-St. Elias National Park and Preserve. The road is owned by the State of Alaska but it is well to remember that most of the land near the road, is privately owned.

One of my favorite spots is the Kuskulana Bridge at Mile 16. It was built in 1911, to cross the 283' gorge over the Kuskulana River. New decking and metal guard rails were added in 1988. When I went through with the Sprinter, people were bungy-jumping off the bridge.

I have decided, if I ever take leave of my senses enough to go bungy-jumping, I want to go off the Kuskulana Bridge. At the very least, I will have magnificent scenery on the way to meet my Maker. None of this jumping off a derrick at a fair!

We stopped at the crinkled railroad trestle over the Gilahina River. It is part of the original railroad bed. Our rest stop included a long enough period to go water a bush (I was used to that after the Yukon River trip). The van dealt with the washboard road better than the Sprinter.

We passed still lakes and beaver dams, with early-morning scenery reflected in them.

Wen said that many of the McCarthy residents were attracted to this secluded place to get away from the world. When tourism began to take hold, they changed their thinking and joined in.

When I drove the Sprinter to McCarthy, I parked in an upper, roughly-dozed, parking space, because signs warned that floods might come swooshing through, if the lake ice gave way. I pulled myself hand-over-hand across the wild, rushing river in two places via an open-sided, two-seated tram, dangling in the air. Except for a few people in tents, truck campers, and small RVs, no one else was around.

After I trammed across one river, I walked a quarter-mile, then trammed across the other river. I walked another quarter-mile into town and paid a $5 fee for a narrated shuttle ride to the Kennecott Mine and the Kennicott Lodge.

This time things had changed drastically. The area at the Kennicott River had been turned into a rough-cut campground. They were charging for parking and camping. I'm not sure whether the combination information-ticket building was makeshift, or just built that way to blend in. If you were going to ride to the mine from McCarthy ($8), you had to buy your tickets there. It was after Labor Day, so there wasn't a choice of times. They didn't charge for using the tram. A telephone booth lived in the parking lot -- amazing. Previously, they used only radiophones.

We crossed on the tram, then went by mini-bus for the five-mile ride to Kennicott Glacier Lodge and the Kennecott Mine. The second tram was no longer necessary because the river changed its course and the bed was reasonably dry. We drove across the rocks on a makeshift road.

We passed the McCarthy Museum (railway depot). It had closed for the season. The driver said a key was available; but, with only a few hours, there wasn't time to pursue it.

Nothing had changed at Kennicott Glacier Lodge. It has a long porch with hanging flowerpots and table views of the mine, glacier, and mountains. Food and lodging are expensive. Everything has to be trammed across the river once the ice has broken. I've seen drums of gasoline, plywood, bikes, and other items, brought across on the trams.

After the discovery of copper in the early 1900s, the Kennecott Mine grew into a community with a general store. Miner's families purchased items, using books of scrip, bought from the corporation. A dairy barn and refrigeration plant also existed. Their hospital had one doctor and several nurses. Pneumonia and head injuries were the most frequent cause of death. They had a school, and a recreation hall, for dances, basketball games, and art shows. It was a company town with strict conduct rules. The cottages used by the foremen and their families, are being fixed up for rentals and private use.

You'll notice the different spellings of Kennecott and Kennicott. You aren't seeing things. The glacier was named after Robert Kennicott, an Alaskan explorer. Due to an error, the mine was spelled Kennecott, and they left it that way.

McCarthy sprang up to provide the miners with what Kennecott didn't: newspapers, restaurants, hotels, pool halls, saloons and a red-light district. The combined area has about thirty-five year-around residents now.

When the mine was closed in 1938, people were given forty-eight hours to pack up and get out. The vital parts of the powerhouse were destroyed and thrown over the side of the cliff in what they call "The Graveyard."

The mine has many interesting faded red buildings perched precariously, in stair-step fashion, on the mountainside. It includes the concentration mill, the ammonia-leaching plant, and the power plant. It is amazing that people are allowed to wander, because of the many open areas you could easily fall through. We couldn't go inside the buildings, but we looked in the windows.

The mine is a National Historic Landmark, but it is all private property. The National Park Service has negotiated for years to buy it. With a tag of nearly five million dollars, it may not happen until the buildings have long gone bye-bye.

With the great piles of rocky gravel in front of the mine, people automatically assume it is tailings. Guides explain that the glacier revises the landscape in its own way, leaving a chaotic, rock, end product.

If you're feeling hardy, there are trails to the glacier, and between Kennicott and McCarthy.

In McCarthy, the McCarthy Lodge still offered sleeping accommodations in the Johnson Hotel, or in the Bunkhouse. I didn't eat in the lodge this time but I know the food is home-cookin' good, and the atmosphere pleasant. Gary and Betty Hickling run the lodge. When I was there before, he had just bungy-jumped three times off the bridge, and swore by the tremendous adrenaline rush (it sounds like Excedrin Headache #493 to me).

My adrenaline rush came from going up in a bush plane with Natalie Bay, who owns Wrangell Mountain Air, with her husband, Kelly. That trip over ghost towns, mines, Dall sheep, the Icefall Stairway, and to see the Wrangell Mountains, was all the adrenaline I needed. I didn't want to come down.

Rumors were rampant that a pizza place was in Beautiful Downtown McCarthy and I couldn't believe it. I thought maybe it was something with neon signs the size of McDonald's golden arches. Jim and Jeannie Miller, long-time residents, have opened a really nice pizza parlor. You can eat inside or outside on the deck. It not only fits into McCarthy decor, but it was a very pleasant place to sit, and discuss our day, and enjoy delicious pizza.

I noticed on the way back to the van that they were putting the finishing touches on the McCarthy-Kennicott Community Church, on what was the island between the two channels of the Kennicott River.

On the way back to Chitina, Wen stopped, and let us walk across the Kuskulana Bridge. Three interesting and friendly young fellow riders, exited the van to go backpacking into the mountains. I wish I had that much adventure in my soul.

A day-long tour isn't enough to explore anything completely. The answer to that is to stay for a while. I can't in all good conscience advise anyone to drive their RV on that road. I wasn't thrilled with the "improvements," but I'll get over it. I just hope they never go as far as paving the road, and it is being discussed. Scuttlebutt says a bridge will soon be built across the river, instead of using the tram. Please visit before "they" ruin everything!

At the same time that I want everyone to experience McCarthy and Kennicott, I want them to stay away in droves. Controversy rages. If the road is improved, amenities increased, and the way cleared for anyone to get there, it will turn into a Yosemite or Denali. If improvements aren't made, a magnificent wilderness will be enjoyed by only a few. I'm selfish.

We boondocked on the banks of the Copper River, and had the opportunity to see several working fish wheels owned by Native Alaskans.

It was Ken's last full day in Alaska and he was treated to fall color at every overlook of the Richardson Highway, and even a few moose. We stopped to hike a couple of times, and drove to Worthington Glacier. This is Alaska's most accessible glacier. Park your vehicle, walk up the hill and you are there, looking down on the glacier.

We stopped for lunch at Blueberry Lake State Recreation Area, then decided to stay. On the ocean side of the mountain pass, we no longer had autumn. We had returned to summer.

The picnickers who occupied the campsite we wanted, not only left the campfire going, but took a stack of wood out of the trunk and left it with us too. The campsite provided an overview of snow-dusted Chugach Mountains, distant waterfalls, and flowers blooming in the meadow at our feet.

Magpies and ground squirrels kept us entertained. We hiked the rocky ridge above the valley, through bushes and wildflowers. The afternoon sun was warm. We picked tiny, wild blueberries that were sweet and delicious in blueberry pancakes the next morning.

It was a perfect evening for a fire, clear and cold.

Valdez is called the "Switzerland of the North." Until this trip, I wouldn't have known it was surrounded by the Chugach Mountains. This was my third trip through Keystone Canyon and the first time I saw it. The only reason I saw Bridal Veil and Horse Tail Falls previously, was because they are in a very narrow canyon, next to the road. I stayed for five days, and ate halibut for five dinners. It was foggy the whole time. I despaired of ever seeing anything but the harbor.

I have also always been there at the wrong time to go to church on the Lu-Lu Belle. From eight to nine on Sunday mornings, the Valdez First Baptist Church sponsors "A different church service," cruising the Port of Valdez. The advertising says, "Everyone Welcome," so I guess they'd let a Presbyterian aboard. Of course, there's always the chance they wouldn't let me off until I became a Baptist!

Valdez is a good place to make arrangements to see the famous Columbia Glacier. It is also part of Klondike Gold Rush History. The Valdez Trail went over the Valdez Glacier to Eagle, and on up the Yukon River to Dawson City.

The original Valdez, died in the tsunami that rolled over the town in the 1964 earthquake. The townspeople rebuilt it four miles away. You can follow gold rush, Trans-Alaska Pipeline (Exxon oil spill), and earthquake history, at the Valdez Museum.

Across the bay from the town, at the gate of the Alyeska Pipeline Marine Terminal, is a monument to the Alaska Pipeline workers. Tours are available there, and at Pump Station #9, Milepost 258. The pipe snakes its way over and under the ground, with great angles and curves, for 800 miles, from Prudhoe Bay on the Arctic Ocean, to its southern terminus at Valdez. Other information and signs are at Visitor Centers, and along the highway.

Ken and I said our good-byes at the Valdez Airport. He was already talking about coming back to Alaska. He flew to Anchorage and back to California.

I turned off the Richardson Highway toward Tok and saw caribou at every curve. I spent the evening wondering which direction I should go. Should I turn right at Tok, and make a beeline for the lower 48? Or turn right, with an immediate left, and go back across Top of The World Highway, toward Inuvik?

The fireweed's sparse petals threatened me. People in the north country use the fireweed flower as a gauge to know when winter is coming. The flowers bloom upward on the stem, and when the last blooms are flickerin' in the breeze, winter is blowin' in the wind. Only two or three blooms were still clinging for dear life.

I called for road conditions on the Dempster Highway to Inuvik. It didn't sound too bad. I decided for the right, and an immediate left.

Independence Mine
State Historical Site
Hatcher Pass Road

Kennecott Mine
National Historic Landmark

Glacier Pudding
Wrangell-St. Elias National
Park and Presesrve

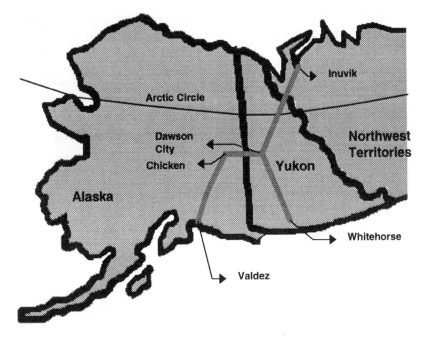

# DOING THE DEMPSTER

The thermometer registered 9º above zero. The weeds were frosted and sparkly in the first light of dawn. It was so cold the roadkill had frost on it. Steam rose from ponds and streams, all reminders that winter was coming.

A stop in Tok provided groceries, money, and someone to replace my ignition switch. It was hot to the touch, depending on if I was using air conditioning, wiper blades, etc. Gasoline was $1.58/gallon.

Since driving from Chicken to Tok in early June, a good bit of the road construction on the Taylor Highway had been finished. Another year and all the kinks and interest will be gone from this heretofore adventurous road. After a quick hello at Chicken, Alaska, I continued on to reach the border before it closed.

The Canadian border guard smiled (nice for a

change) as I drove up. After the usual questions, she waved me on. I proceeded along Top of the World Highway, into Yukon Territory. A cow moose ran across the road in front of me.

Out of habit, I continued to check the ignition switch. It was cool.

I parked on a gravel area off the road. It was a bittersweet evening. The sunset was spectacular, with clouds hovering around the sun, but I knew I would soon be heading "home." It was the sixth of September. Autumn yellows had crawled up the draws and the multi-colored ground cover, carpeted the mountains above the tree line.

I read myself to sleep. I'm not sure what awakened me but when I opened the drapes, I realized I had reached another goal. It was 12:15 a.m., and the Aurora Borealis had come to visit.

It came out of the horizon and made a long, swirling arc to the right of the Big Dipper. I watched it intently. It moved ever so slightly, taking a different shape at the curled end. The front window gave me a panoramic view, when it moved to the left of the Dipper. I went to the back window, took out the screen and propped my pillow in the open window. It danced over my head.

I went outdoors where I could see all of it. The whole sky filled. The night was silent. The air was frigid, but even as I drew my furry robe close to my body, I knew the goosebumps were not all from the cold.

The curtain of lights rippled and became more active as time went on. Just when I thought it was fading; another arm of it brightened. I couldn't hear the crackling some have heard, but I did see very pale green color. I stood with my mouth open, in complete unadulterated awe. Eventually the cold forced me inside.

The lights were magnificent, startling, and completely awe-inspiring. If I hadn't already believed in God and miracles, the Aurora Borealis dancing across a frigid Northern night, would have convinced me.

Twelve days later, while I was in Hyder, Alaska, I heard that a foot of snow had fallen on my lonely spot on Top of the World Highway. It closes during the winter.

No ice chunks huddled on the Yukon River shoreline, but frost was on the pun'kin in Dawson City. The ferry goes downstream first, below the landing, and looks like it will miss the dock by a mile, but it always lands perfectly. After canoeing it, I knew how hard it was to fight current.

When I asked for the latest road conditions to Inuvik at the Northwest Territories Information Centre, Brenda referred me to a man who had just returned. He had nothing good to say. I asked if the roads were washboardy. "Yes." I asked if there were potholes. "Yes." I asked what he had driven. He drove a small car. He had an accent and I thought maybe he was a foreign visitor not used to Northern roads. He was from Whitehorse, 327 miles away! His son looked disgusted. I think the son didn't agree with Dad's assessment. He wished me a safe trip.

This fellow couldn't believe I wanted to drive a motorhome to Inuvik. I asked if he had driven the Denali Highway. He said he had and admitted the Dempster Highway was better. I told Brenda if I decided to make the trip, I would come back and make a report.

The ignition switch was still cool. Just for fun, I felt the wires underneath, and promptly burned myself. I stopped at Northern Superior, and Glen said he was busy and couldn't look at it until three. It was about noon and I said if I decided to wait, I would be back shortly. Prophetic. I was in denial. I wanted those wires to cool off and stay that way and somehow I talked myself into thinking if I drove on down the road, it would all go away. Pathetic.

I touched them again. They were really hot. I stopped in what I thought was a business driveway that was probably closed on Saturday, and got under the dash to check things out. Getting into a position to see under the dash, takes a major contortionistic maneuver. I pulled out a connection. It was burned. I tried to put it back just to get me back to Northern Superior. A horn honked. Someone wanted in the driveway. I explained and apologized, and she said maybe somebody there at the gold camp could help me.

The fellow who answered the door took charge, and rousted his mechanic to help. He couldn't fix it but got the Sprinter started, so I could return to Northern Superior. I could only thank him, since he refused any money. The first fellow followed me back to Northern Superior, "In case anything happens." I cemented the appointment for 3:00.

When the kind fellow asked me to go for coffee in the meantime, and introduced himself as "Dirty Bert," I said maybe I shouldn't go with him. He explained he had played professional hockey for the Detroit Redwings, and one of the fans had called him Dirty Bert. The nickname stuck.

Sipping coffee at the London Grill, I learned Bert was from Manitoba. After a short stint in pro hockey, he went into management and thirty years of dam building for Canada Hydro. He had been working for the last four summers as a surveyor for a gold mining company along Six-mile Creek. The driveway where I stopped, was the gold camp's winter quarters.

Glen put a new connection on the (new in Tok) ignition and charged me only $32.58 ($23.98 U.S.) for an emergency on a Saturday afternoon. Bert invited me for a salmon dinner with his extended family. Although I was an unexpected guest, Violet, Murray, and the guys, welcomed me into the fold.

I mentioned leaving, but they insisted I park in the drive until morning, and get a fresh start. We all went to Diamond Tooth Gertie's for the evening. Bert and I talked, watched the show, and he introduced me to other friends. One couple said they lived in a cabin in the middle of nowhere, and had moose or bear in their yard, regularly.

Bert said the only time they went into town from the mine site was for special occasions, like the Miners Barbecue. Now they were in the process of moving the camp into Dawson for the winter.

I told Bert about seeing the Northern Lights. He said it would be a good night to see them again so we drove up to The Dome. The wait was cold but they finally came out.

We said goodnight, I asked him if he was into hugs. He said, "You bet," and nearly cracked my ribs. He added, "I've been with twelve guys all summer." Hmmm.

## Finally, the Dempster

The following are suggestions from "Dempster Driving Tips" that I received at the information centre.

1. Plan your trip for late June to early September (I missed that on both counts!)
2. Stock your vehicle with the basics: (much the same as I told you in the beginning) extra fluids, spare belts, basic tools (including jack and wrench), and a good full-sized spare tire (no compact or temporary spares).
3. Prevent accidents and flat tires -- slow down (Didn't I tell you?). Don't overload your vehicle and don't exceed the posted speeds. Drive in the worn centre of the road except when meeting or passing. Slow down, and pull over as far as possible, when meeting vehicles, especially large trucks. This will help prevent rock damage to windshields. Mesh, or plastic, headlamp protectors are a good inexpensive investment.
4. Drive with headlights on at all times.
5. Minimize dust by closing windows and using your air conditioner or fan.
6. Protect your trailer. Rock guards and protective covers for wiring, plumbing, and front RV windows are suggested if you plan to tow a trailer or boat.
7. Insects: Take insect repellents and/or protective clothing. (With the snow, I didn't have to worry about insects a whole lot.)
8. Weather conditions can change dramatically (they aren't kidding) and even in midsummer, cold and inclement weather may sometimes be encountered. Warm layered clothing, boots, hat, and gloves are useful items to have.

I had previously read the Dempster Highway information panels at the junction with Klondike Loop (Hwy 2). The road to Inuvik was completed in 1979, and built for supporting oil and gas exploration and development. It would be 914 gravel, round-trip miles before I returned to this spot. The Sprinter and I would actually drive 200 miles beyond the Arctic Circle. I was so excited, I could hardly breathe.

**It was one of those times I wanted to remember
when I am old,
sitting in my rocking chair,
playing the moments of my life
on the TV of my mind.**

A sermon of Sunday sunlight twirled in the autumn leaves. A feast for the eyes and the soul, greeted me at every curve and hill. My heart and the rushing streams, sang a joyful duet. If the colors had been mixed in a carpet, I would have said it was gaudy. In nature, it was beautiful. Being in church that morning couldn't have made me any more of a believer.

My confidence grew when I saw the first of many maintenance camps where I could get help, if I needed it.

Fifty-one miles into the trip, depending on which publication you read, the Dempster Highway reaches its highest point at either 4,229' or 4,265', on North Fork Pass. In the higher elevations, ice coated the trees and bushes. This is "rime," a new word to me.

Hundreds of ptarmigan had already stepped into formal winter wear. I came almost to a complete stop several times. They won't fly until the last second. There was no room to swerve around them. The Arctic fox and hare, were also half-way into their white safety camouflage, for the winter snows.

Three vehicles with flat tires were abandoned along the road. A car, partially in the road, had a broken axle. Nobody was home.

Lakes were still, reflecting snowy mountains and autumn colors. Farther north, the countryside was a study in brown. Gray rock mountains were barren. Red Creek was just that, a red creek.

Weakened muskeg lost its grip. Trees and land slid down the mountains, leaving great brown blemishes. A sign said, "Road closed." I nearly had a conniption fit, until I realized it was temporary while an avalanche was cleared. I napped at the wheel.

The books and brochures tell of golden eagles, great gray owls, Dall sheep, grizzly bear, and caribou. They may have been in hiding because of the weather I was driving into.

I checked several of the campgrounds and they were very nice. At a different time of year, I would enjoy staying a while in each one of them. The scenery is terrific. I suspect bugs would be terrific in hot weather. I was happy with being where I was, regardless of the weather.

True to what you might think in such a place, the wind howled around the Arctic Circle monument. The sun shone, but forbidding clouds gathered to howl with the wind on distant mountain peaks.

Another traveler was alone. We took pictures of each other by the monument. He had gone to Fort McPherson and turned around. He said snow was sticking to the ground a few miles beyond the Circle and "You might as well go back now. There is nothing beyond Fort McPherson. It is boring and flat."

I knew I hadn't come all that distance to turn around on somebody else's opinion of what was boring. Within a couple of miles, snow covered the road. It was the only thing he was right about. I changed my watch to Mountain Time.

At the Yukon Territory and the Northwest Territories border, I drove into a totally different world. It was dark, snowy, and windy. It was more ominous looking than I wanted to admit because I didn't want to turn back. I thought hard for a few milliseconds, then I put the Sprinter in gear, and inched toward Inuvik.

The Dempster Highway is open year around. If I got into trouble, eventually, someone would come along. There weren't that many places to pull off or maybe I just couldn't see them because it was blowing snow. I kept going. I was having no problems, but I had to consciously relax my rigid body now and again. The Sprinter was holding the road just fine, but I also knew if it started sliding, I was in trouble. Obviously my faith was sliding, too.

The Peel River cable ferry operator said he thought I could get gasoline at Fort McPherson although it was already past 5 p.m. The station was closed. As I was looking around for a place to park, the owners returned and opened the pumps ($140.96 C $103.76 U.S.). They were on the way home but somehow, they learned a customer was arriving. I was being well looked after. They asked if I was willing to take their nephew to Inuvik the next morning. I said I was willing, if I could park for the night. They discovered the nephew had found his own ride so I continued on. I stopped for the night at the Mackenzie River.

Two places along the Dempster were widened to accommodate airstrips, with appropriate warnings to watch for planes.

Other signs told other stories. The North West Mounted Police chased "The Mad Trapper of Rat River," for forty-eight winter days. He killed one policeman, and wounded another, after he tampered with Native trap lines. He was killed in February of 1932.

"The Lost Patrol" is another famous story, involving a four-man patrol. They froze to death on their way to Dawson City from Fort McPherson, in December of 1910. Their function was to deliver mail and check on isolated trappers. Even with excellent bush skills between them, they made fatal errors in judgment after becoming lost in a blinding blizzard. Eating their dogs, and some of the trappings and harness to survive, they traveled 620 miles in fifty-three days, perishing from starvation only twenty-six miles from the Fort. The Dempster Highway was named for Sgt. Dempster of the Royal North West Mounted Police, who found the lost patrol in March of 1911.

The ferryboat attendant said, "You're a long way from home." When I explained the Sprinter was my home and that I was living on his boat, he smiled, "Then I'll have to charge you $100." He asked if it was my first time down and I said it was my first time "up."

The ferry went first to the tiny Athabascan town of Tsiigehtchic, beyond the confluence of the Arctic Red River and the Mackenzie River, to pick up fares. It then docked at the mud dock where I drove off toward Inuvik. People who live in Tsiigehtchic, call themselves, Gwycha Gwich'in, "People of the Flatlands."

The next time anyone asks you the name of the largest north-flowing river in North America, you can tell them the Mackenzie River in the

N.W.T. of Canada. It was named after Sir Alexander Mackenzie, who in 1789, was the first non-aboriginal person to travel its entire length. See, that's part of the fun of RVing and traveling. You read all this great stuff, which will make absolutely no difference in your life, except that you may be able to answer a trivia question at a New Year's Eve party.

It was Monday and a great adventure had begun. The sun was bright and the day beautiful. The Campbell uplift, steep cliffs on the other side of Campbell Lake, followed the road.

The road, built high above its surroundings during winter freeze, prevented vehicle damage to the tundra surface. Only the trees were cut down. All other vegetation remained in place. It was covered with thick gravel layers. The vegetation and gravel insulate the road, and keep its warmth from reaching the permafrost layer below.

At Cabin Creek Wayside, I sipped coffee and toasted my buns in front of the heater, watching the sun fade to snow flakes drifting from somber clouds. Nothing to get excited about I guess, except that September and those few flakes sticking to the cold frozen tundra, took on a whole new meaning 200 miles beyond the Arctic Circle.

The last few miles into Inuvik were paved. Wow! Yellow line and all. They even have a McDonalds -- McDonald's Brothers Electric.

I parked at the Western Arctic Visitors Centre ,and as no one seemed concerned with my presence, I stayed there the four days I was in Inuvik. I did not see the two campgrounds, but I know they are open during season.

The architecture of the Visitor Centre, was impressive. Inside, talking displays showed the Gwich'in and Dene cultures, along with the "Mad Trapper" and the "Lost RNWMP Patrol."

I overheard a fellow talking with Andrea, the attendant. He had signed up for a trip to Tuktoyaktuk for that afternoon, but there were no other takers. It was one of the places I wanted to visit.

RC, an electrician and supervisor, with the Ministry of Transportation and Highways near Vancouver, B.C., traveled alone too. We walked to the Arctic Nature Tours but I was only the second name on the list. Fred said tourists were pretty sparse. We needed at least three more.

We talked our way down to "To-gos" for their musk ox burgers (sometimes known as "polar beef"). The chef said, "Nobody has killed one lately." We settled for caribou burgers, a worthy substitute.

It was cold but sunny, and since both of us had been driving steadily, we hiked through the Visitre Centre fish camp and along the river path through the muskeg.

RC was an avid skier and loved the outdoors, too. Exchanging stories and ideas, gave him an interest in learning to canoe and kayak. Though I have no interest in fishing, his being able to get close to birds and otters in a fishing float with waders, gave me a new perspective for photography.

By 3:30, we still didn't have takers for the Tuktoyaktuk trip so we talked about outfitting RC in a sandwich board to advertise. He didn't go for it. We walked around the town and into the residential area. Many houses were newly built, with as many more in progress.

Aklavik was the regional administrative centre, but with constant flooding and erosion, in the mid 1950's, the centre was moved. Inuvik was a replacement for Aklavik. Since not everybody in Aklavik agreed, Aklavik still exists.

Inuvik is, "The first community north of the Arctic Circle built to provide the normal facilities of a Canadian town. It was designed, not only as a base for development and administration, but also as a centre to bring education, medical care, and new opportunity, to the people of the Western Arctic."

Utilidors (hold sewer and water pipes)

You won't find another like it. "Utilidors," holding water and sewer pipes, snake through the town from building to building. Because of the permafrost base, everything is above ground, either on pilings or stilts. Some buildings had skirts around them. A few yards had grass but they looked out of place. A huge log cabin I would have loved anywhere else, didn't fit into that environment. Ingamo Hall, Inuvik's Native Friendship Centre, was built with 1,000 logs rafted 850 miles down the Mackenzie River.

Inuvik means "Place of the people," and is considered a Canadian "Mosaic" of people from a variety of places, traditions and cultures. Koe Park has a triple-arched monument symbolizing the town's dominant triracial character: Inuvialuit, Gwitch'in and Caucasian.

I might have expected the same bland colors I had found in other Arctic villages if I hadn't become friends with Tom Byrne, the fellow who played the Robert Service character in Dawson City. He lived in Inuvik for three years. He created and instituted the colorful plan for the new city. Talk about mosaic. Most of the houses and public buildings are painted bright colors. The hospital is a cheerful yellow. The apartment buildings are deep blues, greens, pinks, reds, and lavenders. Considering how cold it was, Inuvik was a cheerful place for wandering.

In the Boreal Bookstore, I succumbed, once more, to being a grandmother. I bought charming books for Rebecca about children living North of the Arctic Circle.

The lady at Northern Images told us it costs from $800 to $1000 to rent. Utilities were above and beyond that, with heating costs really high.

**The "Igloo" Church -- Our Lady of Victory**

She told us about missing the last Mackenzie ferry the week before, and having to spend the night in her vehicle, without any emergency provisions. She nearly froze. It is surprising that someone from that area didn't carry emergency supplies routinely. We all make mistakes. Up there, it can be fatal.

Festivals are different there in the far, far North. They celebrate the break-up of the Mackenzie River in May, the Midnight Madness summer solstice on June 21, and the Great Northern Arts Festival in early August. I can't imagine any of them more personally celebrated, than the "Sunrise Festival" in January. The sun sets on December 6. It does not rise again until January 6. They thrill to the fifty-nine days when the sun doesn't set at all.

RC treated me to a candlelight dinner at the Eskimo Inn, a pleasant evening with interesting conversation, enjoyed over lots of coffee refills. We agreed it was nice to have someone to share with, but it was the next day before I realized the date was significant. It was what would have been my 40th wedding anniversary. RC was 6' 3" with brown eyes, dark hair, short beard with a touch of gray, and could have been my late husband's twin, at forty something.

RC was driving a truck and camper but opted to stay at the Finto Motor Inn down from the Visitor Centre where I parked. He stopped to walk me to town the next morning. Enough people had signed up for the tour, but it was postponed until eleven. We were ecstatic and went looking for sweatshirts.

The comical ravens didn't seem to mind the weather. Ravens are legends in Native culture, and are protected in the N.W.T. They live year around in the North country, and if you understand their conversations as they raucously squawk to each other, they'll tell you all about it.

At last we were all seated in the eight-passenger plane and the props were twirling. Skies were gray but we were off to a new adventure, Tuktoyaktuk, eighty-five miles farther north, on the Arctic Ocean. We got to the end of the runway, turned around and came back. The pilot explained we had lost the attitude indicator. Aaaagh!!. It didn't help **our** attitudes at all, but we tried to be grateful they found **any** problem while we were still on the ground. We rescheduled for two o'clock.

Our Lady of Victory Church, next to the Arctic Nature Tours building, does not have regular hours. We were never able to get inside. The igloo-shaped church reflects the Arctic lifestyle, and fuses Inuvialuit and Christian cultures. Inside are paintings of the twelve stations of the Cross by Mona Thrasher, an Inuvialuit artist.

After lunch in a distinctly Mexican flavor cafe, we went back for the long-awaited flight to Tuktoyaktuk. One man backed out because his wife wanted to leave town early. The young couple decided they didn't want the expense of staying another night in a hotel. Fred Carmichael, President of Arctic Nature Tours, felt so bad after our dogged but futile persistence, he gave us sweatshirts and Western Arctic Travel Guides.

The weather was getting more frigid by the minute. We walked back to the Visitor Centre, and picked up our certificates proclaiming we had driven across the Arctic Circle. Andrea said Brenda from NWT office in Dawson City, had checked to make sure I got to Inuvik all right. People are good. We spent the afternoon in Inuvik's warm library, reading.

That evening we went to the Aurora Research Centre for a slide show, and program on "pingos." Pingo is an Eskimo word for a conical hill. It is an ice-cored hill that can only grow and persist in a permafrost environment. Roughly 1,450 pingos are in the Tuktoyaktuk Peninsula. They are hundreds of thousands of years old. (A tour is available to visit the pingos.) Professor Mackay said that with a little patience, you can duplicate, in miniature, the natural conditions to grow a pingo in a home freezer. Naturally, I took the instructions for Rebecca and her science teacher father.

Summertime (although they had snow in both July and August in 1996) would be a better time for activities in Inuvik. Boat rides are available on the Mackenzie River Delta, one of the largest deltas in North America, and filled with wildlife.

The Keitels I mentioned from St. Louis, wrote recently and said they took a midnight trip to the delta on the Mackenzie River. Six of them, "Sipped champagne and munched on char sandwiches, while we watched the sun turn the horizons to brilliant orange. I can close my eyes and I'm there." Sounds good to me but I'd have to drive back to experience it...maybe...

Flights to various villages, including Tuktoyaktuk, are available (and more likely to happen) during season. We had a major plus, there were no bugs! No self-respecting bug would be out in that freezing weather. After an evening of sipping coffee, with the north winds whipping fiercely around the Sprinter, RC and I said our good-byes.

The next morning I awakened to a blizzard. I settled in my cozy house, writing post cards. I planned to wait and see what the weather did. I heard a diesel pull in at 8:30. It was RC. He said he thought it would be a good idea to caravan out, since we were both by ourselves.

My first thought was, "No way, Jose." On second, third, and fourth thoughts, I decided if it didn't stop snowing, driving wasn't going to get any better. If it didn't get any warmer, the Mackenzie and Peel Rivers would freeze up and I would be living in Inuvik for the two months it takes the ice bridge to form. The road between Inuvik and the Mackenzie was quite narrow, built up high, and with lots of water on both sides. As much as I liked the adventure of being in Inuvik, my fifth thought was that I really didn't want to spend the winter there. I packed up.

I was leading. I was bigger and more easily seen (he said). I drove in and out of white-out conditions with no tracks to follow. The road was extremely slippery, and scary; but, once we started, there was no turning back. I stuck to the center, except on the rare occasion of meeting a vehicle.

We arrived at the Mackenzie River in time to catch the ferry. After discussing it, we decided due to the weather, and lengthy ferrying time, to skip visiting Tsiigehtchic. We both missed it on the way in. The red-roofed Catholic Church, and the few white buildings on the bank of the Arctic Red River, were quite picturesque

The ferryman told me, "It will soon be time to take the ferry out. When the ice forms, we'll drain the fluids and dry dock it for the winter, probably in October." He did mention it was unusually cold weather for that time of year.

By the time we reached Fort McPherson, thirty-five miles away, we were ready for lunch and a break. The dirt streets were a real mess with the wet snow and mud. Everybody takes their boots off at the door whether it is a restaurant, store, or library. Makes sense to me. People were friendly, but not quite as friendly as in Inuvik.

We parked next to the McPherson Tent and Canvas Shop. If you ever want anything made of canvas, this is the place to go. The factory was small and clean enough to eat off the floor. They were making an order of teepees. With all the fish camps and hunting, big tents are in demand, but they also make backpacks, duffelbags, carrying cases, and other products.

We slopped through the cemetery mud and snow, looking for the grave markers of the "Lost Patrol," but we didn't find them.

At the Peel River ferry, the attendant said if we wanted to wait, they were bringing a snowplow across next, and we could follow him. We waited. The ferry ramp was so irregular, the Sprinter's hitch caught on it. The attendant found a bar to pry me off. He was matter-of-fact. I wondered how many others he had pried off of it.

Waiting for the snowplow was a mistake. He was making more of a mess, than cleaning it. He started up a long, steep hill. I CB'd to RC that I was going to stop and wait. The plow didn't make it. It took him forever to back down again, and when he did, I told RC I was going to make a run for it, otherwise, I wouldn't make it either. I wrestled the RV to the top of the hill. Piece of cake. RC had no problem.

The snow was deeper in the higher elevations. I had set the camera on manual. All I had to do was lift it and aim through the windshield, without adjusting it. Near the summit, the snow was a foot deep. I was literally, pushing it with the motorhome. I couldn't slow down because it would have stopped me. There was no place to pull off.

It was really neat; but when I lifted the camera to get a swift shot, a semi came around a curve, and full tilt up the mountain. I had no idea how far I could drive to the right without going off the mountain, but I pulled over and he shot past me.

I drove in and out of low drifts, deep snow, and areas blown bare by the wind. It took a while. I was relying a lot on the transmission because the brakes weren't working right. I figured the snow was causing problems. The "No Dust Zone" signs looked out of place.

When we hit the Northwest Territories and Yukon Border, it was like cutting the weather with a sharp knife. The sky was clear and blue. We were also grateful to be back on better roads.

During the few short miles to Rock Creek Campground, the mid-afternoon weather became comfortably warm. Both rigs were a mess. RC washed his. I tried to dig the packed snow out from under the Sprinter's front end. It wouldn't budge. It was jammed up around the batteries, and down in front, where the tires wore a slit through it to keep turning.

The next day we stopped again at the Arctic Circle monument for pictures, then continued to Eagle Plains. My brakes were iffy so RC added brake fluid. I filled with gas, and dug a lot of snow out from under the front end, that hadn't already dropped off with the warmer weather. A wire came with it. Hmmm.

RC's time was limited by vacation days and I knew I would have to take it easy because of limited braking power. We hugged good-bye and each continued on, as we were used to doing, alone. I felt a little sad as I watched his yellow and white camper wind through the curves and hills ahead of me but I wouldn't have traded those few days of friendship for anything.

It was a long day, but that was because I pulled in beside a river and read for several hours. I took pictures of a magnificent rainbow after a rainstorm, and sunset pictures, with mountains and clouds and lakes.

Cars blinked their lights at me and I realized I had brights but no low beams. I got off the road for the night.

From the Dempster Corner, it was only twenty-five miles back into Dawson City. Once again I went to Northern Superior. They adjusted the brakes, installed a new low beam, and re-attached that low-slung wire. Because they didn't have new ones the right size, they switched the windshield wiper from the navigator's side to mine. They checked the pressure in all tires, and repaired a flat dual on the back left side. I didn't even know it was flat.

I used a pressure washer to bathe the poor mud-packed Sprinter. I emptied the sewers, filled with water and gasoline, and I was ready to go again. I thought I was.

That evening my friend, Bert, took me to the Jack London Restaurant for dinner. On my way to the Dome, to park in my favorite spot for the night, the newly repaired dual tire, blew. The next morning I drove carefully back down the mountain to Northern Superior. This time they put on the spare.

Bert and I spent the day sightseeing around Dawson, and hiking the l-o-n-g, s-t-e-e-p mountain path to the fire lookout above The Dome. It was a sunny, but cold fall day, with great colorful views of the Yukon River as it turns at Dawson City, and heads for the Bering Sea. He pulled up soft, spongy, pale-green moss, and said it was what they used to use to chink between the logs in cabins.

Afterward we had coffee and cookies at Klondyke Kates. It was their last day of the season.

We had dinner later and said our good-byes. I talked with him on the phone after I got back to Washington. He said within a few days after I left, snow hit big time, and he had snow all the way home to Manitoba.

Between Dawson City and Whitehorse, I stopped three times. My first stop was to see the remains of Montague House, a typical log roadhouse from the turn of the century.

In 1987, when I went to Alaska with Carrs and Cushmans, we found the greatest cinnamon buns, but I despaired of ever finding them again. On my second stop, I found one.

Braeburn Lodge advertised a cinnamon bun big enough to feed four people. It was five inches tall, and definitely as big as a plate. It was so big that I took a picture of it. It was hot from the oven. It was hot, hot. It was served with a tub of butter. Yum! I rolled on out to the Sprinter.

My last stop was in honor of Robert Service.

> As I stood on the marge
> of Lake Laberge
> And admired the snow-covered scenery
> I thought
> What am I doin'
> with winter storms brewin'
> I should have gone south with the greenery
>
> Ralph Waldo Minshall

**Boondocking almost under the Alaska Highway
See those storm clouds brewing?**

## "HEADIN' HOME"

Whitehorse was a good "filling" station. I filled with propane, gasoline, and groceries. After examining my tires thoroughly, the fellow at Canadian Tire was kind enough to tell me that I didn't need all six tires replaced, as I had intended. Four Michelin tires cost $877.40 Canadian ($646.84 US)

Happy Daze fashioned a new U-bolt to hold up the right side of my springs. Considering they gave me priority in the middle of their extremely busy afternoon schedule, I had no quarrel with the $42.44 bill ($31.28 U.S.).

In the late afternoon, I stopped on the Alaska Highway, outside Whitehorse, for one last great view of the Yukon River.

For miles, either direction of Teslin, signs advertise Mukluk Annie's. She offers free RV camping, dump station, RV wash, and a nightly houseboat ride. I have always passed by, either too early or too late in the season. I've never had the honor of staying overnight, or partaking of her All-you-can-eat Salmon Bake and other goodies.

It is 292 miles to the Highway 37 junction, winding in and out of Yukon Territory and British Columbia. Among other beautiful spots, were crossing the Nisutlin Bay Bridge, with views of Teslin Lake at Teslin. The bay bridge, at 1,917', is the longest water span on the Alaska Highway.

I drove until dark and stayed on the Continental Divide. If I cried, one tear would drain to the Arctic Ocean and the other to the Pacific Ocean.

Trans-Alaska Pipeline, Richard son Highway

After a short drive in the morning, I encountered road construction. The genial, smiling sign lady, was from Whitehorse. She and her husband lived in their RV in the construction camp. She had just heard a moose crashing about in the woods. She said sometimes they have grizzlies. I asked what she did if animals came into her "space." She said, "I get into my car. If I had to, I would climb into a passenger car stopped for construction." She described working through the cold winters. She was grateful for the sunny, warm day.

After going through construction, I heard a loud pop. It sounded like a dual had blown. I thumped the tires, but didn't find a problem. I continued toward the Junction, stopping several times to check tires.

"Alaska Highway's Best Coffee" was offered at the Northern Beaver Post. How could I resist, especially since I was surprised to find anything open. The lady who served coffee was restaurant-sitting for the winter. It was closing in mid-October, but she was staying on to write a book about her travels and experiences teaching school in outlying Native villages. A publisher waited in the wings to look at it. That's half the battle.

I asked if she would get lonely. "Watson Lake is only twenty minutes away, and I have plenty of friends there. The Alaska Highway is open all the time, and I hope to persuade the snowplow drivers to take a swipe through the driveway once in a while, so I can get out." Then she mentioned the beaver on the ponds, the token moose, and a white wolf that were hanging around. Part of me envied her.

At Junction 37, many services were advertised, but obviously, for the season only. The gas station and cafe were busy. The "chef" was unavailable for giving my tires a professional "once-over." I decided to trust my own judgement that they were fit as a fiddle.

**Road Woes**

A road grader pulled up for gas while I was filling. I asked the driver about the Cassiar Highway. He said it was pretty good. "I would drive the Cassiar any day, over the Alaska Highway." Personally, I would never pass up a chance to drive the Cassiar one way, and the Alaska Highway the other. (You can call for Cassiar road conditions.)

I drove on and off gravel and seal coat the first day on the Cassiar Highway. it was quite good, with only occasional potholes. Sunshine and autumn reflected in the lakes and streams. Curves and scenery kept my driving to a leisurely pace.

I passed the side road to the town of Cassiar. I had driven the ten miles to Cassiar with a flat dual in April of 1992, thinking I could get it fixed there. I did, but only by the skin of my teeth. Cassiar was a Cassiar Mining (Asbestos) Corporation company town, and they had closed. I had no way of knowing that all the townspeople had been given a really short deadline to get out, and most of them had. Through several people, I found the one soul who had the equipment, know-how, and kindness to fix the flat for me.

Jade City is an interesting stop, but the jade store was closed. Huge jade boulders lying around, in what they call their "Jade Compound," are from the Princess Jade Mine, one of the largest jade mines in the world. This is not a big place, but they have a couple of stores, and a primitive campground. I bought an ice-cream cone next door.

The Cottonwood River rest area is off the highway, on part of the old road. As I often do, I took advantage of this picturesque spot. The rushing river's peaceful sounds, accompanied my lunch, and a few more pages of a good book.

In 1987, the Carrs and Cushmans had pulled into Mighty Moe's campground. Mighty Moe was an eccentric, backwoods Canadian, who entertained the campers in his primitive campground, with questionable stories. He played songs on the back of a frying pan.

Mighty Moe dumped me (and the canoe) in the river, about two hours upstream from his campground, and I had my first solo canoeing experience. Perhaps that short but peaceful, isolated wilderness canoe trip, planted a seed for tackling the Mighty Yukon nine years later.

I made an emergency stop there in 1992, with that above-mentioned flat dual. Mighty Moe wasn't home, but I stayed the night, entertained by moose and beaver in his absence. I thanked him by mail. He had written and asked me to send support letters to the Canadian government regarding a problem he was having with them. I did.

Nothing stays the same. Mighty Moe had gone to a nursing home. The drive was re-routed, and the campground and its facilities were being improved. It is now called Moose Meadows Resort (not surprising since I had seen so many the last time). Hosts, now, are Larry and Lynne Sketchley.

The campground will be nicer, and more people will be tempted to stop. I hope you will, but keep on the lookout. I have a strong feeling that the slightly off-kilter, free spirit of Mighty Moe, who called himself, "The Godfather of Highway 37," will always roam the shores of Cotton Lake.

Moose Country

I guess I'm going to have to go back to Alaska sometime in the next few years. There are still too many places I haven't seen, likeTelegraph Creek. It is not advised for **large** RVs or trailers. It has been described to me as "A lulu of a road," which, of course, explains my interest. It is 140 miles round-trip. The last time I went through, it was snowing and foggy. This time, the weather was great, but snow was coming.

The turnoff is at Dease Lake; and just for the record, Dease Lake is halfway between Seattle, Washington, and Anchorage, Alaska.

We talked about the biggest, bestest, tallest, and widest syndrome, a while back. Dease Lake calls itself the Jade Capital of the province; Jade City says they are the Jade Capital of the North. What it boils down to, is this, there is a lot of green stuff along the Cassiar (not unlike the stuff in my frig, green and too hard to eat).

On previous trips along the Cassiar, I had missed much of the magnificent scenery of the Skeena and Cassiar Mountains, because of foggy or blizzard conditions. I never realized how many lakes and streams, and mountains there were.

The clouds alternately covered Mt. Edziza (9,143'), part of Mount Edziza Provincial Park, and opened, revealing glaciers and new snow. All around me, the skies were blue again, but it looked like it was snowing at the top. I pulled into a viewpoint to feast my eyes and sip coffee.

On the other side of the road is the Spatsizi Plateau Wilderness Park. There are no roads into either of these wilderness areas, but guide services and flightseeing are available.

Many hours had passed, but I had not covered all that many miles, when sleepy time settled in. I backed into the trees in Eastman Kodak Wayside. It was a

**Hello?**

natural considering the amount of film I buy. I must own at least a small chunk, mustn't I?

In the night, I awakened and thought I heard footsteps, sloshing in the mud next to the Sprinter. I froze for a few seconds, then stole quietly out of bed. I peeked outside, and saw an empty parking lot. I turned on the side light and headlights, but didn't see anyone or anything. The noise must have been the rain coming through the leaves, or an animal. I moved the motorhome out into the parking lot, and went back to sleep.

People often ask if I get frightened. Not generally. Although I momentarily had goosebumps, I couldn't quite conceive of anyone being on that lonely road for the purpose of mayhem. I hadn't seen a vehicle for two hours prior to stopping, and the weather had turned really nasty.

About eighty miles of the Cassiar is still gravel. It wouldn't have been all that bad, but the glorious sunshine had disappeared, and it was raining. Potholes reigned, too. Driving was slow. I met two graders. One was in my lane! I did a couple of "switcheroos," and managed to avoid being sandwiched between them. Driving improved for the distance they had graded.

The back end of a black bear disappeared into the bushes, and later, I saw a Mama black bear and a cub crossing the road. With his short stubby legs, Baby bear was having problems keeping up with Mama. He finally made it. He was cuddly looking, but I knew better.

At Bell Irving Bridge, I thought I had finally driven "One mile Beyond." The road was wide, the pavement new, and it actually had shoulders. It didn't last long, but then I instinctively knew it wouldn't.

It was my day for thrills. I drove around a curve and there was Mama black bear and triplet cubs. I pulled well off the highway (on that marvelous new shoulder) and watched them for fifteen minutes. They were undisturbed by the few trucks and cars. My shutting the engine off, only caused Mama to stick her nose in the air and sniff. They continued munching, and ambling in and out of the bushes and trees, as though I wasn't there.

The last thirty miles to Meziadin Junction were a blur of memories. I drove it through a white-out blizzard on May Day, 1992. I also remembered the milk and mustard I cleaned up when the refrigerator contents went topsy-turvy.

### The Friendliest Ghost Town in Alaska
### and
### the southernmost Alaskan community you can drive to,
### Hyder

I hadn't decided for sure whether to go to Hyder but I had no choice, the Sprinter turned right. It was okay. I had warm memories of spending time there before. Don't miss going to Stewart and Hyder. The drive is worth it, just to see Bear Glacier. You can't walk up to the glacier, like you can to a couple of other glaciers, but you can see it very well, from either the road or the rest area. This time the lake wasn't frozen, and I could see a big, blue ice cave at the water's edge.

Waterfalls cascaded down the walls of Bear River Canyon and avalanche warning signs grew in abundance. A few rocks were in the road, but in the early spring in 1992, they were clearing an avalanche.

Crossing from Stewart, British Columbia, into Hyder, Alaska, I saw a portable power wash. At a $1 a foot, Mike and Michael removed several mud layers from the Sprinter. Michael saw the Texas license plate and asked if I was a SKP. He said, "I never believe a Texas plate any more."

At the Home Town Cafe, I asked the lady who was cooking, if she was Laura Lee. I didn't expect her to remember me from 1992, but she said, "I know exactly who you are." She pointed to the bulletin board behind me. One of my yellowed columns was pinned to it. I remembered sending it, but was very surprised that she remembered me.

I told her I wasn't sure if they would still be there. She said, "We've been here twenty-five years and we'll be here forever." I left my copy of *RVing North America* so she could read about Hyder.

Susan, at Northern Stars Gift Shop, had T-shirts designed by the same lady who illustrated the books I bought in Inuvik. I bought one to match Rebecca's books. She said a moose and a bear were hanging around town. The week before, the bear had come halfway through the door of the shop. She yelled, and he scrambled back outside. Mothers have good voices for expected behavior, and he had heard that tone before.

Susan said someone had given her a copy of a magazine cover, with Hyder on it. It was the Escapee magazine, with a Hyder Street scene on it, that I had taken in 1992. I gave magazine copies to both Susan and Laura Lee. They were thrilled. They love their little town and I don't blame them.

I had been on Salmon Creek Road to the mine sites, and above the Salmon Glacier, with the Cushmans. In 1992, I started up with the motorhome and changed my mind (unusual). It is narrow, steep, winding and worth a trip, but it is safer in a car or truck. If the snows are melting or it has been raining, the gravel road has lots of washouts. Tours are available to the mines and glacier.

I parked at Fish Creek Bridge, and worked for a couple of hours, hoping to see bears catching salmon. They must have stayed in for dinner that night, but it is a popular spot for watching bears and bald eagles.

On the way back to town, I picked up a package of mail at the post office. I was lucky, I had forgotten Hyder only gets mail on Tuesdays and Thursdays, and I hit it right. I stopped at Mom's This-N-That Gift shop, to buy a sweatshirt and talk with Dorothy. She gave me some good Christmas tips for gathering with the family.

Stewart and Hyder are at the head of the Portland Canal, a ninety-mile saltwater fjord, and natural boundary between Alaska and Canada. It follows the Misty Fjords National Monument Wilderness, all the way from the Pacific. Hyder is an Alaska State Ferry stop, accessed only by water or through Canada. It is good to remember they use Canadian money.

I went back to the Home Town Cafe for a halibut dinner. I felt like a celebrity. Laura Lee had told her friends about the books. We had a question, answer, and autograph session before dinner.

As on earlier visits, everyone was friendly. I felt warm and fuzzy, and hated to leave, but Hyder winters are legendary. I've heard stories about walking out second story doors and tunneling out at ground level. As nice as they were, I wasn't prepared to stay for the winter. Actually, I'd like to see it in the winter. I filled with gasoline at Hyder's only gas station, and stopped at Canadian Customs. This was something new. Customs were not there at all during previous visits. Who goofed?

Back on the Cassiar Highway, I passed Meziadin Lake Provincial Park, just south of the turn to Hyder. It is a beautiful place to camp but the last time I went on by. It was deep with snow.

The neat thing about the Cassiar is that it hasn't been completely tamed yet. A one-lane bridge crosses 400 feet above the Nass River.

Rest areas along the rest of the Cassiar, were filled with moose

K'SAN LIVING MUSEUM

hunters. I finally found an empty spot by a river. I looked up just in time to see a giant light exploding in the sky...a falling star? If I had been somewhere near a lot of people, I would have said it was fireworks, but it was extremely high. I'm not sure I heard an explosion, or imagined it, but it was forceful. Although it took only seconds, it left a definite impression of heavenly fireworks.

Sunbeams struggled through the fog, and highlighted the fall colors lining the Skeena River, as I made my early morning turn onto Yellowhead Highway. Highway #16 goes all the way from Prince Rupert to Winnipeg, Manitoba.

In 1992, I made side trips to several Indian villages. St. Paul's wooden Anglican Church is at Gitwangak, The separate, original bell tower, dates back to 1893. K'san, the center of Gitksan culture, is a living museum, with longhouses, and an art school. Tours will take you to an archeological dig at Battle Hill in Kitwanga. Kitwancool is the home of the "Hole-in-the-ice" totem pole, "The oldest standing totem pole in the world." No one there when I arrived so early in the season. I'm not sure what, specifically, I was looking at, but I was fascinated with the totem poles. All the villages have authentic totem poles and interesting Native crafts.

Turning onto the Yellowhead, suddenly put me in a completely different world. It was a good, two-lane, paved highway, with no appreciable potholes. Prosperous-looking houses settled permanently on green fertilized lawns. Horses and cattle grazed in fenced pastures on small well-kept ranches. After five months, I wasn't sure I was ready for cities, traffic, impatience, stress, and "civilization."

A big sign at a Petro Canada station, made me wonder about civilization, in their terms. It said, "Worms, free coffee with fill-up." What a combo. I guess I shouldn't knock it if I haven't tried it. After all, I like Pepsi and milk.

The Sprinter's odometer turned 140,000 miles as I drove down the hill into Prince George.

> **I turned right on Highway 97 south.**
> **I had come**
> **full circle.**

Stopping at Cinema Second Hand, north of Quesnel, I took advantage of their free camping again. I popped in to buy a few incidentals and have a conversation.

Over coffee, Vic related the story of buying a canoe for his wife, Theresa. "A fellow drove in with a canoe strapped to the car roof. He hung around until the other customers left. I said, 'It was nice of you to deliver Theresa's birthday canoe.' The guy looked puzzled. I told him, 'I have been wanting to buy her one.' Then the guy really looked startled. He told me he had hung around hoping I would buy it. He needed the money to get back home."

There was no doubt about it. Since I was getting close, I was like a horse heading for the barn. I was anxious to get back to Washington to see family, play grandma, and visit friends. One last new route, Highway 99, tempted me. I had heard about the "Sea to Sky Highway" from several travelers, but in my case, I would be traveling from "sky to sea."

Seven miles north of Cache Creek, I turned toward Lillooet and Vancouver. If you are into following the gold trails, the Hat Creek Heritage Ranch, is just beyond the turn. It is a living museum with one of the original roadhouses. Lilliooet is the beginning of the Cariboo Trail that you will see and hear about so much, as you travel north on Highway 97, toward Prince George.

On this route, except in the narrowest, more avalanche-prone areas, there were many pulloffs, viewpoints, and rest areas. It has lakes, streams, waterfalls, and numerous Provincial parks, Recreation Areas, and private resorts and campgrounds, where you can enjoy them. Remember that as you get closer to Vancouver, especially during season, you are competing with a half-million people.

The other major thing to think about is the road.

> **It is a pretty good road, all of it paved, some of it narrow, most of it winding, but the grades are from 6 to 14%.**

My brakes heated up considerably coming down the mountains. I stopped at more than one view to enjoy the scenery, while they cooled down.

I stopped at the Pavilion General Store and Gas Bar. They advertised they were British Columbia's Oldest Store, built in 1862. I bought a book and talked with Barry. We exchanged cards. When I said how pretty the route had been thus far, he said, "You hadn't seen anything yet." He was right. It was a neat spot. They had campsites, souvenirs, and a post office.

The first night, I stopped at Seton Dam Campsite. It was a BC Hydro campground. It was free, but only a few campsites were big enough to accommodate my 27' rig.

The next morning, I stopped at Seton Lake Recreation Area, overlooking the lake, and stayed for a while. It was just too pretty to leave without soaking it in.

The town of Whistler is a famous ski resort, but in truth, it offers something any time of the year. In the midst of such beauty, and within a very short driving distance of Vancouver, it is another Aspen or Vail and traffic is thick.

As I continued on, I heard a weird roaring noise, even when I wasn't on an appreciable grade. It sounded like I was in second gear all the time. I suspected it might be the clutch fan, although I didn't know that was what it was called, until I had it fixed back in Leavenworth. Good guess.

Certainly, the views driving through the mountains were fantastic, but, starting at Squamish, I was driving along the fjord. The combination of mountains, islands, and the sun filtering through the clouds, was really awesome. I think I would always prefer the "sky to sea" direction.

Scenery, Sea To Sky Highway, British Columbia

My last night in Canada was at Porteau Cove Provincial Park. It has water access, making it a popular park. Even though I stopped earlier than usual, since I didn't want to drive through Vancouver at rush hour, the park was packed. It was $15.50/night Canadian, with no amenities.

It was peaceful until 3:00 a.m., when the woman in the tent behind me, had a fight with her "whatever." For about fifteen minutes, she raved and ranted and yelled and cursed. I thought about firing up and running over the tent.

The Sea to Sky Highway officially ends at the Lions Gate Bridge, at the edge of Vancouver. Even after all the really spectacular scenery I had experienced over the previous five months, Highway 99 has to be one of the most beautiful 209 miles that I have traveled.

Unfortunately, I had the city to drive through, since I somehow, had gotten off my route. I arrived at Peace Arch Park and the Canadian/United States border, at Blaine, Washington.

I thought about continuing on through, and not bothering with the Canadian GST tax, but it was worth the $61 US refund stop.

As I passed through the border, the guard asked, "Did you buy anything in Canada today?" I repeated, "Today?" and then said, "No." He asked, "Did you buy anything yesterday?" Again, I said, "No," and told him I had been in Alaska and Canada for five months, and I still hadn't bought enough of anything to declare. That was it. Now that I have satisfied my curiosity of crossing at Blaine, I would choose a less busy route in the future.

It was fun sharing my love of Canada and Alaska with you. Honest, I have only a few more comments to pass along...in the last chapter. You wouldn't want to be shortchanged, would you?

**Nobody knows the puddles I've seen
Nobody knows,
Nobody**

# PARTING THOUGHTS

Before I left for Alaska the last time, I tried to talk my friend, Linda Bassett, into flying up for a couple of weeks. I said, "Linda, it is a fantastic place. It is not only incredibly beautiful, but there are places still so wild, that if you get off the beaten track, you could very well become something's breakfast." Her reply, "Well, that certainly makes me want to come."Sometimes my enthusiasm gets the best of me.

I have always lived a sheltered life. I love being in an isolated place, surrounded by magnificent scenery; but, at the same time, I like knowing natural dangers lurk in the wilderness. It is a smidgen of "Walking on the wild side." With making you aware of the dangers, I hope I haven't discouraged you.

I've contemplated flying up for a month in the wintertime, but after hearing a few, "It was so cold..." stories, I may change my mind on that. My friend, Doreen Woodall, whom I met in Dawson City, wrote and told me about her winter there:

"Your breath tells you immediately how low the temperature has sunk. When you take your first breath outside, your nose seizes up. You can't get a deep breath. You open your mouth. The air splinters your throat. Another breath and your teeth turn into small white ice cubes and a dagger stabs into your chest. You feel as if you might shatter into a thousand pieces. The more shattered you feel, the colder it is."

With as dreadful as that sounds, she ended her letter this way, "By Monday, February 3, the sun had risen high above the hill, and it was actually giving warmth. I sat reading, with my back to the window for a half hour. **The sun warmed my shoulders like a remembered blessing.**" Maybe I'll just go for a couple of weeks.

Everybody has their own idea of what excites them. I have given you the big picture as far as distances, activities, and accommodations, throwing in costs once in a while, so you get an idea of what they are. You might say, "Whew!" Remember, you don't **have** to go off the main roads, or spend $3,000 for a side trip, to have a perfectly exciting trip to

Canada and Alaska. If you did want to do everything I've done, it would probably take you three trips, as well. I pack a lot into my travels.

Now, to some of that "Packing," just in case you're looking askance, costwise, at some of my adventures. I am single; I am paying one fare. I realize the expense is doubled for couples who want to do the same thing.

Think it over carefully, if expenses make you "gulp." Do you both really, truly, want to do this activity, above all others? Must you do it together? Are **you** absolutely dying for a chance to pull in a 450-pound halibut or observe Native culture in a bush community? Is it only a mediocre desire for your spouse? Maybe your spouse would rather capture iceworms on a glacial expedition. Remember the Australian lady who played with the grizzlies, sans her mate, because he was going to indulge in a guided hunting trip? Consider doing different activities, at least once on your trip.

I can hear you saying (male or female), "But..but...but, I never do anything without my Snookie Wookums." Give me a break! Tours are groups of people. You won't be alone. It is easy to make new friends, if you open your mouth, ask a few questions, then shut it again, and listen. You'll probably make friends that you'll hear from for years. Just think how exciting it will be to share it with your mate later.

Yes, I know, you haven't done anything separately for forty years. Maybe it's about time -- you might just appreciate each other more.

Okay. Supposing you absolutely must do everything together, and whitewater rafting or taking a terrific five-day cruise to the Aleutian Islands, is just plain too expensive. I'm well aware that the expense is on top of gasoline, campgrounds, etcetera, etcetera, etcetera.

Look at it this way. A trip to Alaska is expensive, but it is also the trip of a lifetime. Allow extra money for an activity that **you may not even know about** when you leave your driveway. The desire may surface as you travel or read (Whoa, Tex, we're talking about traveling here).

If you spend $1,000 above and beyond what is already in the pot for "known expenses and possible problems," will its absence make a significant difference in your life over the next year? If it will, would it be worth it? Are we talking the actual loss of food from your mouths or not buying season tickets to whatever?

My side trips this year were very expensive, but you will notice I mentioned house-sitting in Washington, over the winter. First of all, I needed the time to write two books, but secondly, my investment income was accumulating, or more truthfully, **recuperating**. I would rather have had those few quiet winter months, than give up the adventure of a lifetime (or several lifetimes!) that I had last summer.

Don't be afraid to treat yourself **once in a while,** and this is one of those times, even if you are a young family with kids. Have a family meeting, and decide a year (or two) in advance, who can contribute what? Who can give up what? How can you gather the kind of money it takes for a trip of this magnitude?

There are a great variety of tours. Interests range from diving, cruising, boating, fishing, hiking, biking, golfing, flightseeing, horseback riding, mountain climbing, tennis, shopping, restaurants, nightlife, bird watching, bear watching, whale watching, or a llama trek trip.

Maybe you'd like to do what I did a lot of last summer. I watched the tide go in and out, eagles soaring, fish struggling upstream, storm clouds settling over mountain tops, and bear families playing. I panned for gold, hiked in high mountain meadows, and walked through the mud puddles of historical sites. I listened to rushing streams and flowers growing. I smelled the fragrance of spring and the dust of summer. I crunched through the broken leaves of autumn and thrilled to the Aurora Borealis of winter. I observed people. It was all free. I only had to be there.

If none of this floats your boat, study the human migration from Siberia, across the land bridge of Beringia, to North America 40,000 years ago. If that doesn't go back far enough, dig into (so to speak) the mammoths and mastodons. The trip will be, **whatever you make it.**

What is the Land of the Midnight Sun? You didn't know there would be a quiz, did you? The correct answer is? It is a lot more than salmon and moose poop jewelry. It is isolated villages, wild animals, wild rivers, and wild-erness. It is glaciers, bald eagles, and northern lights. It is gravel roads with no shoulders and paved roads with the heaves. It is pleasantly warm in summer, and frigid enough in winter, to shatter your spit when it hits the ground. (You never know what cultured activities you'll read about in my books.)

The challenge of driving to Alaska has pretty much been eliminated, except for the distances involved, providing, of course, that you use your head about slowing down when necessary.

Alaska, northern British Columbia, Yukon Territory, and the Northwest Territories are excitement, romance, intrigue, and incredible beauty. I hope you'll be as fascinated with them as I continue to be.

What's next for me?

Immediately after my return to Eagle from the Yukon canoe trip, Bill was bragging on me to two German canoers. They had started at Lake Bennett and were going all the way to the Bering Sea. I exchanged business cards with Winfried. I have since heard that his young partner had a frighteningly close encounter with a black bear. Apparently, it bothered him enough, that they pulled out at the Dalton Highway, where we did.

That brief association has brought about several communications. In leaving my arms open to adventure, as I do, this may result in our doing a kayak trip on the Porcupine River (above the Arctic Circle). On the other hand, maybe my next trip will be with the Little Lynx, on a big "blue canoe," on the Inside Passage.

Often, people ask if I get lonely traveling solo. No, I like stopping at **my** whim to take photographs, sip a cup of coffee, absorb the scenery, and thank God I'm alive. I like to meet people. If I'm fortunate enough to run into a local character, so much the better. If an adventure hits me head on, I'm all for it. If it's snowing, I pray it doesn't get too deep before a thaw. If it's raining or foggy, I curl up with a book. If I'm lazy, I just curl up. If it's sunny, ah, it's time to enjoy the glories of RVing.

It's time to say good-bye (Have you notice I do that a lot?). Again, I'm not an expert about everything in Alaska and Canada, because I haven't done it all (yet!). My intention was to give you a taste of the North country through my experiences, with enough details to give you approximate costs, guidance, and I hope, a little inspiration. My personal adventures won't parallel yours; but, perhaps, they will serve as a whetting stone for planning your trip.

I want to end the book with this thought, again. If you want to make a trip to Alaska, find a way to make it happen now (legally!). I can almost guarantee, you will make memories that will fall into the following category.

> **It was one of those times I wanted to remember when I am old,
> sitting in my rocking chair,
> playing the moments of my life
> on the TV of my mind.**

## Go for it!

The very thought of your adventures in Canada and Alaska, as my friend, Doreen, would probably put it, "warms my heart like a remembered blessing."

**Send me a post card!**

**God Bless**

**"Charlie"**

# RESOURCES
## http://www.state.ak.us/

**Alaska Ferry Information**
Department of Transportation and Public Facilities
Division of Marine Highways
P.O. Box 25535
Juneau, AK 99802-5535
1-800-642-0066 U.S.
1-800-665-6414 Canada

**Alaska Ferry System**
Homer Ferry Terminal
P. O. Box 166
Homer, AK 99603
1-800-382-9229, 907-235-8449

**Alaska Marine Highway**
P. O. Box 703
Kodiak, AK 99615
1-800-526-6731
907-486-3800 (907-272-4482)
http://www.dot.state.ak.us/external/amhs/general/resinfo.html

**Alaska Public Lands Information Centers**
605 W. 4th St., Suite 105
Anchorage, Alaska 99501
Anchorage: 907-271-2737

P.O. Box 359
Tok, Alaska 99780
Tok: 907-883-5667

250 Cushman St., Suite 1A
Fairbanks, AK 99701
Fairbanks: (907) 456-0527

Ketchikan: (907) 228-6220
http://www.nps.gov/aplic/

**Canadian Customs**
Excise & Taxation Information Service
613-993-0534

**Alaska Railroad Passenger Services**
P. O. Box 107500
Anchorage, AK 99510-7500
1-800-544-0552
(Alaska and AAA magazine 2/96)
http://www.alaska.net/~akrr/

**Wheelers RV Resort & Campground Guide**
(Also have a Jumbo Road Map Atlas)
1310 Jarvis Avenue
Elk Grove Village, IL 60007
1-800-323-8899

**Creative World Rallies & Caravans**
4005 Toulouse Street
New Orleans, LA 70119
1-800-732-8337

**Dawson Celebrations:**
Klondyke Centennials Society
Bag 1996
Dawson City, Yukon, Canada, YOB 1GO
Ph: 403-993-1996
FAX 403-993-2002

**Denali National Park and Preserve**
Box 9
Denali Park, AK 99755
907 683-1266 or 1267
Denali reservations:
1-800-622-7275
http://www.alaska.net/~denst1/

**Escapees RV Club**
100 Rainbow Drive
Livingston, TX 77351
1-888-757-2582

**Family Motor Coach Association**
8291 Clough Pike
Cincinnati, OH 45244-2796

**Firearm Laws:**
Division of State Troopers,
Headquarters
5700 E. Tudor Rd., Dept. P
Anchorage, AK 99507
907-269-5511

**Friends of the Musk Ox**
P. O. Box 587
Palmer, AK 99645

**Gary Ault**
**Inlet Charters**
P.O. Box 2083
Homer, AK 99603
907-235-6126, 1-800-770-6126

**Good Sam**
2575 Vista Del Mar Drive
Ventura, CA 93001
1-805-667-4100
e-mail: goodsam@tl.com
http://www.tl.com

**GST Information**
1-800-668-4748 (Canada)
or 902-432-5608 in the US.

**Harry's Auto Repair Ltd.**
(Towing, Wheel Alignment, General Auto Rep)
Fort Nelson, B. D. VOC 1R0
604-774-2826, 604-774-6545

**Klondike Gold Rush**
National Historic Park Visitor Ctr
Second Avenue and Broadway
P. O. Box 517
Skagway, AK 99840
907-983-2921

**McCarthy Kennecott Tours**
Backcountry Connection
P. O. Box 243
Glennallen, AK 99588
Phone: 907-822-5292

**N.W.T. Tourism "Hot line"**
1-800-661-0788
Western Arctic Regional Visitors Center-
Inuvik: 403-979-4727
Road and Ferry Report:
1-800-661-0752

**Revenue Canada**
Customs and Excise
Visitor Rebate Program
Ottawa, Ontario, Canada K1A 1J5
1-800-66-VISIT (In Canada)
613-991-3346 (Outside)

**Revenue Canada Customs and Excise**
Public Relations Branch
Ottawa, Canada K1A 0L5
613-954-7125

**Riverboat Discovery**
Alaska Riverways, Inc.
1975 Discovery
Fairbanks, AK 99709
907-479-6673

**RV Emergency Road Services**
Rapid Response Roadservice Motor Club, Inc.
P.O. Box 5100, Ste 204
Thousands Oaks, CA 91359-9925
1-800-999-7505

**Southeast Alaska Tourism Council**
Box 20710
Juneau, AK 99802
1-800-423-0568

**Trailer Life Campground/RV Park & Services Directory**
P.O. Box 10236
Des Moines, IA 50381-0236
1-800-765-4167, ext 305

**Volunteer in Parks program**
State of Alaska
Division of Parks and Outdoor Recreation
P. O. Box 107001
Anchorage, Alaska 99510-7001

**White Pass and Yukon Route**
P. O. Box 435
Skagway, AK 99840
1-800-343-7373 (U.S.)
1-800-478-7373 (Canada)

**Woodall's World of Travel (caravans)**
P. O. Box 247
Greenville, MI 48838
1-800-346-7572

**Wrangell Mountain Air Taxi Service**
McCarthy Post Office Box MXY
Glennallen, AK 99588
Radio Telephone: 907-345-1160
1-800-478-1160 (Booking agent)

**Yukon Raft Adventures**
Elmore Enterprises
P. O. Box 145
Eagle, AK 99738
907-547-2355
FAX: 907-547-2208

# ALL NON-FICTION TITLES

Sharlene "Charlie" Minshall

## RVing Alaska! (and Canada) (1997)

A **"How-to"** and **"Why-not"** book, that gives vehicle and mental preparation, map information, where-to-stay, when-to-go, what to take, and road conditions. Add to the practical suggestions and strong comments, the misadventures of playing with the grizzlies in Katmai National Park, and canoeing the Mighty Yukon River, and you'll get information plus entertainment.

**Excerpt:** Please remember, speed is directly relational to anguished springs, broken axles, chipped windshields, and creative alignment.

**Excerpt:** ...at the Yukon Territory and the Northwest Territories border, I drove into a totally different world. It was dark, snowy, and windy. It was more ominous looking than I wanted to admit because I didn't want to turn back. I thought hard for milliseconds, then put the Sprinter in gear, and inched toward Inuvik.

## Full-Time RVing: How to Make it Happen (1997)

A **"How-to"** book that lets you in on the mobile lifestyle that millions are enjoying! What does it take to get started? What should I keep? What should I take? How do I keep relationships with family and friends intact? How do I cross borders into Canada or Mexico? What type of vehicle or health insurance is needed by a full-time RVer? What happens if I break down? How can I prevent breaking down? What is the daily life of a full-time RVer really like?

Full-time RVing doesn't have to be driving the Interstates. Now you'll be able to spend extra time in the most beautiful parts of our country. Let Charlie tell you about volunteering in the Snowmass-Maroon Bells Wilderness or house-sitting in the snowdrifts of a beautiful Bavarian Village. Paraglide with this silver gypsy off a mountain in Colorado or go cattle herding on a family reunion. This book is much more than a "How-to," it's a "Why not?"

## RVing North America, Silver, Single, and Solo

Follow the Silver Gypsy in her adventures into Mexico, Alaska, Canada, and all around the "lower 48." This is the daily life of a full-time RVer.

**Excerpt:** Tim maneuvered (ultralight) so I could look directly into a mining camp...He really didn't need to accommodate me so well. With no windshield for protection, I felt my age regress as the G's smoothed my wrinkles....Instead of landing, he flew a few feet off the ground between startled RVers...I got pictures of the plane's shadow on the ground....I felt like a hawk. Have you ever noticed they don't have wrinkles? There's a reason.

## In Pursuit of a Dream

Find out how and why "Charlie" began her full-time RVing lifestyle. (She started almost eleven years ago, and hasn't stopped yet!)

**Excerpt:** I went into Baja (Mexico) with no idea I would find whales, petroglyphs, Seventeenth Century missions, and cave paintings. The bourgainvillea...sunrises, sunsets, and grande moonlit nights...were a delight....wild furry burros roamed the roads...and I saw the Pacific and the Sea of Cortez mingle at "Land's End."

## Freedom Unlimited: The Fun and Facts of Fulltime RVing

(Co-author - Tech Writer Bill Farlow)     Published by Woodall's Publishing Company
Points of view from all sides of the full-time spectrum by two long-time, full-time RVing writers.

Book Description

# ORDER FORM

For AUTOGRAPHED copies, complete form and send a check or money order (US Funds) to:

Sharlene Minshall
% Gypsy Press
Suite AKBK-5024
101 Rainbow Drive
Livingston, TX 77351-9330

FULL-TIME RVING How to Make it Happen .................................$12.95

RVING ALASKA! (and Canada)...................................................$14.95

RVING NORTH AMERICA Silver, Single & Solo.........................$12.95

IN PURSUIT OF A DREAM........................................................$ 9.00

FREEDOM UNLIMITED The Fun and Facts of Fulltime Rving
(Co-authored by Bill Farlow) ....................................................$ 9.00

Name _____

Address _____

City, State, Zip _____

|  | Price | Qty | Total |
|---|---|---|---|
| FULL-TIME RVING: HOW TO MAKE IT HAPPEN | $12.95 | _____ | _____ |
| RVING ALASKA! (AND CANADA) | $14.95 | _____ | _____ |
| RVING NORTH AMERICA (Silver, Single & Soldo) | $12.95 | _____ | _____ |
| IN PURSUIT OF A DREAM | $ 9.00 | _____ | _____ |
| FREEDOM UNLIMITED | $ 9.00 | _____ | _____ |
|  |  | Subtotal | _____ |

$2 **DISCOUNT** on combo of three books

Discount - _____
Subtotal _____
P&H + _____
**Total** _____

Postage & Handling
Up to $10          $2.25
$10.01 to $20     $3.50
$20.01 to $40     $4.50
$40.01 TO $60    $6.00

**Canadian orders please add $1/$20.**
(Please allow six weeks for delivery)
Prices subject to change without notice.